ANNALS OF THE FAMINE IN IRELAND

Asenath Nicholson
by Anna Maria Howitt

ANNALS OF THE FAMINE
IN IRELAND

Asenath Nicholson

Edited by
Maureen Murphy

THE LILLIPUT PRESS
DUBLIN

First published 1998 by
THE LILLIPUT PRESS LTD
62-63 Sitric Road, Arbour Hill,
Dublin 7, Ireland.

A CIP record for this
title is available from
The British Library.

ISBN 1 874675 94 5

Frontispiece: A drawing of Asenath Nicholson by
Anna Maria Howitt (*The Bookman*, November 1926)

*The Lilliput Press receives financial assistance from
An Chomhairle Ealaíon/The Arts Council of Ireland.*

Cover design by Jarlath Hayes
Set in 10 on 13pt Times by Sheila Stephenson
Printed in Dublin
by Betaprint of Clonshaugh

INTRODUCTION

In January 1847, during the worst winter of the Famine, the American reformer Asenath Hatch Nicholson began her one-woman relief operation in Dublin: a soup kitchen in Cook Street and visits to the poor in the lanes of the Liberties. Apart from a sojourn in Scotland, she had been in Ireland for nearly three years, walking through the countryside reading Scripture and distributing Bibles in Irish and in English, drawn from the depths of the large black bearskin muff that she carried.[1]

Nicholson's account of her travels, *Ireland's welcome to the stranger; or, An Excursion through Ireland in 1844 and 1845, for the purpose of investigating the condition of the poor* (1847), is one of the most valuable records we have of Ireland on the eve of the Famine. *Annals of the Famine* (1851) is the extraordinary narrative of Nicholson's work and witness in Dublin and in the west of Ireland. To understand this remarkable woman – teacher, reformer, writer and traveller – it is necessary to look at three shaping forces in her life: her parents, her vocation as a teacher and her active advocacy of reform through temperance, vegetarianism, abolitionism and peace.

Nicholson was born on the New England frontier, in the village of Chelsea in the White River valley of eastern Vermont. While Nicholson's parents, Michael Hatch (*c*.1747-1830) and his wife Martha (1745-1837), were not named among Chelsea's first settlers who arrived in 1784, Michael Hatch of Ackworth, Cheshire County, New Hampshire arrived in Chelsea on 7 June, 1788 (Russell, *Founders*).

Asenath Hatch was born on 24 February 1792 in Chelsea. Her name was common enough in the Hatch family; the Genealogy and History of the Hatch Family lists four other Asenaths in her generation alone (Hatch-Hale, 135, 143, 144). It was a prophetic name for her, for the Asenath of Genesis 41 was the Egyptian daughter of the priest of On (Heliopolis) who was given as a wife to Joseph. She shared Joseph's life while he managed the famine food supply. In her own time, Asenath Nicholson would manage her own scanty resources to feed and clothe the Irish poor.

Nicholson's parents were probably members of Chelsea's first Congregational Church, the branch of American Protestantism that emphasised the Bible, individual freedom and local congregational autonomy. The conservative, zealous Revd Lathrop Thompson was pastor during

5

Nicholson's childhood (*Chelsea*, 16). The Hatches' Christianity was bound not only by the Congregationalist doctrines of covenant and personal salvation; they provided examples of tolerance and charity to their children – David (1776-1851), Benjamin (b. 1782) and Asenath. Michael Hatch '... hung no Quakers, nor put any men in a corner of the church because they had a colored skin'. Martha Hatch '... remembered the poor and entertained strangers, hated oppression, scorned a mean act and dealt justly by all' (*Welcome*, iii).

Nicholson also took on her father's reputation for frank speech. A local Chelsea legend recalls Mike Hatch's confrontation with a traveller who got himself buried in snow, rescued and buried again. After a scolding by Hatch, the man identified himself as the Governor of Vermont. Hatch replied, 'I can't in conscience take a word back' (Chelsea Archives). That habit of direct speech lived in his daughter who reported that her outspoken ways frequently got her into trouble, including expulsion from the Protestant missionary colonies at Ventry and at Achill. With her self-deprecating humour she warned the unnamed recipient of her 30 October, 1847 letter from Belmullet that she would be '... applying some of those "offensive points" in my character which I so eminently possess' in her call for land reform and better economic opportunities for the Irish poor (*Annals*, 100).

Her candour could be a trial to those she met, but her forthrightness and her integrity made her a reliable observer of the Famine in Ireland. Her friend the Quaker printer Richard Davis Webb (1805-72) spoke of those qualities when he wrote to his friend and confidante, the American abolitionist Maria Chapman (1806-85), from Dublin, 16 September 1847: 'I know no more impartial-minded, scrupulous, truth-loving person than Mrs Nicholson' (Webb, Richard, Letters).

Nicholson's mother, aptly named for the Martha of the New Testament, died in 1837 at the age of ninety-one, leaving her daughter her example of persistent hard work and self-sufficiency, qualities essential to survival in the early days of a pioneering community that practised 'warning out' those who might prove to be a burden to the settlement (*Chelsea*, 8).[2] Nicholson recalled her mother saying, 'The sun never looked down upon me in bed, when I was well' (*Nature*, 1846, 35).

In the spring of 1847, working on her own for the poor of Dublin, Nicholson was grateful for her mother's schooling:

Never before in all my privations in Ireland, had I tested the value of being early trained under the discipline of a rational mother, who fitted me, when a child, for the exigencies of life, who not only by precept taught me, that in going through the journey of this world I should meet with rough roads and stormy weather, and not always have a covered carriage, that sometimes I should have a hot supper and sometimes a cold one, sometimes a welcoming greeting and sometimes a repulsive one, but she had instructed me too, by precept and example, that my hands were to be employed in all that was useful and that idleness was both disgraceful and sinful (*Annals*, 53-4).

It is not surprising then, that 'indefatigable' appears as Nicholson's favourite term of approval for those who worked unremittingly for the poor. It is the adjective that she uses to describe some curates of the Established Church and some rural Catholic priests, the South Presentation nuns in Cork and the Belfast Ladies' Association, individuals like the Quaker Abraham Beale (1793-1847) of Cork, the Belfast worker for social and cultural causes Mary Ann McCracken (1776-1860), the poet/curate Charles Wolfe (1791-1823), the improving landlord George Hill (1801-79) and even the master and matron of the Galway Work-house '... who do not make merchandise of the poor for gain' (*Annals*, 146).

Nicholson was critical of what she considered the idleness and indulgence of many middle and upperclass Dublin women who left the management of their households to servants (*Annals*, 40). She must have pressed this point with Richard Webb's sister-in-law, Maria Waring (1818-74), who found Nicholson 'repulsive' but fascinating. Waring must have taken up some of her views about domestic economy, because she wrote to Lydia Shackleton at that time saying, 'I believe we ought to do our own housework, make our own fires, dress our own food, do the work of servants, instead of having others do it' (Harrison, 56-57).

Nicholson admired the women of the Belfast Ladies' Association for the Relief of Irish Destitution and contrasted their active work among the poor with Dublin women who were inclined to alms-giving and to excusing themselves from personal labour. 'But *giving* and *doing* are antipodes in her who has never been trained to domestic duties' (*Annals*, 57).

To the example of her mother, Nicholson added the biblical models of Solomon and Paul's 'virtuous women and housekeepers' whose only ornaments were their good works. Nicholson believed such a virtuous woman was one who used her skills of household management for her community as well as for her family.[3] Nicholson praised the work of Mrs Susan Hewitson of Rossgarrow, County Donegal, who dispensed her Central Relief Committee grants from her kitchen and who knew how to prepare Indian meal properly. 'Had the Irish mothers throughout Ireland managed as did this woman, their task in the Famine would have been much lighter – the poor, many more of them, would have been saved, and multitudes who have gone down might have retained their standing' (*Annals*, 62). Nicholson could have pointed to her own mission as another illustration of what the effort of one woman could accomplish.

While Nicholson came from Congregationalist New England stock, her own later non-denominational Bible Christianity emphasised charity, equality and the capacity of individuals to reform themselves. These beliefs informed her life and her vocation. Trained as a teacher, Nicholson taught first in Chelsea, perhaps in the school-house in her own District #2 where Michael Hatch was listed as living in 1807 when Nicholson was fifteen (*Chelsea*, 280).

In the second edition of *Nature's Own Book* (1835), she says she started teaching at sixteen and describes long days in the summer terms. It was customary in Chelsea, as in other New England school districts, to employ women for the summer term only so that they did not have to endure the difficult travel and fire-building chores of the winter term (*Nature*, 1835, 53; *Chelsea*, 48). Nicholson was effective in the classroom, for, two generations later, when she was long gone from Chelsea, Thomas Hale remembered her as a 'famous teacher' in his address celebrating Chelsea's Centennial in 1884 (Hale, 78).

Nicholson turned from teaching to reform when the Nicholsons opened their Temperance Boarding House in 1832, but she continued to take a keen interest in schools. The local school was a standard by which she judged the condition of the Irish poor. In the course of her famine journeys, she describes visits to some two dozen schools and reports visiting others. She brought Indian meal to the Presentation nuns for their school at George's Hill; she distributed clothes to children in some of the eleven schools operated by Revd Edward Nangle's (1799-1883) Protestant Missionary Colony in Achill; she enrolled a little boy in a school in Newport where he was fed and taught to read in the winter of 1847; she praised Dr John Edgar's (1798-1866) industrial schools as she travelled through Connacht for their instruction in knitting and sewing which would bring their pupils employment; she exposed the government for the spoiled, black bread they gave to starving children in Mayo schools; she approved of the school for convicts at Spike Island, and she celebrated the Presentation nuns in Tuam for a school where children still retained their normal affect and appearance. The good school appeared to her 'like some humble violet or flower, springing in the desert or prairie, where a scathing fire had swept over the plain, and withered all that was most prominent to the beholder' (*Annals*, 145).

Nicholson remained a teacher at heart, but she became an active reformer in her thirties. The transformation had something of a religious conversion about it. She had been a teetotaller from her childhood (*Loose Papers*, 109).[4] A poor diet, lack of rest and exercise and coffee drinking had led to poor health: digestion problems, nervousness, heart palpitations and high blood pressure (*Nature*, 1835, 53). She thought she would never recover.

There may have been more going on in her life to bring on the clinical symptoms associated with the kind of illness, often labelled as hysteria, that was common among middle class women in the nineteenth century. A sensible physician advised a change, so Nicholson went to New York, opened a school, married merchant Norman Nicholson (*c*.1790-1841) and, in June 1831, heard a series of lectures by Sylvester Graham (1794-1851), the New England temperance advocate turned diet crusader whom Ralph Waldo Emerson (1803-82) called 'the poet of bran and pumpkins'. Nicholson recalled the moment. 'I *heard and trembled*. The torrent of truth poured upon me, effectually convinced my judgment and made me a convert' (*Nature*, 1835, 53).

While temperance and vegetarianism were the core of Graham's regime, the programme also prohibited stimulants such as coffee and tea and animal fats. Alfred Webb (1834-1908) recalled her warnings about butter and the mischief his cousins practised on their eccentric American visitor:

Butter was her peculiar aversion. She told a story of her or some friend examining the intestines of some deceased patient and finding them choked with butter. Our 'Dunville' cousins there in the North considered she ate too many gooseberries in their garden and used to pull them, fill them with butter and replace them on thorns on the trees in hopes she would light on them (Webb, Journal 126).

Graham also advocated cleanliness including weekly bathing, regular rest and exercise, sensible dress and sexual hygiene (Shyrock, 174).

Grahamite boarding-houses opened to house and feed the faithful. The movement flourished in the late 1830s, a decade when the Nicholsons operated Grahamite boarding-houses in a neighbourhood of offices of moral and religious societies that included the American Anti-Slavery Society, the American Tract Society, the Temperance Union and the New York and Brooklyn Foreign Missionary Society. The Nicholsons opened a boarding house as early as 1832 because William Goodell (1792-1878), editor of *The Genius of Temperance,* sent his family out of town during the cholera epidemic that summer and he stayed with the Nicholsons:

It was at that time that Mr. Godell, together with Lewis and Arthur Tappan, and the other temperance reformers became interested in the lectures of Sylvester Graham and partially followed his teachings, giving up tea, coffee, meats, and high seasoning and using unbolted (or Graham) flour bread. They boarded for a considerable time at the Graham boarding-house kept by Mrs. Nicholson, at which Horace Greely, then a bashful young man, saying little or nothing imbibed anti-slavery principles from the conversation of those around him (*Memoriam* 25).

The link with the Tappan brothers is significant. The wealthy silk merchants were major benefactors of many Christian evangelical societies. They endowed Oberlin College which followed Graham's principles for a time. Arthur Tappan was founder and president of the New York and later American Anti-Slavery Society, and the Tappan brothers organized and financed the defence of the slaves who seized the *Amistad* (1839). The Tappans were so despised by southern slave-owners that they offered a price of $100,000 for the brothers' bodies.

Horace Greely, remembered today for his advice, 'Go West, young man!', became the editor of the liberal New York *Tribune*, the paper that would later find its way to Nicholson in Dublin. The *Tribune* publicized the work of the New Yorkers of the General Relief Committee who organized American relief for Ireland. It was the *Tribune* that carried the notice of Nicholson's death and her obituary, probably written by Greely (Fitz McCarthy, Asenath Hatch Nicholson, 63).

A letter from William Tyler, a tutor at Amherst College, to his brother Edward Tyler, written 10 October 1833, described the atmosphere of the Nicholsons' boarding-house:

The Boarders in this establishment are not only Grahamites but Garrisonites – not only reformers in diet, but radicalists in Politics. Such a knot of Abolitionists I never before fell in with. Slavery, colonization, constitute the unvarying monotonous theme of their conversation except [those] that give place to an occasional comment on their peculiar style of living (Le Duc, 190).

The New York Directory lists Norman Nicholson as proprietor of boarding-houses at 79 Cedar Street (1833), Wall Street and Broadway (1834), and Asenath Nicholson of the premises at 118 Williams Street (1835-37) and 21 Beekman Street (1838-41). In 1842, Nicholson, described as a widow, moved her boarding-house across the street to 26 Beekman Street.

The reformer Henry Clarke Wright (1797-1870) lived at Nicholsons' Temperance House at 118 Williams Street in 1836 with other agents of the American Anti-Slavery Society which was located around the corner at 48 Beekman Street (Perry, 29). Wright and Abolitionist William Lloyd Garrison (1805-79) had close ties with the Irish Friends and chances are it was through them that Nicholson made her Quaker connections.

While Nicholson ran her boarding-houses, she visited the poor of New York in the Five Points, the notorious slum nearby in New York's Sixth Ward where cholera had raged in 1832. During those years Nicholson met the poor Irish. 'It was in the garrets and cellars of New York that I first became acquainted with the Irish peasantry and it was there

that I saw that they were a suffering people' (*Welcome*, iii). Although
Protestant missionaries were working in the district – the Central and
Spring Street Presbyterians in the late 1830s and the Congregationalists
in the 1840s – Nicholson chose to work alone as later she would work on
her own in Ireland.

Nicholson talked of visiting Ireland in those years (*Welcome*, iv), so
that in 1844 when she was not only widowed, but otherwise alone, she
felt a divine calling to work among the Irish:

The world was before me and all mankind my brethren. 'I have made you desolate. I want you for other purposes. Go work in my vineyard,' was the word. I
conferred not with flesh and blood.[5]

Her mission? To bring the Bible to the Irish poor.

Nicholson spent six months 'investigating' conditions in rural Ireland
before she filled two bags with Bibles, attached the bags to a stout cord
twisted under her polka coat, picked up her parasol and bonnet and set
off in her Indian rubber boots to distribute Bibles to those who could read
and to read herself to those who could not. Her work was not easy. Catholics suspected any Bible-reading stranger of proselytism while Protestant missionaries rejected her tolerance and democratic ideas.

Her travels through rural Ireland, stopping with the poor in their cabins and sharing their meals of potatoes with them, leave us an account of
the cottier life that would be all but swept away by the Famine before the
end of the decade. While *Ireland's Welcome to the Stranger* is not a jere-
miad, Nicholson senses the gathering storm in a country with an improv-
ident and, for the most part, absentee land-owning class and a tenantry
desperate for work. There is no record that Nicholson ever met Maria
Edgeworth (1767-1849), but she too could have written *Castle Rackr-
ent*.[6] When the Famine came, Nicholson once again heard the call to
work among the Irish poor. Paraphrasing Luke 22:42, she asked, 'Father,
if You are willing, remove this cup from me, never the less, not my will
but Yours be done'. Having taken up what she considered a divinely appointed mission, she never complained about her personal hardships; she
only complained that she did not have the resources to do more for those
who suffered.

Nicholson began her relief programme in January 1847, the month
that the Central Relief Committee of the Society of Friends established
their soup kitchen in Charles Street, Upper Ormond Quay. Until July,
when the government's Temporary Relief Act which provided for the
direct distribution of food to the poor was passed, the Quakers sold an
average of 1000 quarts of soup a day for a penny a quart and soup tickets
that could be distributed to the poor.

Nicholson admired the work of the Quakers and numbered many of them among her friends, but she went her own way and located herself, as usual, among the poor themselves. She describes herself in the early months of 1847 living in a tall house overlooking the Liffey and setting off each morning with a large basket of bread to distribute as she made her way to Cook Street and on to the homes of the poor. Crowds of hungry followed her. Although there were bread riots in the city, she did not fear for her safety but minded the 'dreadful importuning' (*Annals*, 45).

Unlike the Quakers, she did not sell her food; she distributed it *gratis*. She was sensible enough, however, to realise her resources would better be applied to relieving a limited number of people, so she devised a system of triage and until July she fed a small group of Dublin poor. The English Quaker William Bennett provides a glimpse of Nicholson when he met her in April 1847, at the house of Richard Webb:

I found her with limited and precarious means, still persevering from morning to night in visiting the most desolate abodes of the poor, and making food – especially of Indian meal – for those who did not know how to do it properly, with her own hands. She was under much painful discouragement, but a better hope still held her up. Having considerable quantity of arrow-root with me, at my own disposal, I left some of it with her, and five pounds for general purposes (Bennett, 96).

In July 1847 Nicholson left Dublin for the west of Ireland. She knew Mayo from Westport to Achill from her earlier visit, but she was unfamiliar with the area of greatest destitution from Ballina west to the Erris peninsula. She followed the route of the Quakers William Forster (1784-1854), James Tuke (1819-96), William Bennett and Richard Webb. Webb was probably the most helpful to her. She does not mention his tours to the west in May 1847, and in February, 1848, but his letters to the Central Relief Committee identify the people and places that Nicholson describes in the *Annals*. In fact, it is likely that Webb and Nicholson met in Ballina in February, 1848. Webb wrote to the CRC on 18 February 1848 and again on 2 March (*Transactions*, 208; 210); Nicholson spent February in Ballina and left for Castlebar on the 28th.

Through her Quaker contacts and her friends from her earlier visit, Nicholson was able to stay with many of those who were administering local relief: the Savages of Achill Sound who acted for the Quakers, Mrs Margaret Arthur, the widowed Postmistress of Newport, and Samuel Bourne (c.1790-1864), a landlord with a small estate of about seventy tenant families. Located in the midst of suffering, she set about to bear witness, first in letters and then in the *Annals*, to the Famine and fever and to the heroic efforts to bring comfort to the hungry and dying.

Her *Annals* differ from the accounts of her Quaker male counterparts which focus on the logistical problems of famine relief. Nicholson concentrates on the nature of human suffering. On 28 November,1847 she described a scene that anticipated John Millington Synge's *Riders to the Sea*. A fisherman's widow journeyed twenty miles to 'prove' her husband who had been washed ashore and buried without a coffin. She went to the spot where he was buried. With her own hands, she dug him from his grave, 'proved' him by the leather button she had sewn on his clothes and buried him in the white coffin that she had brought with her.[7]

She combined her documentary with other forms of discourse including parables, dramatic scenes and dialogues written in the cadences of the Old Testament in an attempt to find the language to describe the suffering of the Irish poor. She also drew on the Bible, lines from hymns and literary allusions to record scenes which were beyond the experience of her reader. Christopher Morash, discussing the challenge of finding such appropriate language in his Introduction to his collection of famine poetry *The Hungry Voice*, observes that 'images from the prophetic books of the Bible provided a central means of comprehending the accelerated change brought on by the Famine' (Morash, 21).

In evoking images from the prophets herself, Nicholson made it clear that she believed that the Famine's devastation was not a divine judgment, but the failure of man to use God's gifts responsibly. Nicholson considered herself as 'acting entirely as a passive instrument; moving because moved upon', but there was nothing passive about her indictment of those in power, the government and the Established Church, for failing in their stewardship of their relief resources. She distinguished between hired relief officials, whom she dismissed as bureaucratic, hierarchical and self-serving, and local volunteer workers, including clergy of all denominations, coast guardsmen and some resident landlords, whom she praised as compassionate, egalitarian and selfless.

She sneered at Sir Charles E. Trevelyan's (1807-86) *Irish Crisis* assertion that there was not a single case of embezzlement among the two thousand hired relief officers (*Annals*, 106), charging that there were some who lived well while those they were engaged to care for went hungry, and she described the upper classes picking through the clothes collected for the poor for the better garments for themselves (*Annals*, 107).

She also indicted the same class of Dubliners for their indifference to the Famine pointing out that 'the winters of 1847 and 1848 in Dublin were winters of great hilarity among the gentry' (*Annals*, 106).[8] Scrupulous herself about her own expenses, she lived on a diet of cocoa and bread and continued to ask herself whether she was doing enough to economize.

Nicholson denied having interests other than those of administering aid and giving comfort, including prayer and Bible reading, to the poor; however, she criticizes government policies and protocols that interfered with relief to the suffering. Two places in the *Annals* where she directly addresses the issues are in a letter written from Belmullet on 30 October 1847, and in her short Chapter VI where Nicholson interrupts her narrative in order to speak her mind about 'Poor-Houses, Turnips and Black Bread'.

The recipient of the letter is not identified, but the text suggests that he is an English Quaker familiar with famine conditions in the West of Ireland, that he is an abolitionist and that he is probably a radical in his political views. The English corn factor and philanthropist Joseph Sturge (1793-1859) of Birmingham would have been such a person and he had provided Nicholson with a letter of introduction to use during her first visit to Ireland and with funds for her famine efforts; however, her letter appears to address a Member of Parliament ('you who are statesmen') and Sturge was never a successful candidate. Sturge worked closely, however, with another Quaker industrialist, John Bright (1811-89), who was an MP between 1843 and 1889, so Nicholson may have written her letter to Bright.

In her letter, Nicholson pleads for employment instead of relief, arguing that work will save Ireland for England. She calls for a radical like the English abolitionist George Thompson (1804-38) to come and see the degraded conditions of people fed on a programme of government relief and then to lift his voice for Ireland. Thompson's campaign against slavery in America was so inflammatory that he was denounced by President Andrew Jackson (1747-1845) in 1835 and he had to leave the country.

She argues for land reform:

Give her a little spot on the loved isle she can call her own where she can 'sit under her own vine and fig-tree and none to make her afraid' and force her not to flee to a distant clime to purchase that bread that would be sweeter on her own native soil (*Annals*, 102).

She also urges England to call upon America, if necessary, to help feed the Irish. Saying that even those hands fouled with slavery would feed the Irish poor suggests that Nicholson, though a firm abolitionist, would have agreed with the Irish Quakers who opted to accept donations from the slave-holding cities of Charleston and Baltimore when the question of their gifts was debated in Dublin (Goodbody, 24).

In 'Poor-houses, Turnips and Black Bread', Nicholson treats these government schemes with barely-concealed contempt. The building costs of workhouses, 'these splendid monuments to Ireland's poverty', exceeded those of providing each family of inmates with a cottage and a plot of land (*Annals*, 108). She exposed some of the food distributed as nutritionally deficient. A diet of turnips alone led to death in weeks. Other food, the putrid black bread given to the poor of Mayo, was simply a way to dispose of spoiled surplus.

While Nicholson was a pacifist who would travel as an American delegate to the International Peace Conference in Frankfurt in 1850, she advocated radical reform, expressing her sympathy for Young Irelanders William Smith O'Brien (1803-64) and John Mitchel (1815-75) who, she believed, were driven into the Rebellion of 1848 by their 'philanthropic love of country and deep sense of justice' (*Annals*, 119). She had little time for Daniel O'Connell's (1775-1847) Repeal campaign because she believed that Ireland needed employment and land reform more than Repeal. She recalled a gathering around a bonfire to celebrate O'Connell's release from prison when a countrywoman said to her:

It's many a long day that we have been working for that same to do somethin' for us, but not a hap'orth of good has come to a cratur of us yet. We're atin' the pratee to-day, and not a divil of us has got off the rag since he began his discoorse (*Welcome*, 113).

Nicholson was as critical of government relief officers who sent the hungry away until their paperwork was completed and of other bureaucratic requirements which interfered with or delayed getting aid to the poor. Even the Quakers were not exempt from some criticism. When Nicholson received some barrels of meal through their auspices, she was billed for sacks sold by the government to defray the cost of their guarantee to cover the expense of shipping any food for famine relief.

Nicholson balked. Her letter to the Central Relief Committee written from 45 Hardwick Street on 7 July 1847 began with an apology for troubling them but went on to say firmly:

Your clerk told me when I received your order that I must pay for the sacks but if they are returned in good order, this money would be refunded. When this was refused, he denied the engagement saying I should pay freight, if not pay for the sacks. This I am willing to do if it is just, but the donors in New York sent me notice that all they sent me was freight free and sent in barrels and I quite prefer them because sacks will not keep the meal so well as much that I had was seriously injured (Nicholson, National Archives of Ireland, Society of Friends Relief of Distress Papers, Letter 3198).

She did not have to pay.

Nicholson was as critical of Established Church charity as she was of official government relief schemes and practices. She particularly condemned proselytisers supported by the evangelical wing of the Church:

It requires the Irish language to provide suitable words for a suitable description of the spirit which is manifested in some parts to proselyte, by bribery, the obstinate Romans to the church which has been her instrument of oppression for centuries (*Annals*, 181).

A Bible reader concerned with saving the Irish from the superstitions of Rome, Nicholson was, in principle, supportive of Protestant missionary colonies; however, she wanted conversions to be the result of conviction not hunger, and she exposed the Achill Mission for its lack of Christian charity.

She predicted that the proselytisers' gains would be short-lived, citing the voices of children who told her, 'We are going back to our own chapel or our own religion when the stirabout times are over' (*Annals*, 205). She observed that their priests frequently were quiet about their parishioners who accepted food from the proselytisers or 'soupers':

They held these favoured ones of their flock by a cord while the stomach was filling, as the traveller does his steed that he is watering, and turns it away when its thirst is assuaged, caring little at what fountain he drinks if the water be wholesome (*Annals*, 182).

Nicholson's observations have been validated by contemporary historians like Irene Whelan, whose examination of the evidence concludes that the conversions in areas of intense missionary activity never amounted to more than a few hundred, and that the Protestant establishment was the real loser, for all of its clergy working among the poor were suspect (Póirtéir, 149, 153).

Nicholson was very careful to single out clergy, like the curate of Binghamstown, who were not proselytes. Over and over she points to cooperation among members of the clergy of different denominations who worked together to help the poor. In her assessment of the various religious denominations at the end of *Annals*, Nicholson judges each, in part, on its famine work as a way of measuring its Christian charity. As for the Catholics themselves, Nicholson approved that 'where their religious faith is concerned, they call no man master' (*Annals*, 188). Her anti-Catholicism mediated by her experience among the Irish poor, she concluded, 'The Roman Catholic who turns to God with full purpose of heart, and has been really born of the Spirit, is indeed a spiritual Christian' (*Annals*, 185).

Central to Nicholson's spirituality was compassion and generosity, and she celebrated those qualities in those she admired: some relief officers, landlords and clergy; the volunteer relief workers recruited by the Quakers and others who followed their own summons and especially the poor themselves. The hospitality in the Irish countryside was a theme of

Ireland's Welcome to the Stranger: in *Annals*, it was the generosity of the Irish to one another.

Nicholson left Ireland in 1848 when she thought that her work was finished. Her long stay in Cork in the summer of 1848 speaks to the heroic work of her great friend Father Theobald Mathew, whose famine work is less well-known than his crusade for temperance, and to the work of other volunteers like the Quakers and the South Presentation nuns, but she also brings the reader on some sightseeing excursions. The somewhat lighter tone of these pages suggests Nicholson believed that the worst was over. In fact, famine conditions were to continue until 1852, the year she finally returned to America, where she lived in obscurity until her death from typhoid fever in Jersey City, New Jersey, on May 15 1855 (Fitz Mc Carthy, Asenath Hatch Nicholson, 63).

She departed from Dublin without a fuss. The 'lone Quaker' who accompanied her to the boat was probably Richard Webb. An exile now, she promised herself that she would not forget this Jerusalem. She did not. She left us a record of the suffering of the Famine Irish. Content to celebrate the work of others – coastguardsmen and their families, women managing food and clothing depots from their kitchens, selfless curates – Nicholson took their stories to the wider world. It is a record of grace, of those who served. The blessing of those she served was her reward.

EDITOR'S NOTE

Years ago, when I was a student in Dublin, Roger McHugh suggested I look at *Ireland's Welcome to the Stranger*, the travels of the American reformer Asenath Nicholson who walked through Ireland just before the Famine. *Ireland's Welcome to the Stranger; or, An Excursion through Ireland in 1844 and 1845 for the purpose of personally investigating the condition of the Poor* was published in London by Gilpin in 1847; an American edition was issued the same year by Baker and Scribner. An abridged edition called *The Bible in Ireland* edited and introduced by Alfred Tresidder Sheppard (London: Hodder and Stoughton, 1925 and New York: The John Day Company, 1927) brought Nicholson's account to the twentieth-century reader. Sheppard's Introduction also provided valuable biographical clues for one to begin to piece together the facts of Nicholson's life. He also published the drawing of Nicholson by Anna Maria Howitt that has been reproduced as the frontispiece for *Annals*. It was the start of a thirty year interest in Nicholson's life and work and a determination to write her biography. The staff of the Irish Folklore Commission, Kevin Danaher, Anraí Ó Braonáin and Seán Ó Súilleabháin gave me a good start and when the Commission became the Department of Irish Folklore the staff continued to support the project.

In the course of my research, I found Nicholson's *Annals of the Famine*, the account of her work among the Irish during the Famine. It was first published as the third part of her *Lights and Shades of Ireland* by two different London publishers in 1850: by Gilpin and by Houlston and Stoneman. The following year she expanded her Famine account and published it as *Annals of the Famine in 1847, 1848 and 1849* with E. French in New York. Generally overlooked, I believe its unique voice is a major contribution to Famine literature.

Many people have had a hand in making this edition possible. A Hofstra Presidential Research Grant and a School of Education Research Grant provided funds to consult the Irish Architectural Archive, the Society of Friends Library at Swanbrook House, the National Archives, and the National Library of Ireland. I am grateful to those institutions and to Sister Rosario Allen, archivist of the South Presentation Convent.

Closer to home, the American Irish Historical Society, The Haviland Reading Room of the New York Society of Friends, The New York Historical Society Library and the New York Public Library provided sources for Nicholson's life and for Famine-related material, especially the American response to the Famine. The Richard Davis Webb Letters in the Manuscript

Division of the Boston Public Library supplied details about the work of the Dublin Quakers. I am especially indebted to Hofstra University librarians Domenica Barbuto, Eleana Cevallos, Joan Cooney and Janet Wagner.

R. Dudley Edwards and T. Desmond Williams and their essayists in *The Great Famine* and Cecil Woodham-Smith's pioneering study, *The Great Hunger* were my introductions to the Famine. I have benefited from the work of the Famine historians of the current generation: Mary E. Daly, James S. Donnelly, Cormac Ó Gráda, Robert Scally and Kevin Whelan and from collections compiled by John Killen, Noel Kissane and Cathal Póirtéir.

Mrs Jean Hatch Farnham, a descendant of Nicholson's brother David Hatch, kindly supplied me with the Hatch family history and the staff of the Records Office of the Town of Chelsea and the Chelsea Library and Archives provided information about local history. I am grateful to Connie Hendren Fitz whose M.A. thesis has provided valuable information about Nicholson's later years and details of her death.

Friends who joined me on the Hatch/Nicholson hunt include Joan De-Staebler, Henry Farrell, Margaret MacCurtain, Eilis McDowell and Donla Uí Bhraonáin, and the usual suspects gave me advice and encouragement: Francis and Janet Carroll, Anne Francis Cavanagh, Adele Dalsimer, Emmet Larkin, Robert Lowery, Larry McCaffrey, James MacKillop, Lucy McDiarmid, Rhoda Nathan, Janet Nolan, Frank Phelan, Norma and Robert Rhodes, Ginny and Roger Rosenblatt, Catherine Shannon, Mary Helen Thuente, and Maryann Valiulis. I owe a special debt to Jude Uí Fhatharta who taught me Irish, which gave me access to Famine *béaloideas*. Gus Martin, Roger McHugh, Máire and Jack Sweeney and especially Don Murphy were earlier encouragers who did not live to see this project completed.

The Hofstra Office of Special Secretarial Services helped produce the manuscript and Karin Spencer was my editorial adviser. As always Diana Ben-Merre was my most patient and attentive reader. Róisín Conroy, Ruth Burke-Kennedy and Feargha Ní Bhroin of Attic Press realised what a remarkable contribution Nicholson makes to the study of Irish women's history. Antony Farrell, Brendan Barington and Siobán O'Reilly brought this edition of *Annals* to Lilliput's standard of bookmanship.

My final thanks and deepest gratitude is to my parents and to my brothers, to whom I dedicate this work.

MAUREEN MURPHY
Sea Cliff, March 1998

ANNALS

of the

FAMINE IN IRELAND,

IN 1847, 1848 AND 1849.

BY MRS A NICHOLSON,

Author of *Ireland's Welcome to the Stranger*.

NEW YORK
E. FRENCH, 135 Nassau Street
1851.

CONTENTS

CHAPTER I   25

Object of the Work – General Remarks on the Condition of Ireland before the Famine – Coachman's reasons for Murder – Difficulties of Writing a Correct Work on Ireland – Position of the writer, &c.

CHAPTER II   32

Cup of Trembling – Irish Housekeeping – Indian Meal – First News of the Famine – Kind Judge – First Starving Person, and Means of Preserving Him – Unexpected Assistance from New York – Joseph Bewley – Soup-shop – Manner of Carrying Bread Through the Street – Cook Street Labors in Dublin – Central Relief Committee in Dublin – Amount of Moneys – God's Promises and Dealings

CHAPTER III   50

Stewards – Meal from New York – Sacks, and Government Arrangements for Distribution of Meal – Donation from Pauper Children of New York – Convent – Going to Belfast – Doings of the Women There – Hirelings and Voluntaries – Hon William Butler – William Bennett – Mrs Hewitson – Visits to George Hill – Patrick M'Kye's Letter

CHAPTER IV   69

George Hill's Movements and Success – Facts of Gweedore – Visit to Dungloe and Arranmore – Mr Griffith – Sports of Children Gone – Roshine Lodge – Return to Belfast by Derry – Visit to Antrim – A Cave – Return to Dublin – Journey to Connaught – Mistake in Character of a Starving Man – Misery at Newport – Orphan Boy – Abraham and Sara – Sara's Bed and Burial – Abraham's Death and Burial – Drinking Habits – Moderate Drinking Clergy

CHAPTER V   91

The Sound – Tour to Belmullet – Landlords – Tenantry – Walk on the Sea-coast – Burying-ground – Ship-wrecked Sailors'

Burial – *Manner of Burying the Starving* – *Soldiers of Belmullet* – *Appearance of the People* – *Passport* – *Mr Carey* – *Samuel Bourne* – *The Girl of the Mountain* – *Miss Wilson* – *Return to Belmullet* – *Scene of the Cattle Drivers, and Courage of a Boy* – *Letter to a London Friend* – *Return to the Sound* – *Dreadful Storm* – *Drowning of Fishermen* – *Reading with Servants* – *Achill* – *Bad Management of Grants* – *Disposition of Children.*

CHAPTER VI   108
   Poor-houses, Turnips, and Black Bread

CHAPTER VII   115
   Newport – *Pulling down Houses* – *Mr Pounding* – *Gildea* –
   Burial at Newport – *Molly Maguires, &c.* – *Rebellion of 1848* –
   Croy Lodge and Ballina – *The Self-denying Child* – *Hunting,
   and Habits of a Hunting Lady* – *Visit to Ballina* – *Hospitality of
   Peter Kelly* – *Character of Mr Kinkead* – *Captain Short, and
   the People in General Leaving the Town* – *Stop at Pontoon and
   Arrival at Castlebar* – *Trial for Murder* – *The Feelings of the
   Jury* – *Patrick's Day* – *Widow Fitzgerald* – *Visit to Partra* –
   Ballinrobe – *Scene in the Mountains* – *Old Parish Priest* – *Visit
   to Ballinrobe* – *To Cong* – *Industry of the Curate* – *Visit to
   Ballinrobe Work-house* – *Old Head* – *Distress There* –
   Louisburgh – *Excursion to the Killary Mountains, &c.* –
   Excursion to Adelphi – *Incidents* – *Good Landlady* – *Shepherds
   – Romantic Scenery* – *Return* – *Rockery* – *Adieu* – *Westport
   and Castlebar* – *Soup-shops* – *Soyer's Soup* – *Journey to Tuam
   – Children in the Convent* – *Happy Results* – *Sad Treatment on
   a Car* – *Arrival at Cork* – *Description of Cove and Cork* –
   Scenery up the Lee – *Deaths in the Famine* – *Blarney* –
   Castlemartyr – *Potato Blast* – *Spike Island* – *Mathew Tower* –
   Letters

CHAPTER VIII   161
   Grave of Charles Wolfe – *Water Cure* – *Friend's Funeral*

CHAPTER IX   192
   Leaving Cork – *Passage to Dublin* – *New Trials There* –
   Reflections on Past Labors, &c. – *Last Look of Ireland* –
   Summing up – *Landlords* – *Clergymen* – *Relief Officers* –
   Going out of Ireland

INTRODUCTION TO THE AMERICAN EDITION

Mrs Asenath Nicholson, the author of the following pages, is a native of Vermont, where she is extensively known (by her maiden name of Hatch) as an able teacher. She is also widely known for many years as the keeper of a boarding-house in this city (on the Vegetarian principle) which used to be the resort of hundreds of choice spirits from all parts of the country, including most of the names of those who were engaged in measures of social reform. She is a woman of great acuteness of intellect, and of the most self-sacrificing benevolence, with great independence of mind and force of character.

Her visits to Ireland and labors there are but the workings of her character; and those who are best acquainted with her wonder neither at her courage nor at her adventurous and untiring charity.

Her first work on Ireland – *Ireland's Welcome to the Stranger*, narrates her travels and observations prior to the Great Famine of 1847.[1] It was republished in this city some years ago. The present work recites some of the scenes which she witnessed during that calamitous season. Her heart was in a continual agony, and her limbs wearied by incessant toils to relieve if it could be only a small part of the misery she witnessed. In answer to appeals on her behalf, some funds were placed at her disposal from this country, by friends who knew how effectively they would be employed in her hands.[2] The tale of woe should be read by the whole American people; it will have a salutary effect upon their minds, to appreciate more fully the depth of oppression and wretchedness from which the Irish poor escape in coming to this land of plenty.

For the sake of giving a wider circulation to the material facts of the Famine and its effects, the American publisher has thought it advisable to omit some chapters which were contained in the English edition, giving a history of Ireland from the conquest by Henry II of England; as this information can be obtained in other works.[3]

J. L.[4]
New York, *April* 1851.

PREFACE

The reader of these pages should be told that, if strange things are recorded, it was because strange things were seen; and if strange things were
seen which no other writer has written, it was because no other writer has
visited the same places, under the same circumstances. No other writer
ever explored mountain and glen for four years, with the same object in
view; and though I have seen but the suburbs of what might be seen,
were the same ground to be retraced, with the four years experience for a
handmaid, yet what is already recorded may appear altogether incongru-
ous, if not impossible.[1] And now, while looking at them calmly at a distance, they appear, even to myself, more like a dream than reality,
because they appear out of *common course*, and out of the order of even
nature itself. But they are realities, and many of them fearful ones – *realities* which none but eye-witnesses can understand, and none but those
who passed through them can *feel*. No pretensions to infallibility either
in judgment or description are made – the work is imperfect because the
writer is so – and no doubt there are facts recorded which might better
have been left out. In such a confused mass of material, of such variety
and such quality, I am not so vain as to suppose that the best has always
been selected or recorded in the best way.

CHAPTER I

'Stript, wounded, beaten, nigh to death,
I saw him by the highway-side.'[1]

Those who have read the volume called *Ireland's Welcome,* have been informed that I left New York in the spring of 1844, for the purpose of exploring and ascertaining, by eye-witness, the *real* condition of a people whose history has been mixed with fable, and whose *true* character has been as little understood as their sufferings have been mitigated.

In pursuing this work, the object is not precisely the same as in the preceding one; *that* was but the surface – the rippling of that mighty sea, whose waves have since been casting up little else but 'mire and dirt', and whose deep and continual upheavings plainly indicate that the foundations, if not destroyed, are fast breaking up. I then aimed at nothing more than giving a simple narration of facts, as they passed under observation, leaving the reader to comment upon those facts, as their different features were presented to the mind.

Some, and possibly *many,* have been grieved that so much 'plainness of speech' has been used: but *here* emphatically 'flattering titles' should have no place. Opiates have served no other purpose for diseased Ireland than to leave undisturbed the canker-worm that was doing more effectually his deadly work within. 'Peace, peace,' where there is no peace, eventually brings down the chastenings of the Almighty, and He has shown in language that cannot be misunderstood, for the last three years, that He sitteth in the heavens, overturning and overturning the nations of the earth, and, in his own due time, He whose right it is to rule will rule. The stone is rolling, and its velocity increases as it proceeds. The potato has done its work, and it has done it *effectually:* it has fed the unpaid millions for more than two centuries, till the scanty wages of the defrauded poor man have entered into the 'ears of the Lord of Sabboth', and He is now telling the rich that their gold and silver is cankered, and that their day is coming speedily.[2]

We are gravely told that the year 1844 was one of great abundance, and that the peasantry were *then* a contented and happy people; but listen! the year 1844 *was* a year of abundance, but did the poor man share in this *abundance*? Was he contented and happy? Why then was the whole country rocking 'to and fro' with the cry of repeal? And, why was O'Connell in prison? Were the people all singing in their chains, not feeling the galling of the fetters, till he aroused them from their contented sleep? Did his fiery breath fan up embers that had lost all *power* of life? And were there no heartburnings beneath the tatters of the degraded cabiner, that strongly prompted to make a struggle for that liberty, which God has by birthright bestowed upon all bearing his image? A struggle they *would* have made, had one nod from the prison grates of O'Connell given the signal. Though there was no clamor, yet the leaven was silently leavening the whole lump, and they appeared anxiously waiting for some event, which they felt *must* come, they knew not *whence,* nor cared not *how.*[3]

But the year of abundance. From June 1844 to August 1845, I visited the middle and southern part, including all the sea-coast, *always* on foot in the most destitute regions, that I might better ascertain the condition and character of the peasants in their most uncultivated state.[4] What I then saw of privation and suffering has been but partially sketched, because the 'many things' I had to say the world was not *then* able to bear, neither are they now able to bear them *all;* but posterity will bear them, and posterity shall hear them. Please read the partial sketch of Bantry, Glengarriff and the sea-coast of Kerry, given the years 1844-5, and enter into some floorless, dark, mud cabin, and sit down upon a stool, if haply a stool be there, and witness the 'abundance' of those happy fertile days.[5] Again and again did I partake of a scanty meal of the potato, after a day's walk of miles, because I knew a full repast would deprive the family of a part of the supply in reserve for the meal, which by multitudes was then taken but once a day.

Mark! These are not isolated cases, but everywhere in the mountainous regions, upon the sea-coast, and in the glens; from Dublin to the extreme south did I daily meet these facts. Nor was this privation of short continuance: from Christmas to harvest the poor peasant must stint his stomach to one meal a day, or his seed for the coming crop would be curtailed, and the necessary rent-payer, the pig, not be an equivalent to keep the mud cabin over the head of his master.[6]

So much for 'abundance', now for 'content'. That there was an unparalleled content, where anything approached to tolerable endurance, cannot be denied, but this was their *religious* training; however imperfect their faith and practice may be, in patience they *have,* and *do* exemplify a pattern which amounts almost to superhuman.[7] 'We must be content with what the Almighty puts upon us,' was their ready answer when their sufferings were mentioned. Yet this did not shut their eyes to a sense of the sufferings which they felt were put upon them by man, and their submission seemed in most cases to proceed from the requirements of the

Almighty, rather than from ignorance of their wrongs; for in most
instances the parting question would be: 'Don't ye think the government
is too hard on us' or 'do ye think we shall ever git the repale, and will
Ireland ever be any better', &c. That they are a happy people so long as
any ray of hope remains, or when they share in common the gifts of
Providence, must be allowed; yet their quick perception of justice often
manifests itself, where any loop-hole is made which promises amendment to their condition, and when the flickering spark of life is kindled
within them. They have committed bold and wicked acts, which revenge
prompted by a sense of injustice alone would do. Justice long withheld,
and oppression multiplied proportioned to uncomplaining endurance,
sometimes awakes to a boldness almost unequaled by any but the savage
of the wilderness. Nor do they wait for the night, or seek any other con-
cealment, than to make sure of their prey – they care not who sees them,
or on what gallows they are hung, if the hated victim be out of the way.

> Hark! from yon stately ranks what laughter rings,
> Mingling wild mirth with war's stern minstrelsy.
> His jest – while each brave comrade round him flings,
> And moves to death with military glee.
> Boast, Erin! boast them tameless, frank and free,
> In friendship warm, and cool in danger known,
> Rough Nature's children, humorous as she.
> And he, great chieftain, strike the proudest tone
> Of thy bold harp, green Isle, the hero is thine own.[8]

Seldom do they murder for money, and in no country where oppression has ruled have the oppressed plundered and robbed so little as in
Ireland, yet they can plunder and rob; and these crimes are multiplying
and will multiply till a new state of things places them in a different condition.[9]

I was riding upon a coach in the second year of the Famine, in a lonely part of the west, when the coachman pointed me to a corner around the
wall, and remarked, 'When I passed this place to-day, a man lay dead
there who had been killed some hours before by one of the tenants living
upon the land here.' 'Why did he do the shocking deed?' I inquired. 'A
good deed, by dad,' was the answer. 'Why lady, he was the greatest
blackguard that ever walked the airth; he was agent to a gentleman, and
he showed no mercy to a poor man that was toilin' for the potato; but as
soon as the Famine was sore on the craturs, he drove every one into the
blake staurm that could not give the rent, and many's the poor bein' that
died with the starvation, without the shelter; and wouldn't ye think that
such a hard-hearted villain better be dead, than to live and kill so many

poor women and helpless children, as would be wanderin' in the black mountains this winter, if he should live to drive 'em there.' Now, this is certainly unChristian logic, but it is resentful nature's logic, and in accordance with all the principles of national killing. In vain I preached and held up a better principle: 'A great good had been done to all the parish, and all the parish should be glad that so many lives had been saved by this one which had been taken.'

It was night, and I felt a little relief when a policeman ascended the coach, who was going in quest of a coroner; a sad deed, he added, but the murdered man was hard-hearted, and no doubt that it was some of the tenants on the land of which he was agent who did the work, yet not one has escaped. 'And why', retorted the driver, 'should a hap'orth of 'em take up the heel; they have done a good deed, and if they're hung, it will be better than the starvation.' The policeman was silent, and I was not anxious to pursue the fruitless argument with one who saw no light, but through the medium of doing unto others as others do to him. And where this principle prevails, as it does in the hearts of *all* the unsanctified, the wonder is that so few have been the lawless deeds that have been transacted in that oppressed country for centuries gone by. The mischief is all laid at the door of the Papists; and when I speak of the Christianity of Ireland, I would do it with caution. I would not 'hurt the oil or the wine'; I would not 'judge nor set at naught my brother', but I would say deliberately and conscientiously, that if those who call themselves the only true light of that benighted land, the only safe lamps to guide to the heavenly country, were more careful to show mercy and walk humbly, they might long ago have seen a better state of things. Yes, had Bible men and Bible women possessed that love in *heart* which has been upon the *tongue*; had they manifested that tenderness for Christ, as they have for a party, a name, or a church; had they been as assiduous to win souls to Christ by love and kindness, as they have to gather in their tithes by law and violence, many who are now scoffing at a 'truth held in unrighteousness', might have been glorying in one producing holiness and peace. But I forbear: 'murder will out', wrong will be righted, however painful the process, and though judgment long delay, yet it must come at last. The wheel of Providence is ever rolling, and every spoke belonging to it must in turn be uppermost, and the oppressed cannot always be at the bottom.[10]

The object of this volume is to place before the world a plain and simple outline of what is called the *Famine of Ireland,* in 1846-7-8-9.

But before I take the reader down the sides of this dreadful gulf, before I uncover to him the *bowels* of that loathsome pit, on the margin of which he often may have tremblingly stood, I will gird up his mind for the conflict by taking him, in the autumn of 1845 and the spring of 1846, through the more fertile and happy north, where we are told that better management has produced better results. There we shall find mementos of deep interest, when, ages now passed away, this people stood out to surrounding nations not as a 'by-word and hissing', but as a noble example of religion, industry, and prosperity, which few if any could then present. And though its early history is quite obscured by fiction, and interlarded with poetical romance, yet all this serves to prove that the remains of a true coin are there, or a counterfeit would not have been attempted.

Not only in the north, but scattered over the whole island, are found inscriptions on stone, some standing above ground and others buried beneath, which, by their dates and hieroglyphics, tell you that centuries ago men lived here, whose memories were honored, not only for their valor in war, but for their purity of life. It was not till I had faithfully explored the interior and southern coast, that the early history of this people had been much studied, as my object *then* was to see them as they are found in the nineteenth century, without investigating *particularly* their age or pedigree. In my later excursions, facts so startled and convinced me that their pretensions to former prosperity and greatness were not fabulous, that I regretted for my supineness on the subject; for I found by well-authenticated history, that the common saying among the peasantry that Ireland was once 'a land of saints', was founded in more truth than her enemies or even *friends* are ready to acknowledge; and the belief is quite confirmed in my mind, that when searching for truth concerning a nation 'scattered and peeled', as the Irish have been, the true ore can better be found in the unpolished rubbish, in the traditions of a rude nation, retained from age to age, than among the polished gems of polite literature, written to please rather than instruct, and to pull down rather than build up.

It has never been my lot to meet with a straightforward, impartial, real matter-of-fact work written on that devoted country till since the Famine commenced. It has been suggested that an Irishman *could* not write an impartial book on his country, and an Englishman or Scotchman *would* not.

The last three years have abundantly proved that there are many Englishmen, who can not only *feel,* but *act* for that poor despised island, who would rejoice to see her rise, yes, who would and do take her by the hand, who not only *talk* but make sacrifices for her welfare; and let me record it with gratitude that posterity may read the efforts they have made and are still making to place this down-trodden people among the happiest nations of the earth. Gladly would I record, were the privilege allowed me, the names of those Quakers, those Dissenters of all denominations, and many of the Churchmen too, who have done much in the days of darkness for the starving poor of that land. Yes, let me record as a debt of gratitude *I* owe to England, the scenes I have witnessed, when some box of warm clothing was opened, when the naked, starving women and children would drop upon their knees, and clasp their emaciated fingers, and, with eyes raised to heaven, bless the Almighty God for the gift that the kind English or blessed Quaker had sent them; and while I was compelled to turn away from the touching view, my heart responded *Amen and Amen*. Let this suffice, that when in these future pages truths may be recorded that will not always be so salutary, yet be assured these truths are such as should be told, and they will not meet any cases mentioned in the above – in other language, they will not fit where they do not belong.

My position in regard to the condition and feeling of Ireland during the Famine, was different from all others. I must necessarily look at things with different eyes, and different sensations from what others could do. I was a foreigner, could not *expect*, and did not *ask*, any reward either in praise or money for the interest I might take in that country. I was attached to England, as the race from which I descended, and pitied Ireland for her sufferings, rather than I admired her for any virtues which she might possess. Consequently, my mind was so balanced between the two, that on which side the scale might have preponderated, the danger of blind partiality would not have been so great.[11]

Besides, the country had previously been traversed, the habits and propensities of the cabiners been studied, they had been taken by surprise when no opportunity was given for escape or deception. I was always an unexpected guest, and gave them no time to brush up their cabins, or put on their shoes, if happily they might have any. When the Famine came over them, they were placed in a different position to draw out their feelings toward others, and the pangs of hunger induced them necessarily to act unreservedly; all party feeling was lost, and whoever gave them bread was the object to which they most closely hung, and to those who rudely sent them empty away, the answer was often made, 'May the blessed God never give ye to feel the hunger'.

And here it must be written that, though *some* might be ungrateful, yet such were the *exceptions*; as a people they are grateful, and patient to a proverb. Not a murmuring word against God or man did I once hear among all the dying, in those dreadful days, and the children were taught by parents and teachers to fall on their knees morning and evening, to pray to Almighty God to 'bless their kind benefactors and keep them from the hunger', and many have died with these prayers on their lips. I must not enlarge: these things are not mentioned to probe afresh the painful sensations which philanthropists have felt for Ireland, but to bear a testimony to facts which deserve to be recorded. And should any of these facts appear exaggerated, let it be said that no language is adequate to give the *true*, the *real picture*. One look of the eye into the daily scenes there witnessed would overpower what any pen, however graphic, or tongue, however eloquent, could portray.

As my eye was single to one object, as I have ever peculiarly felt that I was acting for eternity, in acting for Ireland, the candor I use must be forgiven, and the pronoun *I* can make no other apology but sheer necessity, as no *we* had a part in anything essential which will be recorded in these pages.

When the hand that pens these pages, and the heart that has been lacerated at these sufferings, shall have ceased together, may Ireland and her benefactors 'live before God'.

CHAPTER II

'Afar we stand, a gloomy band,
Our worth, our wants neglected,
The children in their fatherland
Cut off, despised, rejected.'

Allow me to say to the reader that the cup I now hold in my hand is a 'cup of trembling', and gladly would my sickening heart turn away from its contents, 'but "for this cause was I sent" and the cup which my Father has given me shall I not drink it?'[1] Yes, *for this cause was I sent*, for *this cause*, in the face of all that was thought consistency or prudence, *unprotected* by mortal arm or encouraged by mortal support, was I bidden to go out and to go 'nothing *doubting*' into a strange land, and there do what I should be bidden, not knowing what that might be nor inquiring wherefore the work were laid upon me.

I came, the island was traversed, stormy days and dark nights, filthy cabins and uncomfortable lodging-houses were my lot, evil surmises from the proud professor, and the cold neglect of many, were all alike to me. The 'tower' into which I ran was always safe and always open, the 'rock' under which I sheltered was indeed 'higher than I', and the tempest passed harmlessly by.

From June 1844 to December 1846, though I could say with the disciples returning from Emmaus that 'my heart burned within me', yet with them I must add, my 'eyes were holden', that I had not *yet* seen the *ultimate* object nor had the slightest curiosity been awakened as to the result of the researches which had been made, who would understand or *misunderstand*, who would approve or *condemn*.[2] Ireland's pride and Ireland's humility, her wealth and her poverty, her beauty and deformity, had all been tested in a degree, and the causes of her poverty stood out in such bold relief that no *special* revelation, either human or divine, was requisite to give a solution.

'Will not God be avenged on such a nation as this?' was the constant question urging me, and the echo is still sounding as the mighty wave is now rolling over the proud ones who have 'held the poor in derision', and the only answer is, 'What will ye do in the end thereof?' What avails the multiplicity of prayers while the poor are oppressed? The surplice, the gown or the robe will not hide the stain; the 'leprosy lies deep within. For all this his anger is not turned away, but his hand is stretched out still'.

Too long have ye 'dwelt in your ceiled houses', while the poor, who have 'reaped down your fields for naught', have been sitting in their floorless, smoky cabins, on the scanty patch where they have been allowed to crouch till your authority should bid them depart, to eat their potato on some bog or ditch elsewhere. And more fearful than all, *now* that the root on which you have fed them for centuries is taken away, famished and naked you drive them into the pitiless storm. Ye withhold from them labour, and then call them 'idle'; ye give them work without any just equivalent, and then cry out when the scanty food is blasted, '*Improvidence, Improvidence!*' – that had these 'idlers' put by anything for a 'rainy day', they might have had money to have bought bread! That idleness and improvidence (which are generally companions) are two great evils of Ireland, must be acknowledged. The rich are idle from a silly pride and long habits of indulgence; and the poor, because no man 'hires them'.

'Would you have us work,' said a shopkeeper's wife, 'when we can get scores of girls, glad to do it, for 10s. a quarter?' Here is one of the sources of evil: 'the ways of the household', which are specially allotted to the 'prudent wife', are made over to the uninterested servant; because this poor servant was 'glad' to work for a little more than nothing. The keys of the house are peculiarly the care of the mistress, and with these well pocketed she prevents all inroads into her larder, and the servant may eat her potato at option, for in but few families is she allowed bread and butter or tea. This keeping everything locked, we are told, is to keep servants from theft – the surest method of making them thieves. Their late hours of rising and of meals necessarily unhinge all that is good in housekeeping; and where all is left to servants, economy *must* come in by-the-by.

The middle class, such as shopkeepers, good farmers and tradesmen of all kinds, live on a few articles of diet, and the mistress seldom taxes her ingenuity to apply the useful proverb, 'To make one thing meet another'. Bread, butter, tea and an egg are the ultimatum of a breakfast at nine and often ten in the morning; then a yawning about, or perhaps a little fancy knitting till lunch, which is a piece of cold meat and bread, and in the higher classes' wine; a dinner from four to six, and tea often brought on before leaving the table, or in an hour after. The dinner is, among farmers and tradesmen, mostly pork, put upon a platter with cabbage, and potatoes served in two ways: first, brought on in the jackets, as they are boiled; next dish, which is the dessert in most houses, the potatoes are browned upon a griddle which gives them a good flavor. Bread is seldom or never taken with potatoes, and a pudding is rarely seen, except on special occasions. Pies are often made; but these are the chief commodities, and always ended by 'hot whiskey punch'. This accompaniment is so necessary, that in genteel families a handsome copper kettle is kept for the special purpose, which is put upon a frame in the centre of a table. The 'lower order' only are teetotalers, because, as the reason is often given, 'it was necessary for them, they were so ignorant and vulgar'.

Now what, must it be expected, could the daughters of such a family be? Why, the *exact copy of the mother*; the servant must do for her what would be for her own health, and what is actually her duty to perform. She is sent to school, and goes the routine of a genteel education. She can work Berlin wool, perhaps read French, and possibly German, play the piano, and write a commonplace letter, in *angular* writing, made *on purpose* for the ladies; but with all this her mind is not *cultivated*, her heart is not *disciplined*. She looks pretty, walks genteelly and talks sometimes quite enchantingly; but with all these appurtenances, the inquiry *must* and *does* arise – 'What are you good for?' The little, *common, necessary* daily duties which belong to woman are unheeded; and when any exigencies fall upon her she has no alternative. A mind always accustomed to the same routine, and that a *frivolous* one, cannot, when unexpected adversity comes, plunge into new difficult duties and perform them efficiently. If she had always had a dressmaker to fit her apparel and a waiting-maid to put it on, how can she, should her husband become a bankrupt, be qualified to make and repair the garments for herself and children, which probably she *must* do, or her children be in a very untidy state.

Now, as trifling as these things appear to many, yet Ireland has suffered, and is still doomed to suffer deeply, on these accounts. Many of these genteel ones are reduced to the last extremity, the mistresses not being able to give even the 10s. per quarter to a servant. She knows not how *economically* to prepare the scanty food which her husband may provide; and multitudes of this class are either in the walls of the union or hovering about its precincts.

When the Famine had actually *come*, and all the country was aghast, when supplies from all parts were poured in – what was done with these supplies? Why, the *best* that these inefficient housekeepers *could* do. The rice and Indian meal, both of which are *excellent* articles of food, were cooked in such a manner that, in most cases, they were actually unhealthy, and in *all* cases unpalatable.[3] So unused were they to the use of that common article, rice, that they steeped it the night before, then poured the water off, without rubbing, and for three and four hours they boiled, stirred, and simmered this, till it became a watery jelly, disgusting to the eye and unsavoury to the taste, for they never salted it; besides unwholesome for the stomachs of those who had always used a dry pota-to for food. The poor complained that it made them sick; they were accused of being ungrateful, and sometimes told they should not have any more; and the difficulty, if possible, was increased by giving it out uncooked – for the starving ones in the towns had no fuel and they could not keep up a fire to stew it for hours, and many of them ate it raw, which was certainly better, when they had good teeth, than cooked in this un-savoury way.

But the Indian meal! Who shall attempt a description of this frightful formidable? When it first landed, the rich, who had no occasion for using it, hailed it with joy, and some actually condescended to say they beli-eved they could eat it *themselves*. But the poor, who had not yet slid down the precipice so far as to feel that they were actually dying, could be heard on the streets, and in the market-place, interrogate one another: 'And have ye seen the yaller Indian, God save us awl? By dad and "Peel's brimstone" has come over again, to scrape the maw of every divil on us.'[4]

The reader must be content to take the Famine just as I saw it; and though the language may be sometimes startling, to refine it by any sub-stitution or seasoning of my own invention would be weakening its force, and oftentimes frittering away the truth. In justice it should be said that they often use the word devil in a quite different meaning from how others do, always applying it to a poor neglected creature, however deserving he may be, as well as to those who are wicked. Thus they would often say, 'The breath is cowld in the poor divil's body, he'll no more feel the hunger, God bless him!' And the yaller Indian was called by all manner of epithets, and went through all manner of ordeals but the right one. The Indian meal by some was stirred in cold water with a stick, then put quite dry upon a griddle, it consequently crumbled apart, there was no turning it; and one desponding woman came to me saying that the last bit of turf had died on her, and 'not a ha'porth of the yaller Indian would stop with its comrade'. Others make what they call 'stirabout'. This was done, too, by first steeping in cold water, then pouring it into a pot, and immediately after swelling it became so thick that it could not be stirred, neither would it cook in the least. The 'stirabout' then became a 'standabout', and the effect of eating this was all but favourable to those who had seldom taken farinaceous food. They were actually afraid to take it in many cases, the *government* meal in particular, fearing the 'Inglish intinded' to kill them with the 'tarin' and scrapin'' but when hunger had progressed a little these fears subsided, and they cared nei-ther what they ate or who sent it to them.

Had the women of the higher classes known how to prepare these articles in a proper manner, much money might have been saved and many lives rescued, which are now lost.

When the first clamour had a little subsided, there followed the recipes for cooking Indian meal. One of these, highly celebrated for a while, was from Italy, and called 'Polentia'. Whether spelt correctly the learned must decide, but this same Polentia would do for gentlemen and ladies too.[5] The recipe cannot precisely be given, but enough to know that it was turned and overturned, covered and uncovered, boiled and steamed in a pot and then came out genteelly, in a becoming shape, according to the form of the pot used. Now this was often on the tables of the gentry, for the recipe and meal were from Italy; the poor would only hear of this at a distance – the cooking they could never attain. Next came American recipes. These, with all due credence, were accepted as the one thing needful, for they possessed these redeeming qualities: first, they were from America, the land which they loved for many of their 'kin' were there; next, that though they thought that nobody but negroes ate it – yet negroes *lived* on that food and 'sure the Americans wouldn't hurt em'.

These recipes were prepared in due form, and made up with suets, fats, sweets and spices, so that the Laird John Russell himself could 'ate 'em'. A great and grand meeting of lords and nobility was held, called by the poor 'the yaller Indin maitin', and a *bona fide* sanction put on to the Indian meal cake. Here again was a difficulty – the meal was for the hungry. Where could they procure spices, sweets and fats for such delicacies? And as they thought that these were necessary to make it safe to eat, then their fears were awakened anew. But a few weeks adjusted all these difficulties, for when the number of the slain had increased in every parish, all murmuring at the quality of the food ceased – they suffered in uncomplaining silence.

It was on the evening of December 7, 1846, when about stepping into the train at Kingstown for Dublin, I heard a policeman relating to a bystander a case of famine at the south.[6] The potato, I knew, was partly destroyed, but never thought that actual famine would be the result. The facts were so appalling that had they not come from a policeman, who, it should be said, are in general men of veracity, my mind would have doubted; and when he added that 'I got this information from a friend who was present in the court, and who wrote the circumstances to me', all queries were removed.

A man had died from hunger, and his widow had gone into the plowed field of her landlord to try to pick a few potatoes in the ridges which might be remaining since the harvest; she found a few – the landlord saw her, sent a magistrate to the cabin, who found three children in a state of starvation and nothing in the cabin but the pot, which was over the fire. He demanded of her to show him the potatoes. She hesitated; he inquired what she had in the pot – she was silent; he looked in, and saw a dog, with the handful of potatoes she had gathered from the field. The sight of the wretched cabin, and still more the despairing looks of the poor silent mother and the famished children, crouched in fear in a dark corner, so touched the heart of the magistrate that he took the pot from the fire, bade the woman to follow him, and they went to the court-room together. He presented the pot, containing the dog and the handful of potatoes, to the astonished judge. He called the woman – interrogated her kindly. She told him they sat in their desolate cabin two entire days, without eating before she killed the half-famished dog; that she did not think she was stealing to glean after the harvest was gathered. The judge gave her three pounds from his own purse; told her when she had used that to come again to him.

This was a compassionate judge, and would to God Ireland could boast of many such.

I heard that story, heart-rending as it was, and soon found that it was but a prelude to facts of daily, yes, hourly occurrence, still more appalling. The work of death now commenced; the volcano, over which I felt that Ireland was walking had burst, though its appearance was wholly different from anything I had ever conceived. A famine was always in Ireland in a certain degree, and so common were beggars, and so many were always but just struggling for life, that not until thousands were reduced to the like condition of the woman last mentioned did those who had never begged, make their wants known.[7] They picked over and picked out their blackened potatoes, and even ate the decayed ones, till many were made sick, before the real state of the country was known; and when it fell, it fell like an avalanche, sweeping at once the entire land. No parish need be anxious for neighboring ones – each had enough under his own eye and at his own door to drain all resources and keep alive his sympathy. It was some months before the rich really believed that the poor were not making false pretenses; for at such a distance had they ever kept themselves from the 'lower order', who were all 'dirty and lazy', that many of them had never realized that four millions of people were subsisting entirely on the potato, and that another million ate them six days out of seven entirely; they did not realize that these 'lazy ones' had worked six or eight months in the year for eight pence and ten pence, but more for sixpence, and even threepence in the southern parts, and the other four months been 'idle' because 'no man had hired them'. They did not realize that the disgusting rags with which these 'lazy' ones disgraced their very gates, and shocked all decency were the rags which they had contributed to provide; and such were often heard to say that this judgment was what they might expect, as a reward of their 'religion and idleness'.[8] But the wave rolled on; the slain were multiplied; the dead by the way-side, and the more revolting sights of families found in the darkest corner of a cabin in one putrid mass, where, in many cases, the cabin was tumbled down upon them to give them a burial, was somewhat convincing, even to those who had doubted much from the beginning.

There were some peculiarities in this Famine which history has not recorded in any other. It may be scrupled whether any were heard to say that they did not deserve it – that they had not been such sinners above all others, that they must suffer so much – and so little plundering was never known in any famine as this; scarcely ever was a bread-shop disturbed, though the poor creatures have been found dead under its window in sight of it; the old proverb that 'hunger will break through a stone wall' was never exemplified during the Famine. Some carts laden with meal have been pillaged, and some boats have been robbed, but these were not common occurrences; occasionally, in the cities, would a man throw a stone at a street lamp, or do some other trifling mischief, always in presence of a policeman, that he might be put in jail where the law must feed him. This was certainly an alternative for a starving man not so much to be censured as admired. Let it be stated that these men had applied for work in vain.[9] I will descend to particulars and state what my eyes have seen and my ears have heard, and be answerable for whatever statements are thus made.

The first starving person that I saw was a few days after the story of the woman and dog had been related. A servant in the house where I was stopping at Kingstown said that the milk woman wished me to see a man near by that was in a state of actual starvation; and he was going out to attempt to work on the Queen's highway. A little labour was beginning opposite the house, and fifteen-pence a day stimulated this poor man, who had seven to support, his rent to pay, and fuel to buy.[10] He had been sick with fever; the clothes of his family that would fetch any price had been pawned or sold, and all were starving together. He staggered with his spade to the work; the overseer objected; but he entreated to be allowed to try. The servant went out and asked him to step into the kitchen; and, reader, if you have never seen a starving human being, *may you never!* In my childhood I had been frightened with the stories of ghosts, and had seen actual skeletons, but imagination had come short of the sight of this man. And here, to those who have never watched the progress of protracted hunger, it might be proper to say that persons will live for months, and pass through different stages, and life will struggle on to maintain her lawful hold, if occasional scanty supplies are given, till the walking skeleton is reduced to a state of inanity – he sees you not, he heeds you not, neither does he beg.[11] The first stage is somewhat clamorous – will not easily be put off; the next is patient, passive stupidity; and the last is idiocy. In the second stage they will stand at a window for hours without asking charity, giving a vacant stare, and not until peremptorily driven away will they move. In the last stage the head bends forward and they walk with long strides and pass you unheedingly.

The man before mentioned was emaciated to the last degree; he was tall, his eyes prominent, his skin shrivelled, his manner cringing and childlike; and the impression *then* and *there* made never *has* nor never *can* be effaced; it was the *first,* and the beginning of these dreadful days yet in reserve. He had a breakfast, and was told to come in at four and get his dinner. The family were from home; the servant had an Irish heart, consequently my endeavours were all seconded. Often has she taken the loaf allowed for her board-wages (that is, so much allowed weekly for food), and sliced nearly the whole away – denying herself for the suffering around her. It must be mentioned that labourers for the public, on roads, seldom or never ate more than twice a day, at ten and four; their food was the potato and oatmeal stirabout, and buttermilk, the luxury which was seldom enjoyed. This man was fed on Indian meal, gruel, buttermilk or new milk and bread in the morning; stirabout, buttermilk and bread at four.

Workmen are not paid at night on the public works, they must wait a week; and if they commence labour in a state of hunger they often die before the week expires; many have been carried home to their wretched cabins, some dead and others dying, who had fallen down with the spade in their hands. The next day after this wretched man was fed, another, in like condition, at work in the same place, was called in and fed; he afterward died when the labour was finished, and he could get no more work. The first man gradually gained strength, and all for him was encouraging, when my purse became low – so many had been fed at the door that a pot was kept continually boiling from seven in the morning till seven at night. Indian meal was then dear, the Americans had not sent their supplies, and much did my heart shrink at the thought that my means must be exhausted.

Let me here speak of the virtues of Indian meal; though always having been accustomed to it, more or less, not till December 1846, in the Famine of Ireland did I know its value. It was made into gruel, boiled till it became a jelly; and once a day from twenty-five to thirty were fed – some who walked miles to get it, and every one who had this privilege recovered without tasting anything but that, once a day. They always took it till they wanted no more; and this too without bread. One old man daily walked three miles, on his staff for this and he grew cheerful; always most courteously thanking me, saying, 'It nourishes my old heart, so that it keeps me warm all the night.'

I had told these two labourers that when they found the gate locked they must know that I had no more to give them and they must go home. The sad hour arrived; the overseer sent me word that he thanked me for feeding them so long; they must otherwise have died at their work. The gate was shut, and long and tedious were the next two days. One child of the poor man died, and he buried it in the morning before light because if he took an hour from labour he would be dismissed. When the poor creatures that had daily been fed with the gruel came and were told there was no more for them, I felt that I had sealed their doom. They turned away, blessing me again and again, but 'we must die of the hunger, God be praised'.

I would not say that I actually murmured, but the question did arise: 'Why was I brought to see a famine, and be the humble instrument of saving some few alive, and then see these few die, because I had no more to give them?'

Two days and nights dragged on. News was constantly arriving of the fearful state of the people, and the spectres that had been before my eyes constantly haunted me. My bedroom overlooked the burying ground.[12] I could fancy, as I often arose to look into it, that some haggard father was bringing a dead child lashed to his back, and laying him on some tombstone, as had been done, and leaving it to the mercy of whoever might find it a grave!

I was sitting in solitude, alone, at eleven o'clock, when the man of the house unexpectedly arrived. He had a parcel; in that parcel there was money from New York, and that money was for me!

No being, either Christian or pagan, if he never saw a famine, nor possesses a feeling heart, can understand what I then felt. I adored that watchful Hand that had so strangely led and upheld me in Ireland; and now, above all and over all, when my heart was sinking in the deepest despondency, when no way of escape appeared, this heavenly boon was sent! The night was spent in adoration and praise, longing for the day, when I might again hang over the 'blessed pot', as the Irish called it. I lay below on a sofa and saw no tombstones that night.

The morning came – the pot was over the fire. As soon as shops were opened, meal, bread and milk were purchased. The man of the house went early to his business in Dublin.[13] The gate was unlocked – the breakfast was prepared. The quantity was well-nigh doubled, though enough had always been provided before. The sight of the man was more than I wished to abide; he was again sinking – had taken nothing but a 'sup', as he termed it, of some meagre slop but once in the day, because his children would all die if he took it from them. The other soon followed, and while they were taking their breakfast I was reading from New York the result of a meeting there in behalf of the Irish.[14] This awakened gratitude toward my country unknown before; and now, should I not be unmindful of the Hand that had led me through this wilderness thus far, and in every emergency carried me almost miraculously through, if what I am about to record of the few following months, so far as self is concerned, should be withheld?

That day my mind was most active, devising how the greatest good might be effected by the little which God had intrusted to me. Indian meal, when cooked in a suitable manner, was now becoming a great favourite; this I knew how to do, and determined to use the money for this object, always cooking it myself. When this was adjusted in my mind, the remainder of the day was devoted to writing letters to America, mostly for the two objects of thanking them for what they had done and giving them, from eye-witness, a little account of the Famine. In this, the desire and even the thought was entirely withheld of receiving anything myself to give; acting entirely as a passive instrument; moving, because moved upon. Here, afterward, was the wisdom of Him who sees not as man seeth, peculiarly manifest; for had I that day, by the parcel put into my hands from New York, been in possession of a hundred pounds, the day would have been spent in going into the cabins of the starving, and distributing to the needy – the money would have soon been expended, and then no more means would have been in my power to do good.[15] But my weakness was God's strength, my poverty His riches; and as He had shown me, all the journey through, that my dependence should be entirely on Him, so now, more than ever, it was to be made manifest. The letters crossed the ocean, found the way to the hands and hearts of those to whom they were sent, and, when in the multitude of other thoughts and cares they were by the writer forgotten as a past dream, they were returned, embodied in a printed parcel, accompanied with donations of meal, money and clothing; and this, like the other, reached me when all means were exhausted.

When the rumour of a famine had become authenticated in Dublin, Joseph Bewley, a Friend, possessing both a warm heart and full purse (which do not always go together), put in operation a soup-shop which fed many hundreds twice a day.[16] This soup was of the best quality, the best meat, peas, oatmeal, &c.; and when applications became so numerous that a greater supply was requisite and funds failing, mention was made to this benevolent man that the quantity of meat must be reduced, his answer was that not one iota should be taken off, but more added, if even it must be done entirely at his own expense.[17] It shall, he added, be made rich and nourishing as well as palatable. The poor who could, were required to pay half-price for a ticket; and benevolent people purchased tickets by the quantity, and gave to the poor. The regulation of this soup establishment was a pattern worthy of imitation. The neatness and order of the shop; the comely attired Quaker matrons and their daughters, with their white sleeves drawn over their tidy-clad arms, their white aprons and caps, all moving in that quiet harmony so peculiar to that people; and there, too, at seven in the morning, and again at midday.[18] All this beauty and finish contrasted with the woe-begone, emaciated, filthy, ragged beings that stood in their turn before them, was a sight at which angels, if they could weep, might weep, and might rejoice too.[19] Often have I stood, in painful admiration, to see the two extremes of degradation and elevation, comfort and misery, cleanliness and filth, in these two classes made alike in God's image, but thrown into different circumstances developing two such wide and strange opposites.

My task was a different one – operating individually. I took my own time and way – as woman is wont to do when at her own option; and before the supplies, which afterward came through the letters mentioned I marked out a path which was pursued during that winter until July when I left for the North.[20] A basket of good dimensions was provided sufficient to contain three loaves of the largest made bread; this was cut in slices, and at eight o'clock I set off. The poor had watched the 'American lady' and were always on the spot, ready for an attack, when I went out; and the most efficient method of stopping their importunities was bread.[21] No sooner well upon the street, than the army commenced rallying; and no one, perhaps, that winter, was so regularly guarded as was this basket and its owner. A slice was given to each till it was all exhausted; while in desperation, at times, lest I might be overpowered – not by violence, but by number – I hurried on, sometimes actually running to my place of destination, the hungry ones, men, women, and children who had not received the slice in pursuit till I rushed into some shop-door or house, for protection, till the troop should retire; sometimes the stay would be long and tedious, and ofttimes they must be driven back by force.

Cook street, a place devoted almost entirely to making coffins and well known by the name of Coffin street, was the field of my winter's labour.[22] This was chosen for its extreme poverty, being the seat of misery refined; and here no lady of 'delicate foot' would like to venture; and beside, I saw that a little thrown over a wide surface was throwing all away, and no benefit that was lasting would ensue. Ten pounds divided among a hundred, would not keep one from starvation many days; but applied to twenty, economically, might save those twenty till more effi-cient means might be taken. So much a day was allowed to each family, according to their number – always cooking it myself in their cabins till they could and did do it prudently themselves. The turf was provided and the rent paid weekly, which must be done, or, in many cases, turning upon the street was the consequence. For it is no more than justice to observe that there are some kind slaveholders in the United States, and there are some kind landlords in Ireland, but in too many cases both are synonymous terms, so far as power may be equal.

One of these miserable families was that of a widow. I found her creeping upon the street one cold night, when snow was upon the ground. Her pitiful posture, bent over, leaning upon two sticks, with a lit-tle boy and girl behind her crying with the cold, induced me to inquire, and I found that she was actually lame, her legs much swollen, and her story proved to be a true one. She had been turned from the hospital as a hopeless case, and a poor, sick, starving friend had taken her in, and she had crawled out with a few boxes of matches to see if she could sell them, for she told me she could not yet bring herself to beg. She could work, and was willing to, could she get knitting or sewing. I inquired her number. 'I will not deny it again,' she replied. 'I did so to a lady, soon after I came out of the hospital, for I was ashamed to be found in such a dreadful place by a lady; but I have been so punished for that lie, that I will not do it again.' Giving her a few pence, and meaning to take her by surprise if I found her at all, an indirect promise was made to call at some future day. At ten the next morning my way was made into that fearful street, and still more fearful alley which led to the cheerless abode I entered.

The reader may be informed that in the wealthy, beautiful city of Dublin, which can boast some of the finest architecture on earth, there are in retired streets and dark alleys some of the most forbidding, most uncomfortable abodes that can be found in the wildest bogs of that wretched country.[23] Finding my way through darkness and filth, a sight opened upon me, which, speaking moderately, was startling. When I had recovered a little, I saw on my right hand the miserable woman before-named, sitting in a dark corner on a little damp straw, which poorly defended her from the wet and muddy ground-floor she was occupying. The two ragged, hungry children were at her feet; on the other side of the empty grate (for there was not a spark of fire) sat the kind woman who had taken her in, on the same foundation of straw and mud, with her back against the wall. She was without a dress – she had pawned her last to pay her rent; her husband likewise had pawned his coat for the same pur-pose. He was lying upon the straw, with a fragment of a cotton shawl about him, for he had no shirt. They were all silent, and for a while I was a mute.

The woman first mentioned broke the pause, by saying, 'This, I believe, is the kind lady I met last night. You have found the way to our dark place, and I am sorry we cannot ask you to sit down.' There was not even a stool in the room. The young woman had been sick for weeks, and was now only able to sit up a little; but having neither food, fuel or covering, nothing but death stared them in the face; and the most affecting part of the whole to me was the simple statement of the widow who said, in the most resigned manner, 'We have been talking, Mary and I, this morning, and counting off our days; we could not expect any relief, for I could not go out again, and she could not, and the farthest that the good God will give us on earth cannot be more than fourteen days. The children, may be,' she added, 'God would let her take with her, for they must soon starve if left.' This had been a cool calculation made from the appearance of the present condition, and without the least murmuring they were bringing their minds to their circumstances. 'You are willing to live longer,' I said. 'If the good God wills it,' was the answer, 'but we cannot see how.'

They did live. Daily did I go and cook their food, or see it cooked, and daily did they improve; and in a few weeks many an apronful of shavings and blocks were brought to me from the coffin-shops by the young woman who was sitting almost naked on the straw. They both were good expert knitters and good seamstresses; and my garments, which were approaching to a sisterhood with many of the going-down genteel ones, were soon put in tidy repair by this young woman. Often, late in the evening, would I hear a soft footstep on the stairs, followed by a gentle tap, and the unassuming Mary would enter with her bountiful supply of fire-kindling; and when she was told that less would do very well, and she should keep more for herself, she replied, 'I can do with little, and you would not like to go to the shop for any.' She watched my wardrobe, kept everything in the best repair, and studied my comfort first, before she seemed to know that she needed any. I had saved her life, she said, and that was more than all she could do for me; and the day that I sailed from Dublin for England, as I was hurrying along the street, someone caught me by my dress, and turning about, Mary stood before me, whom I had not seen for months, having been absent in the mountains.[24] She had a basket on her arm, was comfortably clad, said she was selling fruit and vegetables and doing well; the other was still with her, in ill health, but not suffering for food. 'Farewell, Mary, we shall meet no more on earth; may God fit us both for a better world!' 'Shall I never see you again? God be praised that he sent you to us!'

The man whom I found on the highway at Kingstown, having heard that I was going from Ireland, walked seven Irish miles that day to see and thank me, and leave his blessing. I was out and regretted much, for his sake as well as mine, that he was disappointed. These testimonials were more grateful to me than would have been a donation of plate from the government. They were God's testimonials – the offerings of the poor; and that heart is not to be envied that does not know their blessings.

Another feeble dying woman I found upon the street one rainy day, who had reached a state of half idiocy, and for two years was fed and partly clothed, whether I was in Dublin or not; and though she had a tolerable supply of food, her mind never rallied; yet she always knew and acknowledged, even to a weakness, her benefactress.[25] She never has yet been made in the least to rely on herself; what she is bidden to do is done like a child, and then she is satisfied.

These few cases are given as specimens, not wishing to be tedious with such narrations, only to show the character of the Famine and its effects in general on the sufferers with whom I was conversant. The distribution of the bread in the street was continued, not even Sabbaths excepted; my basket was often taken near the chapel door, and left in some house till I came out. So pressing at last was the crowd, that I dare not go into a shop to take out my purse to buy the most trifling article, and a bread-shop above all was avoided. There was no fear of violence, but the dreadful importuning, falling upon their knees, clasping their emaciated hands, and their glaring eyes fixed upon me, were quite too much. Sometimes I endeavoured to steal into a shop in the evening unperceived, but never succeeded. Hunger, in its incipient stages, never sleeps, never neglects its watch, but continues sharpening the inventive faculties, till, like the drunkard's thirst, intrigue and dissimulation give startling proof of the varied materials which compose the entire man.

From the first look that was presented me by the starving man in Kingstown a common desire for food never returned, so that through the winter but little was necessary for my wants. Twopence halfpenny worth of cocoa for a week, threepence halfpenny for milk, threepence for sugar, and fourteenpence for bread; making in all twenty-threepence, was the most ever used; but in a few weeks necessity compelled a reducing of the expense, from which not the least inconvenience was felt. My practice was to pay the mistress for lodgings weekly, in advance, that she might feel no uneasiness; and after doing this one Monday morning my purse promptly told me that Saturday night would leave my poor pensioners, one in particular, without a shelter, if the usual quantity of food were taken.[26]

Something must be done: money was exhausted, and from no human source could I that week look for more. In a paper I had a pound of Indian meal – the cocoa, milk and sugar were stopped, and the meal made into gruel, twenty-three pence was reduced to fourteen; and when the meal was expended a penny roll was taken into my muff as the day's excursion commenced, and eaten when and where opportunity best presented and inclination most strongly prompted. The widow's rent was paid, no inconvenience felt, and before the next demand was made, an unexpected call for a few books which I had published in Scotland put me in possession of a little more, so that the cruise of oil never failed.[27] The pensioners were fed in the meantime from their own industry, for the women had been provided with knitting, which though poorly paid yet kept them from actual hunger. Another expedient I never omitted when available.

The people of Dublin, among the comfortable classes, whatever hospitality they might manifest toward guests and visitors, had never troubled themselves by looking into the real home wants of the suffering poor.[28] Enough they thought that societies of all kinds abounded, and a poor-house besides, were claims upon their purses to a full equivalent for all their consciences required, and to visit them was quite unlady-like if not dangerous. To many of these I had access as a matter of curiosity to hear from me the tales of starvation, which they were now to have dealt out unsparingly; and so kind were the most of them that the interview generally ended by an invitation to eat, which was never refused when needed, and the meal thus saved was always given to the hungry. These people would not have given a shilling in money, but many and many a meal of gruel was provided from these haphazard lunches through that sad winter; and, more than this, a kind woman who is now in her grave, and with whom I had once lodged, gave me an invitation, which was to continue during my labours in Dublin, of coming to dine with her every Sabbath; and then a bountiful, well-cooked dinner of vegetables and a pudding were always provided.[29] These kind Sabbath dinners were all I tasted that winter; two meals a day for the other six made me quite satisfied. Something better was now in reserve.

The Central Committee of the Society of Friends, which was organized in November 1846, had effectually and untiringly begun and carried on one of the most extensive and noble plans that probably had ever been known under any circumstances of distress by private individuals. And their first circular should be stereotyped and kept that future generations may read.[30] One or two sentences only are here recorded, as specimens of the spirit which moved this faithful body of men:

Many of us partake largely in the Lord's outward gifts; and it is surely incumbent on us to be prompt in manifesting our sense of His unmerited bounty, by offices of Christian kindness to our suffering fellow-creatures. May we prove ourselves faithful stewards of the substance intrusted to us.

Let none presume to think that the summons to deep and serious thoughtfulness, and to a close searching of heart, does not extend to him. Which of us has ever experienced what it is to want food? May none of our hearts be lifted up by these things, or betrayed into forgetfulness of our dependent condition, and of our utter unworthiness of the least of the Lord's mercies; for surely to each of us belongs the humbling inquiry, Who maketh thee to differ from another, and what hast thou that thou didst not receive?

Other committees soon co-operated with this; Waterford, Limerick, Cork, Youghal, &c., were moved to like exertions.[31] Nor did these exertions rest on the British side of the Atlantic.

In March 1847, an extract from the Central Relief Committee's [correspondence] says: 'In consequence of a letter addressed by Jacob Harvey of New York, to Thomas P. Cope, a meeting was held in Mulberry Street House, committees appointed to make collections, &c;' and what was the result?[32] The report says: 'Considering the short time which had elapsed at the period of our latest accounts, since sufficient information of the distress of Ireland had reached the American public; that from the great extent of the mission no opportunity had then been afforded for the full development of public feeling; that the supplies of money and food already received and on the way, are but the first fruits of their liberality, the movement must be regarded as one of the most remarkable manifestations of national sympathy on record.' And in another report, after two years and a half labour, this same Committee say that, referring to their circular, 'it was responded to, not merely by those to whom it was addressed; but by many unconnected with our religious societies in these countries, and also by the citizens of the United States, to an extent and with a munificence unparalleled in the history of benevolent exertions.[33] The contributions confided to us, in money, food, and clothing, amounted to about £200,000, of which more than half was sent from America.' The Committee added, that 'the contributions intrusted to them were but a small proportion of the whole expenditure for the relief of the country'.

America sent much money and many ship-loads of provisions, which did not pass through the hands of this committee. The British Relief Association dispensed about £400,000.[34] The distribution by other relief associations may be estimated at fully £200,000, and the collections by local committees in Ireland exceeded £300,000. The aggregate of the whole, taking remittances from emigrants, private benevolence, &c., was not less than one million and a half sterling. Government relief, ten millions sterling.

To return to individual exertion. The New York people opened a fund, appointed a Treasurer, and devoted the avails to me to be used at my discretion; and sent these donations, at first, through the channel of the Central Committee in Dublin.[35] This favour to me was more than can be described or imagined by any who never witnessed what I had, and who had never been placed in the same condition to act. I now ascended an eminence which was a lofty one; and on which I hope I may never again stand – such a mission, however honorable it may be to be able to rescue our fellow-creatures from death, has an unnatural cause for its claim; and when famine is allowed to progress till the slain are multiplied, it says one of two things: First, that the promise of a 'seed-time and harvest' did not embrace a sufficiency of food for every mouth in the world; or else that man has not done his duty in securing that food. Now God never deals vaguely with man, His promises are clear and definite, His demands rational and peremptory – 'Do this and live; neglect it, and die'. When He said 'seed-time and harvest', He said, by that, food shall always be sufficient for man: and never was a famine on earth, in any part, when there was not an abundance in some part to make up all the deficiency; and if man is not warned by some dreamer, like Pharaoh, of a seven years' famine, to secure a wise Joseph, to provide in advance for a seven years' destitution; yet if he is a wise husbandman, a good steward, a discerner of the signs of the times – when the skies drop down 'extra fatness', and the harvests are doubly laden with rich fruit, he hesitates not in believing that tithes and offerings will be called for somewhere, into the storehouse of the Lord, proportionable to the seventh day's manna that was rained from the heavens, to be gathered on the sixth.[36]

Thus Ireland's Famine was a marked one, so far as man was concerned; and God is slandered when it is called an unavoidable dispensation of His wise providence, to which we should all humbly bow, as a chastisement which could not be avoided.[37] As well might we say to the staggering inebriate that he must be patient under a wise dispensation of Providence, that the Lord does not willingly afflict him, &c., as to say that the starving thousands in Ireland must submit patiently, because God, for wise purposes, had turned from all natural laws to send this affliction upon them. For in the first place, the potato had been, everywhere in Ireland, an indirect curse, and in many parts a direct one. For centuries the poor had been oppressed and degraded by this root – for oppression is always degradation; they had not the privilege even of the beasts of the desert in variety. For the brutes, where instinct or pleasure demand, can select their food; the bird, if it cannot find a corn, may select a seed; the lion, if he cannot find an opportunity to capture any nobler game, may secure a sheep or calf; the cat, if the mouse be not in reach of her stealthy step, may secure the unwary bird, or if the wing of the bird be too lofty she may put her quick paw and fasten the nails into the darting fish; the horse or cow, if grass from the meadow or hay from the stack be wanting, may be supplied from the full granary. But the Irish must masticate the potato every day in the year, either boiled or roasted, with or without salt; and if his churlish, dainty, grumbling palate should show any symptoms of relishing food like other men, he is told that, lazy, dirty and savage as he is, the potato is a boon which is quite too good for him.

Now when God gave the 'herb-bearing seed, and the tree bearing fruit' to man, He said not that one portion of mankind shall be confined to a single root; and though his patience long continued to see him fed on this root, by his masters, yet, in his own time, He 'came out of his place', and with one breath blackened and blasted this instrument of torture and cruelty; and though puny man has attempted to resuscitate and bring it to its old use, this breath blows upon it, and it shrinks back into its insignificance, abashed and deadened, as if cognizant of the degrading use to which it had been applied. But the care of God, at the same time that this fatal work was done, had before filled the granaries of the husbandman, at least over the civilized world, to an overflowing abundance; and while He had been doing this He also prepared the hearts of these husbandmen, all over the Christian world, to rise in one simultaneous mass and pour into this famished land the fruits of their harvests; so that – shall it be said, for future generations to read – that it rotted in the harbors while the dying were falling in the streets for want of it? Yes, unhesitatingly may it be said, that there was not a week during that Famine but there was sufficient food for the wants of that week, and more than sufficient.[38] Was there then a 'God's famine' in Ireland, in 1846-7-8-9, and so on? No! it is all mockery to call it so, and mockery which the Almighty will expose, before man will believe, and be humbled as he ought to be. It is therefore I say, may I never be on such an eminence again, from such a cause, from one which, if its breaking forth could not have been foreseen or prevented, need never have resulted in the loss of a single life.

The principle of throwing away life to-day, lest means to protect it to-morrow might be lessened, was fully and practically carried on and carried out.

CHAPTER III

'Man's a king – his throne is Duty
Since his work on earth began.'[1]

The responsibility of a stewardship is a great one, and doubly so where
the results are connected with life as well as property; and where the last
is in the hand of the steward, who at option may save or destroy the former. Had a commission been intrusted to me, under certain restrictions,
and a salary paid, on condition of a right performance of duty, the path
would have been open and plain. But working for no reward, under no
restrictions but conscience, in the midst of the 'valley and shadow of
death', emphatically, where some would stumble and fall, and where all
had an equal claim upon the bounties which were to be applied, was a
fearful task.[2] This task must be entered upon, and the first duty, after
securing a room for a deposit, was to find suitable objects – by this is
implied objects which were not only needy, but which, in the jumble of
so much machinery as was attached to so many different Associations,
were overlooked. These Associations had now multiplied to such an
extent that the time in getting the varied instruments into harmonious
action was considerable; many died in sight of boilers preparing to feed
the hungry, or when prepared they must wait till the 'Relieving Officer
had time to enter their names on the books'.[3]

I stopped for no books, knowing that a faithful unerring record would
be kept in the council chamber above, where the rich and the poor would
soon meet before the Maker of them all; and my only prayer was, that
when that book should be opened, I should not find there noted the name
of any who had gone before as a witness of my neglect.

Cook street furnished a tolerable supply; and the remainder I found
scattered in desolate places. Some who had despaired of relief, because
having neither courage nor strength to make their way through the tumultuous revolting crowds which congregated about every place of public
relief, submitted to their fate with a patient coolness and apparent resig-
nation which I have never been able to comprehend. One woman I found
sitting in her chamber, looking respectably clean; upon inquiry into her
real condition, the facts proved to be these: she had heard of the
Government Relief and had exhausted the last farthing for food, and

when hunger became pressing she sought her way timidly to the Relieving Officer's station, and made her wants known. She was then suffering extremely but she was sent away with the promise that he would call in the morning and make inquiries, and if he found her worthy she should have her name entered into the 'books'. She went to bed supperless, and arose the next morning, waiting for the officer – he came not. She feared if she should go out he would call, and then she should lose her opportunity. That night she went to her bed without the least relief; the next day she did the same; the third morning I found her in that state of patient suffering, with her mind fully made up to die, without making any further effort.[4]

These facts are recorded to show the incomprehensible features of that Famine; and to inquire of the Christian, the philosopher and the physiologist what is the nature of that kind of suffering, which could bring the mind into such a cool passive frame, especially to operate so upon a nation naturally impetuous in their passions and keenly alive to the tenderest sensibilities of the heart. Was it their hereditary suffering that had become a second nature, was it the peculiarity belonging to hunger alone or was it their religion that had produced that submissiveness which overcame the natural propensities, and brought them into passive obedience, when the hand of affliction pressed them sore?

My first donation was Indian meal, with a few pounds of money. A store-room was made of my lodging apartment which was three floors from the ground. The carpet was removed; the meal which had been put in sacks, by the order of government, was getting heated, and much of it must be emptied. The government had, for reasons which are not fully understood by all, sent to Ireland sacks which were sold for half-a-crown each. The meal was taken from the barrels and deposited in them, which answered two purposes – it made sale for thousands of sacks, at a tolerable profit, and was an effectual method of heating the meal, which soon gathered dampness, then became mouldy and wholly unfit for use.[5] The hungry, in some cases, took it gladly. The consequences in many instances were fatal, producing a state of the system often beyond the power of nature or medicine to cure.

The meal sent from New York was of the best kind, the hull being taken off and the meal kiln-dried, which had it been left in barrels would have remained for a year or more in good order. This, the government, being unacquainted with the nature of the article, probably did not understand. If the inquiry be made – why did the government interfere with donations sent to the 'Dublin Central Committee', as donations – the answer can only be that they must have acted upon one of two principles: that as they paid the freight of the American grants, they had a right to use a little dictation in the arrangement in order to secure a partial remuneration; or, they must have acted upon the principle that their interference would forward the exertions making in behalf of their subjects. Is the inquiry made – what became of the barrels? Why every commercial man knows the use of these articles in trade, and every housekeeper who has ever had a broken one knows the convenience of making a rapid fire to hasten her dinner. What became of all the tens of thousands of sacks, or in other words, who paid for them? For one, I must answer, that when mine were delivered through the 'Central Committee', a promise was made that the money paid for them should be refunded when the sacks were returned. This was immediately done but the money was withheld with no other explanation but that I must sell meal enough to pay for them. This meal was property of the poor, and a property most sacred because life was suspended on it, and the meal was sent in the best manner to preserve it, and taking it out injured it most seriously and sometimes fatally, and the article taken from their hungry mouths to pay for sacks, was, besides, robbing them of their own, deducting so much from life. I could not, I dare not, and I did not comply.[6]

This circumstance is important, not only because it involves a great principle, but as furnishing a solution, as far as it goes, why the poor were so little benefited by the bounties sent them from abroad. The hungry, it should be borne in mind, for whom these donations were sent, had no control of what was virtually their own exclusively, but must be content to receive it by proxy, in great or small parcels, in a good or bad state at the dispenser's option. Consequently, they did not always have what belonged to them, and if the meal and rice paid for the sacks, as mine were required to do, a great deduction must be made from the original amount. I once heard a woman observe, whose husband had large donations intrusted to him, that they had £200 worth of sacks, which must be paid for out of the meal, as they could not do it.

These two facts are the only tangible ones on this subject which came under my cognizance. I name them not to expose faults which should be concealed, nor to find fault for the gratification of doing so; but reading in a book often quoted for its veracity, that 'on the side of the oppressor there was power, but they had no comforter', conscience compels me to throw into the scale every particle of truth which belongs to the poor, who have been so much accused of ingratitude toward their benefactors.[7] They never were ungrateful to their real benefactors but second-handed ones, like me, who had power intrusted, did not all of them act wisely nor for the best good of the poor at all times. Some of this was ignorance; some who did not know how to prepare the food sent it to them in the most economical way; and others, who had never felt hunger, took care to guard their own stomachs in good time against its attacks which necessarily required much free feeding and drinking to keep up health and strength for the arduous work. Consequently all this caused delay, and twenty-four, forty-eight and often more hours were the starving obliged to wait till their time should come to be served.

My labours were constant, but not complex, having arranged that eight in the morning must be the time for giving the donations, and that a delay till nine on the part of the beneficiaries would debar them the twenty-four hours' supply. They had all been lectured and duly trained previously that if any appeared dirty, or brought a fresh beneficiary without my knowledge, they should forfeit their own donations.[8] The requirement of eight o'clock attendance was necessary because my visits in Cook street were requisite through the day, and I was obliged to rise at four in the morning to copy manuscript and correct proof sheets till seven; then my penny roll was taken, and all put in due readiness for the distribution.[9] The rooms below me were occupied as offices, which were opened at nine, and the appearance of bare feet, tatters, and sacks of meal, would not be at all in unison with the refinement of gentlemen; and above all it was done so early that the train of beggars, which would have been drawn at any other hour, was avoided. Thus, every hour was time occupied without the least self-denial. The greatest suffering was during the few hours devoted to sleep, when I was occasionally awakened by hearing some moan of distress under my window. My lodging-places in Ireland had been sometimes of quite a peculiar kind; and here, in the beautiful city of Dublin, in a tall house overlooking the Liffey, was my proud heritage – my bed was a short sofa, or apology for one, placed in the middle of barrels of meal, spread upon blankets on the floor, and one crazy old chair, which served to make out my lodging at night and provide a seat while copying manuscripts; an old deal table, with a *New York Tribune* for a table-cloth, made up the furniture of that happy room. But this bliss was limited, every day the quantity of meal lessened, and my purse grew lighter. The poor looked on, and said, 'Praise God, we shall all be destrawed', but God was better to them than their fears – they did not die.

Mine was more than a happy lot. Never before in all my privations in Ireland had I tested the value of being early trained under the discipline of a rational mother, who fitted me, when a child, for the exigencies of life; who not only by precept taught me that in going through the journey of this world I should meet with rough roads and stormy weather, and not always have a covered carriage; that sometimes I should have a hot supper, sometimes a cold one, sometimes a welcome greeting and sometimes a repulsive one; but she had instructed me too, by precept and example, that my hands were to be employed in all that was useful and that idleness was both disgraceful and sinful. This practical knowledge was never more extensively useful to me than now, knowing how to prepare the Indian meal and rice so that it was palatable, and no waste. Yet with these appliances, the meal at last failed. No skill in cooking would make it last like the widow's barrel; and though I had learned not to distrust, yet it cannot be said that I felt the same animation in giving out the *last* day's mess as the *first*.[10] I had a little money left, and the weather was getting warmer: a portion, at least, of what had been wanted for fuel could be reserved for food. I hoped that on the ocean there might be something destined for me; though not the least intimation was given to these poor ones, but they were urged to apply to some of the Relief Associations.

One unfortunate man was the only one that died who had received any aid from me and his life was forgetfully left to go gradually out, when it might have been saved. A curate called and found him recruiting from the last stage of starvation in which I first found him, and kindly gave him a little money and food, promising that he would provide for him in future, and relieve me, as so many were on my hands. The curate forgot him. Three weeks after I called to see him. A girl of two years was dying on a litter of straw in the corner, nestled by the emaciated father, who was too weak to know the suffering of his child; and in two days they were both dead. He had been 'forgotten by his neighbours', his wife was in the hospital. He sat waiting, as was common, in patient hope, till death relieved him.

Cases of death were not so common in Dublin as in many cities. The Society of Friends did much to stay the plague, and their work was carried on by different means. Their labourers, in most cases, were volunteers who asked no reward but that of doing good. How many of the poor bless the name of William Forster and Joseph Crosfield, from England, for their labours of love – who, on the 28th of December, 1846, reached Dublin, made their object known to that Committee, whose views and operations harmonized, and thence they proceeded on their mission of love and mercy.[11] Their graphic report is before the world, as well as others of that denomination of Christians – James Tuke, Marcus Goodbody, William Dillwyn Sims, and William Todhunter.[12]

These men, moved by high and lofty feelings, spent no time in idle commenting on the Protestant or Papist faith – the Radical, Whig or Tory politics; but looked at things as they were, and faithfully recorded what they saw. Not only did they record, but they relieved. They talked and wrote, but acted more; and such a lasting impression have their labours left that the next summer, as I followed in their wake through the country, the name of the 'blessed William Forster' was on the lips of the poor cabiners, and it was from their testimony that his name and good deeds first reached me. William Bennett, too, passed six weeks in Ireland, and a clear and concise account was recorded by himself of the state of the Famine. Though his own beneficence, which was not scanty, has not been definitely known, because he acted as an individual; therefore he was not responsible to any society.[13]

As the pestilence followed the Famine, the entire country seemed to be sinking into the vortex, and a knowledge of Ireland was gaining by all classes of people both in and out of the country. An innovation was made, promising good results, into the long-established habits and condition of that people, which nothing before had done. Poverty was divested of every mask; and from the mud cabin to the estated gentleman's abode, all strangers who wished, without the usual circuitous ceremony, could gain access. The landlord, who had long sported at his ease, was beginning to pay a penalty of which he had never dreamed; the tree, which was planted centuries ago, was now beginning to yield an exuberant crop; the starved tenants are driven into the 'Union', or turned defenceless into the storm, and, in either case, the rents were left unpaid.[14] The landlord growls, but growls in vain: the 'lazy dogs', who are not in the poorhouse, drawing enormous rates from his extensive farms, are at his doors, begging bread, or lying dead under his windows, waiting for 'the board to be put on 'em', as they called a coffin. Coffins were now becoming scarce, and in the mountainous regions and islands two rough boards, with the corpse, in the rags which were about it when the breath departed, placed between these, and a straw rope wound about, was the coveted boon which clung to them to the last.

The winter passed, but the spring brought no fresh hopes; onward was the fearful march. Many faces that were ruddy, and limbs that were robust, and hearts that had scarcely had a fear that the wolf would enter their dwelling, now began to fade, stumble and finally sink under the pursuer. My purse was low, my meal gone, when a letter, the choicest and best, arrived, written by a teacher of a pauper school in New York, and signed by the Corresponding Committee there of the Dublin Friends Society, transmitting me a few barrels of meal, from the children of that pauper school.[15] This was an offering richer than all; it was the interest of the widow's mite, coming through the channel of the orphans, whose willing hearts and ready hands had gathered from their scanty comforts a few pounds without solicitation, and begged the privilege to send it to me.[16] It came.

I had previously been informed that a school in the poorest convent in Dublin was in a state of the greatest suffering.[17] These schools were composed of children who had no means of support, many of them orphans, or the offspring of parents reduced to beggary, and gathered into convents and other schools of charity where they were fed once a day. The nuns were of the order belonging to the poor, and in time of plenty had only been able to feed sixteen daily; and when some hundreds were added, the distress was almost overwhelming. This donation, coming from children of the poorest emigrants in New York, particularly belonged to such as were in like condition, for if such children were turned from the schools, many, and most of them, must inevitably perish, notwithstanding the Friends Society were acting with the greatest vigilance. The British Association, too, was in motion; besides the government had been bountiful. America was doing much – private individuals, of the Irish in America, and in all other countries where they were scattered, were sending one continued train of remittances, to the utter astonishment of the postmasters. Yet death sharpened his teeth daily for new victims.

With gladness of heart, I hastened to the committee-rooms, presented the letter, was requested to wait an answer till the next day; the next day another day was demanded; called the third day, and was denied in toto. The clerk returned the letter without an explanation, only saying that 'the committee had concluded not to grant it'.[18] Had I that moment been summoned by a policeman to appear before a court and answer to a charge of swindling or fraud, I could not have been more astonished, and certainly not so disappointed, for my heart had been most intensely fixed on this as the most sacred offering ever sent me. The deep sense of injustice which was felt, drew these remarks – that if the Americans had misplaced their confidence, in sending remittances through that channel, I was sorry that I had requested them to send mine in that way, and would immediately write them to desist. No other explanation was given than a plain decided denial, but when I had passed the door the solution began to open. The fault was mine, God had sent me to Ireland, in His own way, and instructed me to lean entirely on Him; His promises had never failed towards me – nothing had been wanted, but had been supplied to my wonderment; and now, when daily He had been explaining for what purpose I had been sent hither, that I should lean to the creature, and ask aid, which in reality was not needed, and only retarded my operations, He had sent a rebuke upon my unbelief, which silenced the severity I at first felt towards those instruments in whose hands I had foolishly placed myself. I do not censure them, they acted from motives no matter to me; and God might have used them as a corrective most effectual, because in them I had placed both confidence and power, which were in safer hands before. Man may do well, but God can do better; and it would be fulsome flattery to say that the 'Central Committee of Dublin' were infallible; and cruel injustice to assert that they did not act effectually, liberally and, taken as a whole, do the best that was done.

On my way home with my rejected letter in my hand, Richard Webb met me, took the letter, and entered the committee-room. What barriers he removed I know not, but the meal was sent.[19] This was the only co-working that I attempted in Ireland; not because my strength and wisdom were complete, but because they were so inefficient, that an Almighty arm was requisite to effect the object.

The next morning early I went to the convent. They knew not of my object but learning that I was an American, 'Bless God', said the Abbess, 'that I see one of that nation, to say how much we owe in this convent to their liberality.[20] These children here must have died, but for what they have sent them; and this morning they have assembled to receive the last bit we can give, and we have been saying that we should be ashamed to ask from the Americans any more, had we an opportunity to do so.' They then led me into the school-room, and called the attention of the children to see one of that kind nation who had fed them through the winter, and that through me they must send thanks to my people. They were then told what the pauper children of New York had sent – children like them, who were poor, but who saved all the pence they could procure, and had sent the little gathering to them. I have not the least doubt, had the benevolent friends of that 'Dublin Central Committee' witnessed the happy scene of joy and gratitude which was there manifested, they would have better understood my feelings, and rejoiced too.

July 6th, I took the steamer for Belfast.[21] *Here* was a work going on, which was paramount to all I had seen. *Women* were at work; and no one could justly say that they were dilatory or inefficient. Never in Ireland, since the Famine, was such a happy combination of all parties, operating so harmoniously together, as was here manifested. Not in the least like the women of Dublin, who sheltered themselves behind their old societies – most of them excusing themselves from personal labour, feeling that a few visits to the abodes of the poor were too shocking for female delicacy to sustain; and though occasionally one might be prevailed upon to go out, yet but for a few days could I ever persuade any to accompany me. Yet much was given in Dublin; for it is a city celebrated for its benevolence, and deservedly so, as far as giving goes. But *giving* and *doing* are antipodes in her who has never been trained to domestic duties. The faithful John Gregg thundered his powerful anathemas on the indolent in God's vineyard, who laboured not among the poor, nor descended to the duties of women in emergencies like this.[22] They heard it. Some said it was beautiful; some declared he was the most witty man they ever heard; and others said his remarks were quite amusing. But how many ever through the week were influenced to practice his preaching, eternity will best tell.

The Belfast Ladies' Association embraced an object which *lives* and *tells*, and will continue to do so, when they who formed it shall be no more on earth.[23] It was on January 1st, 1847, that the first meeting was held in the Commercial Buildings by ladies of all religious denominations; and they there resolved to form a Society for the purpose of raising a fund to be appropriated to afflicted localities without any regard to religious distinctions. Visiting soon commenced, under the titles of Corresponding Committee, Industrial Committee, Clothing Committee, and Collecting Committee. Without inserting the names of these indefatigable ladies, it may be recorded that more than one hundred and fifty were associated in this work; the highways and hedges were faithfully visited, the poor sought out, their condition cared for, and the children of the most degraded class were taken and placed in a school which continues to flourish on an extensive scale.[24] This school has the benefit of being taught the elementary branches of an education, and the most useful needlework and knitting; and the squalid looks of the children were soon exchanged for health, and that indifference to appearance which the hungry, neglected poor soon wear, was, like magic almost, transformed into a becoming tidiness and self-respect.

Though many had never before known anything of sewing or knitting, yet they soon produced specimens praiseworthy to teacher and scholar, and by this industry earned a little each week which they could call their own. Other schools of the kind multiplied in almost every part of Ireland, especially in Connaught, where the exertions of Dr Edgar, who explored this province, have been a great blessing in this respect.[25] Many a poor child by these schools has been made to look up with a hope which was entirely new – a hope that in after days she might wear a shawl and a bonnet, write a good letter, make a dress, &c. The happy effects of industry on the minds of the children were striking. That passive indifference to all but how a morsel of bread should be obtained was exchanged for a becoming manner and animated countenance, lighted up by the happy consciousness that industry was a stepping-stone which would justly and honorably give them a place among the comfortable and respectable of the earth. And again, to quote Dr Edgar, every look seemed to say, 'They have had in their work a full reward'. And he adds: 'Thus an independent, self-supporting, and useful generation may be raised, who will be less at the mercy of changing seasons; and who, when the day of trouble comes, will have some resources on which to draw.'

My greatest object in writing this sketch of the Famine being to show
its effects on all classes rather than to detail scenes of death by starvation, a few sketches only of this kind in passing along will be given, for
the purpose of illustrating the principle of mind as it develops itself in the
varied changes through which it is called to pass. These Industrial
Schools, which I afterward visited when passing through Connaught in
1847 and 1848, were subjects of the deepest interest; for to me they told
the whole story of Ireland's wrongs and Ireland's remedy. They told me
that when usurpation robbed them of the means of industry, for their own
good, that oppression confined this industry to the personal benefits of
the oppressor, and thus deadened every natural excitement to labour,
which promised nothing but a bare subsistence among the children of
men who looked down with contempt upon them because, by this 'hewing of wood and drawing of water', they had been kept in degraded,
unrequited servitude; but now that an industry, founded on righteous
principles, was springing up – an industry that not only rewarded but elevated – the convenient term, 'lazy Irish', was hiding its slanderous
head.[26]

The Belfast Association felt this more and more, as they received
returns from Connaught of the happy effects of these schools, and their
hearts were more and more encouraged in pursuing these labours of love.
They met often, they planned, they talked together of the best means to
accomplish the most good; and one great beauty of these meetings was
no one said to her sister, 'Stand by, for I am holier than thou'. Different
parties who had never mingled now felt one common interest. She who
had much brought in of her abundance, and she who had little brought in
her mite. While these benevolent women were teaching the practice of
industry to the poor, they found the benefit react upon themselves, for
they too must be industrious. This new, this arduous, long-neglected
work required not only their skill but their energies to put and keep the
vast machinery in motion. Money was not all that was requisite in the
work. The abodes of the most wretched must be visited; and, though
before the Famine they had scarcely dreamed of the suffering that was in
their city, and could not believe that their intelligent, industrious town
was in much real want, when they found that many uncomplaining children of distress has been struggling for life long before the Famine, they
doubled, if possible, their energies, and cheerfully showed by individual
exertion that if they had previously over-looked this pleasing duty, they
would repair as far as possible all that had been neglected before on their
part. The men, too, showed themselves efficient co-workers; they contributed, many of them bountifully, and some visited too. They erected a
bath-house for the benefit of labourers and the poor of all classes, to

which was attached a laundress, that the poor in the most economical way could be provided with materials for this important handmaid to health and respectability – cleanliness.

I loved to linger in Belfast. All seemed to be life, and life to some purpose. All hearts seemed to be awakened to one and the same object, to do good most efficiently; and one peculiar trait was here perceivable – none of that desire for who should be *greatest* seemed prevalent. A mutual confidence prevailed. One would tell me enthusiastically that she did not know how the association could manage without Maria Webb; her judgment was always the turning point in all difficulties.[27] Maria Webb would expatiate on the efficiency of Mary Ireland as a visitor and manager. A third would regret that the indefatigable Miss McCracken, she feared, would soon leave us, as her age had passed the line of three-score years and ten. Another expatiated on the faithful Miss —, who was a Roman Catholic, but whose labours of love had been untiring; and she was quite sorry that difference in religious profession had so long kept so many useful members at a distance, &c.[28] This to a stranger could probably be viewed with a sober, impartial eye, that those moving in the machinery could not; and to me it looked like a heavenly influence distilling unperceived into the hearts of all, like the dew, which falls alike on the garden flower or mountain weed.

Another most valuable principle was illustrated by this Famine, which a God-loving heart must admire, viz., the difference between a hireling and a voluntary worker, and so clear was this difference that whenever, in going the length of Ireland, I met any of either class upon coaches, in trains, visiting the poor or distributing donations in soup-shops or elsewhere, a mistake was not once made in pronouncing who was a paid officer, or who was there moved by an innate voice, to do what he could for the poor. Allow me to dwell a little on this and make it as clear as I can.

An officer paid by government was generally well paid. Consequently, he could take the highest seat in a public conveyance; he sought for the most comfortable inns, where he could secure the best dinner and wines; he inquired the state of the people, and did not visit the dirty hovels himself when he could find a menial who would for a trifle perform it; and though sometimes when accident forced him in contact with the dying or dead, his pity was stirred, it was mingled with the curse which always follows – 'Laziness and filth', and he wondered 'why the dirty wretches had lived so long', and he hoped 'this lesson would teach them to work in future, and lay up something as other people did'. When his plan of operation was prepared, his shop opened and books arranged, and the applications of the starving were numerous, he peremptorily silenced this, and sent away that without relief. Many had walked miles without food for twenty-four hours, and some died on their way home, or soon after reaching it; and when the story was told him, and he was entreated to look into the cases of such, the answer was, that he must be true to the government, and not give out to any whose names he had not entered into the books; if they died how could he help it, &c. If all did not do precisely as has been stated, all manifested a similar spirit, more or less.

The Hon. William Butler, who was appointed as an overseer by government, was an exception, so far as language was concerned. He spoke feelingly, but his personal habits were not brought to that test of many with a lower station. He acted kindly as an inspector, and devised the best means which he could, and I was informed, when making the inquiry respecting his distinguished humanity, that he accepted his appointment from principle, and not from necessity, that he might see that justice was better administered.[29]

Let us now follow the self-moved or heavenly-moved donor. He was found mingling with the poorest, often taking the lowest seat, curtailing all unnecessary expense that he might have more to give, seeking out the most distressed; looking into the causes of distress, that he might better know how to remove them, never upbraiding with harshness, and always seeking some apology for their misdoings when representing their case to the uninformed. Many, both men and women among this class, took most responsible donations without any reward, and acted in the kindest and most judicious manner; always minding to serve first those who needed most and had come the farthest. This kindly spirit was reciprocated at once by the poor, and with an astonishing discernment they often manifested this knowledge; sometimes much to the uneasiness of the party who were guilty. Through the whole of the Famine I never heard any of the poor complain of one who was giving from his own purse, and seeking out his own objects; nor, on the other hand, did I ever hear one say, who gave him true benevolence, that he ever met ingratitude. This might have been, but I speak only from personal observation.

While stopping in Belfast, at the hospitable White House, so called, owned by the family of Grimshaws, I became acquainted with a Miss Hewitson, whose father resided in Donegal.[30] My destiny was to that county; hearing that the distress there was very great, I wished to see it.

William Bennett and his son had visited that part in March, distributing donations at his own expense mostly, and his painful descriptions had awakened a strong desire to see for myself, and though I had no means in hand, I had reason to hope that there might be some on the ocean. I took the coach for Derry, a few miles from that town. The mother of Miss Hewitson was to meet me in her own carriage, and conduct me to her house in Rossgarrow. Derry had not suffered so much as many other towns, and a stranger passing through would not notice any particular change from its condition in the past years. But this little relief was only to make what followed appear the more painful. Mrs Hewitson met me with her son, and we took tea at a delightful little mansion on the sloping side of one of Ireland's green lawns, looking down upon a beautiful lake.[31] 'And is there,' I asked, 'on this pretty spot, misery to be found?' 'Come and see,' was the answer of my kind friend. It was twilight when we stepped into the carriage, and few painful objects met us till we reached her dwelling.

Her paternal cottage was nestled in a pretty wood, its roof thatched, and its windows shaded by the creeping vine in front. On one end, a window gave one of the most beautiful peeps upon a lake that can be imagined; and the back contained a garden which was one of the most pleasant retreats I had met, for the gooseberry was just ripe. Here had this discreet, this virtuous woman lived, and by precept and example trained a family of sons and daughters, which will, which do arise and call her blessed. Her husband had been an officer, and was then receiving a small pension, and during the first season of the Famine had been employed by government as an overseer of the Board of Works. His heart had sickened at the scenes which came under his eye, some sketches of which have been before the public.[32]

The morning lighted up a pretty cottage, well ordered, and the breakfast-table presented a treat unseen before by me in Ireland. Instead of the bread, butter, tea and egg, which are the height of the best Irish breakfast, there was a respectable corn-cake, made as it should be, suitable accompaniments of all kinds, with the best of cream for me; and were it not that the hungry had then commenced their daily usages of assembling in crowds about the house for food, that breakfast would have been a pleasant one. When I ascertained that her husband had been in America, and from him she had been told of the virtues of corn-cake, and that her skill had been exercised till she had brought it to perfection, I valued it if possible still more. Had the Irish mothers throughout Ireland managed as did this woman, their task in the Famine would have been much lighter – the poor, many more of them, would have been saved, and multitudes who have gone down might have retained their standing. Had the higher classes known how to have changed the meal into the many palatable shapes contrived by this economical housekeeper, when the wheaten loaf was so high, immense money might have been saved to all parties. It was brought in such disrepute by bad cooking, that many would be ashamed to be found eating it, and one man who was begging most earnestly for food, when offered some of this prepared in Irish style, turned away in contempt, saying, 'No, thank God, I've never been brought to ate the yeller Indian.'

This industrious woman, like Solomon's prudent wife, had not only risen 'while it was yet dark', to prepare meat for her household, but she had been in her meal-room at four in the morning, weighing out meal for the poor, the Society of Friends in Dublin having furnished her with grants.[33] This I found was her daily practice, while the poor through the day made the habitation a nucleus not of the most pleasant kind. The lower window-frame in the kitchen was of board instead of glass, this all having been broken by the pressure of faces continually there.

Who could eat, who could work, who could read, or who could play in such circumstances as these? Certainly it sometimes seemed that the sunshine was changed, that the rain gave a stranger pattering, and truly, that the wind did moan most dolefully. The dogs ceased their barking, there were scarcely any cocks to be heard crowing in the morning, and the gladsome mirth of children everywhere ceased. O! ye, whose nerves are disturbed at the glee of the loud-laughing boy, come to this land of darkness and death, and for leagues you may travel, and in house or cabin, by the wayside, on the hill-top or upon the meadow, you shall not see a smile, you shall not see the sprightly foot running in ecstasy after the rolling hoop, leaping the ditch or tossing the ball. The young laughing full faces, and brilliant eyes and buoyant limbs, had become walking skeletons of death! When I saw one approaching, with his emaciated fingers locked together before him, his body in a bending position, as all generally crawled along, if I had neither bread nor money to give, I turned from the path; for, instead of the 'God save ye kindly', or 'Ye look wary, lady', which had ever been the salutation to me on the mountains, I knew it would be the imploring look or the vacant sepulchral stare, which, when once fastened upon you, leaves its impress for ever.[34]

The kind Hewitsons seemed not only to anticipate my wants, but to enter into my feelings as a stranger whose heart was tortured with unparalleled scenes of suffering, and they did all to make my stay pleasant, and if possible to draw away my mind a little from the painful objects around me. They conducted me from place to place, and showed me much of the beautiful scenery with which Donegal abounds, as well as all Ireland. Lakes bountifully dot this part of Donegal. Rathmelton, Milford, Letterkenny, Dunfanaghy – all lie in this region – as well as a romantic spot on the sea-shore called M'Sweeny's Gun, so called on account of the report that the sea makes when it rushes with tremendous force under the rock which overhangs it, and through which a round hole has been made and as the waves dash, shooting through high into the air, a loud report, like that of a gun, is heard. But as natural curiosities are not the object of this sketch, they cannot be dwelt upon: curiosities of a most unnatural and fearful kind have fallen to my share. As fond as I had always been of looking upon the grandeur of the sea-coast in Ireland – which has no rival probably, taken as a whole – *now* the interest was so deadened by the absence of the kindly children who were always ready to point out every spot of interest, and give its name, that a transient look sufficed.

At Letterkenny, the Roman Catholic Bishop invited us to his house, and treated us with much courtesy; showed us his robes and badges of honour given him at Rome; and though he knew that we were Protestants, yet he appeared not to suspect but that we should be as deeply interested as though we were under his jurisdiction.[35] Many favourable opportunities presented to become acquainted with the effects of the Famine upon the Romish priests. Some were indefatigable, and died in their labors while others looked more passively on. They had two drawbacks which the Protestants in general had not. First, a great proportion of them are quite poor; and second, they, in the first season of the Famine, were not intrusted with grants, as the Protestants were. These difficulties operated strongly upon the minds of the benevolent class among them. One Protestant clergyman informed me that so much confidence had he in the integrity of the Catholic priest in his parish, that when he had a large grant sent to him he offered as much of it to the priest as he could distribute, knowing, he added, that it would be done with the greatest promptitude and fidelity. No ministers of religion in the world know as much of their people as do the Catholics, not *one* of their flock is forgotten, scarcely by name, however poor or degraded; and consequently when the Famine came, they had not to *search out* the poor, they knew the identical cabin in which every starving one was lying, and as far as knowledge was concerned were in a condition to act most effectually.

My next visit was to the far-famed Gweedore, the estate of Lord George Hill.[36] This gentleman is too well-known to need a description. His works will live when he is where the 'wicked cease from troubling'. His *Facts on Gweedore* are the most amusing of anything I have read on the habits of the Irish; and to understand what Lord George Hill has done, whoever visits that spot should first read these 'facts', and then all objections must be silenced respecting the capacity of the most savage of that nation being elevated. These 'facts' I had never read till some time after my visit there, which I now much regret. It would not be supposed that during a famine this spot could be seen to much advantage; but there was, even then, a degree of comfort which did not exist in any other part I had seen. It lies in the parish of Tullaghobegly, on the north-west coast of Ireland, where the wildest scenery stretches along the bold coast in many places; and where it would seem that man, unless driven from the society of his fellow-being, would never think of making his abode. But here men had clustered, and here they had constructed rude huts of loose stone or turf, and with but little law, they were a 'law to themselves', each one doing as he listed.

The system of Rundale prevailed: 'one tenant had his proportion in thirty or forty different places, and without fences between them'; and the strips were often so small that half a stone of oats would sow one of these divisions; and these 'Gweedore Facts' tell us that one poor man had his inheritance in *thirty-two* different places, and abandoned, in despair, the effort to 'make them out'.[37] There were no resident landlords, the rent was paid any how, or not at all, as the tenant was disposed.[38] Sometimes a little was 'picked up', as they termed it, by some agent going from cabin to cabin and receiving what each might please to give. Their evenings were passed in each other's huts till late at night, telling stories, drinking poteen, &c. Perpetual quarrels arose from the Rundale system. For the cattle, on a certain day, were brought from the mountain, to graze on the arable land; and if Mikey or Paddy had not his crops gathered, they were injured, and then a fight set matters at rest again. The animals, too, were often divided, according to the Rundale system. If four men, for instance, owned a horse, each must provide a shoe; in one case, but three men had a share in one, consequently the *unshod* foot got lame. A dispute arose, one of the two complained to a magistrate that he had kept his foot shod decently, and had shod the *fourth foot twice to boot!* Let modern socialists take a few lessons from these originals.

Their materials for agricultural labour were at one time quite novel. When a field was to be harrowed the harrow was made fast *to the pony's tail;* a rope was fastened to the horse's tail, and then to the harrow; but if the hair of the tail was long it was fastened by a peg into a hole in the harrow. Thus equipped, a man mounted his back and drove him over the field.[39] Whoever lacks invention let him learn from Paddy. The following true description of that district is given by Patrick M'Kye, the teacher of the National School in 1837, in a memorial sent to the Lord Lieutenant; nor was Patrick's memorial in vain, for it not only awakened an Englishman to send these naked ones clothing, but it will be handed down to future generations as a memento of both the suffering state of that people and the faithfulness of the writer; and, above all, it will show in very lively colours what persevering enlightened philanthropy can do, when in the heart of such a landlord as Lord George Hill.[40]

Here follows the document; and if every schoolmaster in Ireland had so turned his parish inside out, many more Lords like George Hill might have long since arisen to their help:

To His Excellency the Lord-Lieutenant of Ireland,

THE MEMORIAL OF PATRICK M'KYE
MOST HUMBLY SHOWETH,

That the parishioners of the parish of West Tullaghobegly, in the Barony of Kilmacrennan, in the County of Donegal, are in the most needy, hungry, and naked condition of any people that ever came within the precincts of my knowledge, although I have traveled a part of nine counties in Ireland, also a part of England and Scotland, together with a part of British America; I have likewise perambulated 2253 miles through seven of the United States, and never witnessed the tenth part of such hunger, hardships, and nakedness.

Now, my Lord, if the causes which I now lay before your Excellency, were not of very extraordinary importance, I would never presume to lay them before you.

But I consider myself in duty bound by charity to relieve distressed and hungry fellow-man, although I am sorry to state that my charity cannot extend farther than to explain to the rich where hunger and hardships exist, in almost the greatest degree that nature can endure.

This I shall endeavour to explain in detail, with all the truth and accuracy in my power, and without the least exaggeration, as follows:

There are about 4000 [see note p.68 over] persons in this parish, and all Catholics, and as poor as I shall describe, having among them no more than –

    One cart,
    No wheel car,
    No coach, or any other vehicle,
    One plow,
    Sixteen harrows,
    Eight saddles,
    Two pillions,
    Eleven bridles,
    Twenty shovels,
    Thirty-two rakes,
    Seven table-forks,
    Ninety-three chairs,
    Two hundred and forty-three stools,
    Ten iron grapes,
    No swine, hogs, or pigs,
    Twenty-seven geese,
    Three turkeys,
    Two feather beds,
    Eight chaff beds,
    Two stables,

Six cow-houses,
One national school,
No other school,
One priest,
No other resident gentleman,
No bonnet,
No clock,
Three watches,
Eight brass candlesticks,
No looking glasses above 3d. in price,
No boot, no spurs,
No fruit trees,
No turnips,
No parsnips,
No carrots,
No clover

or any other garden vegetables, but potatoes and cabbage, and not more than ten square feet of glass in windows in the whole, with the exception of the chapel, the school-house, the priest's house, Mr Dombrian's house and the constabulary barrack.

None of their either married or unmarried women can afford more than one shift, and the fewest number can afford any, and more than one half of both men and women cannot afford shoes to their feet, nor can many of them afford a second bed, but whole families of sons and daughters of mature age, indiscriminately lying together with their parents, and all in the bare buff.

They have no means of harrowing their land, but with meadow rakes. Their farms are so small that four to ten farms can be harrowed in a day with one rake.

Their beds are straw – green and dried rushes or mountain bent: their bedclothes are either coarse sheets, or no sheets, and ragged filthy blankets.

And worse than all that I have mentioned, there is a general prospect of starvation, at the present prevailing among them, and that originating from various causes, but the principal cause is the rot or failure of seed in the last year's crop, together with a scarcity of winter forage, in consequence of a long continuation of storm since October last, in this part of the country.

So that they, the people, were under the necessity of cutting down their potatoes and giving them to their cattle to keep them alive. All these circumstances connected together, have brought hunger to reign among them to that degree, that the generality of the peasantry are on the small allowance of one meal a day, and many families cannot afford more than one meal in two days, and sometimes one meal in three days. Their children are crying and fainting with hunger, and their parents weeping, being full of grief, hunger, debility and dejection, with glooming aspect, looking at their children likely to expire in the jaws of starvation.

Also, in addition to all, their cattle and sheep are dying with hunger, and their owners forced by hunger to eat the flesh of such. 'Tis reasonable to suppose that the use of such flesh will raise some infectious disease among the people, and it may very reasonably be supposed, that the people will die even faster than the cattle and sheep, if some immediate relief be not sent to alleviate their hunger.

Now, my Lord, it may perhaps seem inconsistent with truth that all I have said could possibly be true, but to convince your noble Excellency of the truth of all that I have said, I will venture to challenge the world to produce one single person to contradict any part of my statement.

I must acknowledge, that if reference were made to any of the landlords or landholders of the parish, they would contradict it, as it is evident it would blast their honours if it were known abroad that such a degree of want existed in their estates among their tenantry. But here is how I make my reference and support the truth of all that I have said; that is, if any unprejudiced gentleman should be sent here to investigate strictly into the truth of it, I will, if called on, go with him from house to house, where his eyes will fully satisfy and convince him, and where I can show him about one hundred and forty children bare naked, and who were so during winter, and some hundreds only covered with filthy rags, most disgustful to look at. Also, man and beast housed together, i.e., the families in one end of the house, and the cattle in the other end of the kitchen.

Some houses have within their walls from one cwt to thirty cwts of dung, others having from ten to fifteen tons weight of dung, and only cleaned out once a year!

I have also to add that the National School has greatly decreased in number of scholars, through hunger and extreme poverty; and the teacher of said school, with a family of nine persons, depending on a salary of £8 a year, without any benefit from any other source. If I may hyperbolically speak, it is an honour for the Board of Education!

One remark before I conclude. I refer your noble Excellency for the authenticity of the above statement to the Revd H O'F, Parish Priest, and to Mr Rō, Chief Constable, stationed at Gweedore, in said parish, and Mr P——, Chief Officer of Coast Guard, in same district.

Your most humble and obedient Servant,
 Patrick M'Kye.

NOTE This is an error; the population of Tullaghobegly being 9040 in the year 1841. Paddy M'Kye, however, when he wrote in the year 1837, had no means of ascertaining *this*, as he had all the other particulars in his statement.

This error of the faithful Paddy is certainly a very modest one, and serves rather to brighten than eclipse the picture. It looks as though the mind of the writer was not so perverted, nor so lacking in material, as to be driven to exaggeration to make out a vivid, exciting story.

CHAPTER IV

'I stand alone, without fear, in the midst of thousands,
though the valiant be distant far.' Ossian[1]

Now, reader, summon your forces, collect your strength, and see if you
are prepared to meet such a formidable host and go forth to battle. There
was one in the face and eyes of all the foregoing graphic facts, stood up
single-handed; and, like the shepherd son of Jesse, went forth and boldly
challenged this gigantic Goliath.[2] Yes! Lord George Hill is not a George
Washington, his work was a *mightier* one – *his* was a grapple with *mind*,
with *untutored* mind, gathering strength for ages till it seemed to defy all
attempts of reform; and, like the bolt cliffs which hung over their wild
coast, stood up in their pride and said, 'Dash on, we heed you not'.
Washington had *carnal* battles to fight, and with *carnal* weapons, in the
hands of gallant soldiers, he scattered the foe. But mark! He that by
moral power grapples with the worst passions of men, and lays them
harmless at his feet, has done more than he who has conquered whole
armies by the sword. This, Lord George Hill has done. In 1838 this indefatigable man purchased small holdings, adding to them till the whole
amounted to upward of 23,000 acres: 3000 people then inhabited the
land, and but 700 paid rent. *What did he do*? Did he take a body of
policemen, and arm himself with a pike and pistol and go forth demanding submission or death? He had an efficient agent, and temporary apartments were fitted up on the spot. He then went himself into every hut on
his estate: and, understanding Irish, he soon gained access to their hearts:
they said, he could not be a lord because he spoke Irish.[3]

His first work was to check the illicit distillation of their grain; and he
built a corn store 87 feet long and 22 wide, with three lofts, and a kiln;
then a quay was formed in front of the store admitting vessels of 200
tons, having 14 feet of water at the height of the tide.[4] A market was
established where the same price was paid for grain as at Letterkenny, 26
miles distant. The difficulties of building this store were great indeed –
no masons or carpenters in the vicinity – and the site must be excavated
by blasting a solid rock. But what *will* not, and what *did* not perseverance
do? It was done, and next a wheelwright was employed; timber and iron
brought from Derry. Until the calls multiplied, the store was stocked with

the common necessities of life, and at last it was increased double in size.
The inhabitants, for the first time, began to eat bread; and, can you
believe it? *Savage* as they were, they loved it. The next difficult work
was to place each tenant on his own farm; and to do this every landholder was served with notice 'to quit'. A surveyor had drawn maps, the tenants were assembled and, the new allotments made according to his rent,
all previous bargains were adjusted to mutual satisfaction. But the final
allotments of land took three years to settle: they must look over their
new farms, all in one piece, and cast lots for them. The Rundale system,
when disturbed, brought new difficulties to these people; it broke up
their clusters of huts, and the facilities of assembling nights, to tell and
hear long stories; and they must tumble down their cabins, which were of
loose stones; and the owner of the cabin hired a fiddler, which no sooner
known, than the joyous Irish are on the spot. Each takes a stone or stones
upon his or her back (for women and children are there). They dance at
intervals – the fiddler animates them on while the daylight lasts, and then
the night is finished by dancing.[5]

When the houses were set up anew upon the farms, Lord George
thought it advisable to have a few ten-acre farms fenced in on the waste-
land. This was instantly opposed, for they did not want these divisions
occupied, as by so doing it would thin out the crowds and break up the
clanship too much. They would not be hired to make the ditches, and a
'fearless wanderer' could only do the work. Though sods of turf were
hurled at him he kept on, but the contest was so sharp that it was settled at
last by two policemen, at night, who frightened away the assailants, who
had assembled to 'settle' the ditch. Peace was concluded, ditches were
made, premiums were offered for the best specimens of clean cottages,
which now had chimneys and windows, whitewashed walls, suitable beds
and bedsteads, crockery and chairs, and the *manure heap* at a respectable
distance, and all bearing the appearance of comfort. These premiums
extended to growing green crops, draining farms, good calves, pigs, colts,
&c., and for webs of cloth, best knit stockings, firkins of butter, &c.

The premium day was the wonder of wonders; for they were told that
the noble-hearted Lord George was to dine with them, which the poor
people could not believe, and were afraid to go in till the surveyor
assured them that it was *true*. This was the crowning of the whole, and
puts forever at rest any doubts of the good sense of this well-balanced
mind, which knew how to lay the foundation, set up the walls, and put on
his seal to the topmost stone. Our Saviour explained this principle emphatically, when rebuked for eating with publicans and sinners: 'I came
not to call the righteous,' &c.[6] Lord George Hill knew well the secret
avenue to the hearts of these people; he knew they were *men*, and though

circumstances had made them *degraded ones*, yet if the smothered embers of that image in which they were created could be stirred, living sparks would be emitted. Did this 'familiarity breed contempt?' Did they take undue advantage and say, 'We will not have this man to rule over us'; and was God offended? Come and see the fruits of his decision and condescension – they both stand out in as bold relief as the old mountain Arrigle [*recte* Errigal] which nods its cloud-capped head over this district.

But details must be left: *Facts from Gweedore* should be in the hand and heart of every landlord who may have anything to do in difficulties like these. Let him visit these comfortable cottages, supplied with decencies, to cause the inmates to *feel* that they are *human*; let him see the industry of the women and the becoming clothing of the peasantry; let him visit the store, the mill, the union-house, school-house and dispensary; and while he is doing all this, let his home be for a few days in that well-ordered hotel, and notice the consistency of the whole; and if he *can*, let him go and do likewise. If he *cannot*, let him retrace all his steps, and impartially decide how far his own negligence, improvidence, love of ease and indifference to the real good of his tenantry may have contributed to bring him into this state. If he have not capital, like Lord George Hill, where is his capital? Have horses, coaches, hunting dogs, and hunting dinners frittered it away? Then woe betide him, his day is over, who can help him? The school-house at Bunbeg, near this store, is not a small item in this great work. The room is 25 feet by 15, lofty and well-ventilated. The teacher has a dwelling under the same roof; and when I visited it all was order and comfort. The girls are taught sewing, for of this the people are quite ignorant, and it may safely be presumed that Lord George would not restrict their advance in education to certain bounds, lest their talents should transcend their station in life.

I spent a Sabbath in that quiet hotel, and attended the Church service, which was then conducted in the school-room; a house of worship was in progress, but not ready to be opened. The female tenantry who were at home walking upon the street, or calling into the hotel, always had their knitting-work in motion whenever I saw them, and such a surplus of stockings as amounted to about £200 was then on hand, all of which the females had been paid for knitting. They shall not be idle, said his lordship, though the work is on my hands unsold. His family residence is located about twenty miles from Gweedore, but he and his wife were at the hotel the evening that I reached it, and meeting him in the morning in the hall – supposing him to be some respectable appendage to the house – made inquiries concerning it; and not till he made some remarks respecting my self-denying travels in Ireland did I find my mistake. I saw at once the secret of his mighty achievements; his simplicity was his dignity and strength. He had struggled hard during the Famine to keep his tenantry from suffering without much foreign aid, had sacrificed much, and difficulties were increasing. The next winter the hotel was closed for a time; sickness had made inroads into the house, and death likewise; but it was re-opened the next season, under more encouraging auspices.

This man has proved to a demonstration what can be done even with the most hopeless, and under the most discouraging, circumstances; for if Lord George Hill could transform those wild mountain goats, even to common civilized *bullocks*, what could not be done with any and *all* of the wild game of Ireland? Pity, great pity, that so few have applied the right key to the Irish heart! Still greater pity that so few believe there *is* a key that can find a right entrance; give Lord George Hill a patent right, and let all who will improve it, and Ireland will arise.

Now, in 1850, he writes: 'Say that *no person* died of famine at Gweedore, though many of the aged and infants, from being scantily fed, died earlier than otherwise they would, as well as from change of diet; also that the people are reviving in a great degree, from the potato having held out this year.'

Lord George Hill is an Irishman of the Hillsborough family, in the County Down, brother to the *late* and uncle to the present Marquis of Downshire, a *true Irishman*, who lives and acts for his country.

Two miles from Gweedore an English gentleman had fixed a residence on the woody side of a hill, with a fine lake at a little distance, who was attracted there by the beauty of the scenery and a desire to enjoy the evening of his days in a romantic peaceful retirement among a peasantry which pleased him; and his wife and daughters were quite an acquisition to the scattered intelligent class which dotted the wild scenery there. His family were then in England, and when I met him a few weeks after in Derry he said, 'I waited all day to see you, but when you come again we shall not be disappointed.' He died a few weeks after, and left a sad breach in the hearts of many.

This little incident is named to show how much the English, who go to Ireland because they admire the country, and justly appreciate the people, are beloved. They are always mentioned with the greatest admiration where they have behaved with a proper condescension and kindness to the people.

My next excursion was from Gweedore to Dungloe with Mr Forster, who conducted me to his pretty cottage and lovely family in the parish of Templecrone.[7] It was a wild and dreary waste which led us to it – here and there a cluster of miserable cabins, and still more miserable inmates, met the eye; now and then a hungry being would crawl out and make some sorrowful complaint of neglect by the relieving officer, which could not be remedied; but when we reached the cottage of my guide, all bespoke plenty and comfort. Here, in the midst of desolation and death, his isolated bright spot said, 'Mercy is not clean gone forever'. Here was the minister of Templecrone who had come to dine, for he heard that a stranger who pitied Ireland was to be there, and his heart was made of tenderness and love.[8] Seldom can be met a being where such amiable, tender and sympathetic kindness are united with energy and perseverance, as were in this man. He was alive to every tale of woe, and active to surmount all difficulties; with his own hands he laboured to assist the poor – they have laid their dead around his gate in the night, knowing that the 'blessed minister would not let them be buried without a board on 'em'. We spent a painful-pleasant evening at this hospitable house, talking of the dreadful scenes of death in their midst, and then the kind man rode eight miles on horseback to his home.

The next day we were to visit Arranmore, a pretty sunny island, where peace and comfort had ever reigned. The peasantry here were about 1500 in number, occupying a green spot three miles in length, and had always maintained a good character for morality and industry. They kept cows, which supplied them with milk, sheep with wool, geese with beds, fowls with eggs; and grew oats, potatoes and barley; they wore shoes and stockings, which none of the female peasantry can do in the country places; they likewise spun and made their own wearing apparel, and as the difficulty of crossing the channel of the sea, which was three miles, was considerable, they seldom visited the mainland. When they saw the potato was gone, they ate their fowls, sheep and cows, and then began to cross the sea to Templecrone for relief. What could they find there? One man could do but little to stay the desolation. Hundreds had died before this, and though I knew that painful scenes were in waiting, yet, if possible, the half was not told me. Six men, beside Mr Griffith, crossed with me in an open boat, and we landed, not buoyantly, upon the once pretty island. The first that called my attention was the death-like stillness – nothing of life was seen or heard, excepting occasionally a dog. These looked so unlike all others I had seen among the poor I unwittingly said – 'How can the dogs look so fat and shining here, where there is no food for the people?'[9]

'Shall I tell her?' said the pilot to Mr Griffith, not supposing that I heard him.

This was enough: if anything were wanting to make the horrors of a famine complete, this supplied the deficiency. Reader, I leave you to your thoughts, and only add that the sleek dogs of Arranmore were my horror, if not my *hatred*, and have stamped on my mind images which can never be effaced.

We made our first call at the door of the chapel. The fat surly-looking priest was standing there; and, saying to him, 'Your people, sir, are in a bad state'.[10]

'Bad enough, they give *me* nothing.'

'Why should they? You cannot expect or *ask* anything of the poor starving creatures.'

The curate withdrew, leaving the battle to be decided by the priest pilot and myself, for he had known him before.

'Ah,' said the pilot, softly, 'he's a hard one; *there's* the Christian for you,' pointing to the curate, 'he's the man that has the pitiful heart – not a creature on the island but would lay down the life for him.'[11]

This pilot was a Roman Catholic, but that characteristic impartiality peculiar to the Irish, where justice and mercy are concerned, belonged to him likewise. We went from cabin to cabin, till I begged the curate to show me no more. Not in a solitary instance did one beg. When we entered their dark, smoky, floorless abodes, made darker by the glaring of a bright sun which had been shining upon us, they stood up before us in a speechless, vacant, staring, stupid, yet most eloquent posture, mutely, *graphically* saying, 'Here we are, your bone and your flesh, made in God's image, like you. *Look at us!* What brought us here?'

May God forgive me, and I believe he will, or I would not say it. With Job, I said, 'Let darkness and the shadow of death stain that day when first the potato was planted in this green isle of the sea', to oppress the poor labourer, and at last bring him to a valley of death – *deep, dark intricate* – where slimy serpents, poison lizards and gnawing vultures creep and wind about his wasted limbs, and gnaw into the deepest recesses of his vitals.[12]

In every cabin we visited, *some* were so weak that they could neither stand nor sit, and when we entered they saluted us, by crawling on all fours toward us, and trying to give some token of welcome. *Never, never* was the ruling passion stronger in death. That *heartfelt* greeting which they give the stranger had not in the least died within them. It was not asking charity, for the curate answered my inquiries afterward, concerning the self-control, which was the wonder of all, that he had sent a man previously through the island to say that a stranger from across the sea was coming to visit them, but she had no money or food to give, and they must not trouble her. I gave a little boy a biscuit, and a thousand times since have I wished that it had been thrown into the sea. It could not save him: he took it between his bony hands, clasped it tight, and half-bent as he was, lifted them up, looked with his glaring eyes upon me, and gave a laughing grin that was truly horrible. The curate turned aside, and beckoned me away. 'Did you see that horrid attempt to laugh?'

'I cannot stay longer,' was my answer. We hurried away.

The noble-minded pilot said, 'Will you step into my little place, and I will show you the boiler where I made the soup and stirabout, while the grants lasted'.[13] These grants were mostly sent by the churches in England, and some poor deserving persons selected to give them out, and a very small compensation granted them, from the food they were distributing; and it should be here remarked, that when mention is made of the difference between 'hirelings' and 'volunteers', I mean those 'hirelings' who were paid by government great salaries, and like the slave-overseers, could order *this* flogging, and withhold *that*, according to their own caprices. This does not in the *least* apply to such distributors as these.

The house of this man was a step in advance of the common cabins, and every part as clean as cabin or cottage could be. His young despairing wife sat with a clean cap and apron on, for she knew we were coming, and uncomplainingly answered our inquiries respecting food, that they had not eaten that day, and the husband let us into the next room, opened a chest, took out a small bowl, partly filled with some kind of meal, and solemnly declared that they had not another morsel *in* the cabin or *out*, nor a sixpence to buy any. The curate said, 'I know him well, he is a deserving man, and tells us the truth.'

When we left this cabin we passed a contiguous one, and a decently clad woman, with shoes and stockings and blue petticoat (that was the kind the peasants always wore in their days of comfort) very pleasantly offered me a bowl of milk. Astonished at the sight of such a luxury, I refused, from the principle that it would be robbing the starving. 'I regret,' said the curate, as we turned away, 'that you did not take it, her feelings were deeply injured. A shadow of disappointment,' he said, 'came over her face, as she answered in Irish: "The stranger looks wary and her heart is drooping for the nourishment."'

O, my Heavenly Father! *My heart drooping for nourishment* after having taken a wholesome breakfast, and with the prospect of a good dinner at our return. A second kind woman was about making the same offering, when I begged Mr Griffith, who spoke Irish, to say how much I thanked her; but that I never drank milk, and was not in the least hungry. Inquiring how we came to find milk, the pilot answered that scattered here and there, a comfortable farmer, who had milked some three or four cows, had saved one from the wreck; but that would soon go, and then all must die together. We hurried away. And now for the burying-ground. 'You have seen the living, and must now see the place of the dead.'

A famine burying-ground on the sea-coast has some peculiarities belonging to itself. First, it often lies on the borders of the sea without any wall, and the dead are put into the earth without a coffin, so many

piles on piles that the top one often can be seen through the thin covering; loose stones are placed over, but the dogs can easily put these aside,
and tear away the loose dirt. This burial-place was on a cliff, whose sides
were covered with rough stones, and the ascent in some parts very difficult. We ascended, sometimes keeping erect, and sometimes being obliged to stoop and use our hands. When we reached the top, the painful nov-
elty repaid all our labour. It was an uneven surface of a few perches, with
new-made graves and loose stones covering them. A straw-rope was
lying near a fresh-dug grave, which the pilot said belonged to an old man
who two days before he saw climbing the cliff, with a son of fifteen
lashed to his back by that cord, bringing in his feeble hand a spade. 'I
untied the cord, took the corpse from the father's back, and with the
spade, as well as I could, made a grave and put in the boy,' adding, 'Here
you see so many have been buried, that I could not cover him well.'

This was the burial-place of Arranmore, and here, at the foot, was the
old roaring ocean, dashing its proud waves, embracing in its broad arms
this trembling green gem, while the spray was continually sprinkling its
salt tears upon its once fair cheek, as if weeping over a desolation that it
could not repair. At a little distance was a smooth green field, rearing its
pretty crop of young barley, whose heads were full and fast ripening for
the sickle. 'This,' said Mr Griffith, 'is the growth of seed which was presented by William Bennett, last March; the poor creatures have sowed it,
and if the hands that planted it live to reap the crop, they will have a little
bread.[14] Take a few heads of it, and send them to him as a specimen of its
fine growth, and of their care in cultivating it. Had these industrious people,' he added, 'been supplied in the spring with seed of barley and
turnips, they would not need charity from the public. The government
sent a supply around the coast, the delighted people looked up with hope,
when, to their sad disappointment, this expected gift was offered at a
price considerably higher than the market one, and we saw the ship sailing away, without leaving its contents; for not one was able to purchase a
pound. And we have since been told, that the "lazy dogs" were offered
seed, but refused, not willing to take the trouble to sow it.'

We left without doing *one* favour, and without being asked to do one,
except to drink a basin of milk. We found two little meagre, almost naked
girls, sitting upon the beach picking shells and grinding them in their
clean teeth; they gave a vacant look as we spoke, but answered not.

I gave the six boatmen a shilling each, who had not eaten one mouthful that day, and Mr G. added sixpence each. Their grateful acknowledg-
ments were doubly affecting, when they said, 'This is more than we have
had at one time since the Famine', and they hastened to the meal-shop to
purchase a little for their starving families. We went to a full dinner, pre-

pared in that style which the gentry of Ireland are accustomed to prepare for guests; but what was food to me? The sights at Arranmore were sufficient. What could be done? Mrs Forster said she had written to England, till she was ashamed to tire their generosity again, not once had she been refused from the churches there, and she felt that their patience must be exhausted. She gave the names of some of her donors. A letter was written in the desperation of feeling to an Independent minister there; and God forever bless him and his people, for the ready response. Arranmore was relieved a little.

The next day, a ride of eight miles took me to the house of Mr Griffith; and here was a family made up of that kindness which the husband and father possessed. He occupied a spot among the honest poor indeed. We went over the bleak waste, to visit a romantic pile of cliff, upon the sea-coast, and on our way the laughing sport of children suddenly broke upon the ear, the first I had heard since the Famine; it was from behind a little hillock, and the sound was *mournfully* pleasant.[15] We hurried on to greet the joyous ones and, unperceived, saw two little ragged girls, not wasted entirely by hunger, who had come out of a little dark cluster of stone cabins, and forgetting their sufferings, were playing as other children play. We saluted them, and told them to 'play on, we are glad to see your sports'. We spoke of the allusion of the prophet, when boys and girls are again to be seen playing in the streets of Jerusalem, as a token of its happiness – a happiness which, until the Famine of Ireland, I never valued enough, but *now* it is one of the brightest sunbeams that shines across my path.[16] We at last reached one of the most fearful, sublime and dangerous broken piles of rocks imaginable, tumbled together, and standing almost perpendicularly over the ocean. Deep and frightful caverns yawned between them, and how they came tumbled in this mass never has been made out. They appeared as if shaken together by some sudden crash, and stopped while in their wildest confusion, each seizing hold of its contiguous one to save it from falling. I was glad, quite glad to get away, for had my foot stumbled or slipped, some dark deep gulf might have placed me beyond help or hope. Ossian might have made his bed among these caves, when he says – as two dark streams from high rocks meet and mix.[17]

Rain hurried us to our dinner and poured upon us during the ride of eight miles, in darkness, to the cottage of Dungloe. A little incident occurred this evening, which happily testified to a remark made by Mr Forster in a letter to a committee during the Famine. Speaking of the starving poor, he says, 'They are suffering most *patiently*, and in this parish, where there are ten thousand souls, not one single outrage has ever been committed in the memory of man.'

Mrs Forster and myself in our retreat and hurry had neglected to shut the hall door; in the morning it was quite open and the hall floor covered with water. 'What a dangerous condition,' I said, 'is this, to leave a house at night, especially in a time of hunger, as the present.'

'Not in the least,' was the answer. 'I should not be afraid to leave every door unlocked at night, and every window open, with food or any other property in reach; not the least iota would be touched by one of them.' This was self-discipline, which can scarcely be reconciled with hunger in any stomachs but the Irish.

The letter from Mrs Griffith, in the spring of 1849, says that the people of Arranmore had recovered their former standing, that relief was immediately sent from England, and they had saved as much for seed as they could, and not starve.[18] Five hundred died from famine on that island. The potato was not blasted the following year, and they again looked up with tolerable comfort. The island has since been sold and cultivation will be carried on upon a more extensive and profitable scale. Could a new race of landlords settle up on that coast, and drain and plow the now useless soil, the tenants that are drooping and discouraged would lift up their heads with joy and hope. The air blows as pure as ever breezes did; and were industry encouraged, and food abundant, the inhabitants would cause the grave-digger to have the same source of complaint that once was made in the south, when a poor woman exclaimed, 'The times are dreadful, ma'am, Patrick has not put a spade to the ground this six weeks, not a word of lyin'.'

The comfort and hospitality at Roshine Lodge must be left, and with the kind Mrs F and her friend I turned away *sadly* from the scenes of desolation there witnessed and again went to Gweedore to meet Mrs Hewitson, who was to accompany me to Belfast, and we prepared for the journey. She has distributed her grants and her unceasing labours, often for twenty hours in twenty-four, called for relaxation. We left the pretty spot in sadness, for the starving were crowding about and pressing her for food, following the carriage – begging and thanking, blessing and weeping. We were obliged to shake them off, and hurried in agony away. 'Many of these poor creatures,' she observed, 'will be dead on my return.' On our way we passed the afternoon and night at Derry; it was a day for a flower and cattle show. Here were attracted most of the gentry in the county, as well as nobility; and we had an opportunity of sitting on a seat upon the sloping side of a hill for nearly three hours, in a public garden which overlooks a pretty part of the town, and feasting our eyes with a view of it. It was supposed nearly three thousand ladies had come out in their *best*, on this pleasant day, to see this pretty show of flowers; and though these were almost *surpassingly* beautiful, as Ireland's flowers

are, yet the ladies were *more* so. Their pretty figures (for they are in general of a fine form) and becoming dresses, in all the variety of modern
colours and fashions, brought me, after more than two hours' admiration,
to the conclusion that a more beautiful assemblage of females of the like
number could not be found.

Had the women been educated after the model of Solomon and Paul's
'virtuous women and housekeepers', what a crown of glory would they
be? But alas! The most of the fine material of which woman is composed,
is made up for *ornament* rather than use, in that unhappy country.[19] A few
Mrs Hewitsons and Forsters are sprinkled here and there, and many can
be found in Belfast who have arisen to a higher standard in this respect
than the country in general; and the Famine, which has been the proof of
all that is praiseworthy and all that is deficient in females, has shown that
Belfast has a capital which when employed can be worked to a great and
good advantage. But their late rising and late breakfasts wasted the best
part of the day; and their foolish custom, which made it approach to vul-
garity to give a call before twelve, retarded much that might have been
done more easily and effectually. It is much to be scrupled whether *one*
arose 'while it was yet *dark*, to prepare meat for her maidens'.

I spent a day in the Library, which was instituted in 1788, and now
contains 8000 volumes, without *one* of fiction.[20] Is there another library
on the globe that can say this? It speaks more for the good sense and cor-
rectness of principle in the people of Belfast than any comments or praise
whatever *can* do. I felt, while sitting there, that here was an atmosphere
of truth, entirely new. What would the reading community of all nations
be, if youth had access to such libraries as these, and to no others?

From Belfast I went up the coast of Antrim, visited many beautiful
towns and places, but all was saddened by the desolations of the Famine.
Industrial schools were everywhere showing their happy effects; and
often by the wayside, in clusters upon a bank, or under a tree in some village, were young girls with their fancy knitting, sitting pleasantly together, busy at their work; and this was a striking fact, that in *no* case where
they were thus employed did they look untidy; though their garments
were of the plainest and poorest, yet they appeared cleanly. I visited a
school at Larne of this description, conducted by a pious widow woman;
and the arrangements in all respects reflected honour on the superinten-
dents and teacher. Their reading, writing, working and knowledge of the
Scriptures manifested great wisdom and faithfulness in the teacher, as
well as aptness in the scholars. The most useful work was done there, and
the finest fancy material, much of which has been sold in London, at a
fair price, for the benefit of the poor children. One little girl of twelve, by
her industry in that school the preceding winter, had kept a family of

three or four from the poorhouse by her fancy knitting, occasionally working nearly all night. The father came to the window with a load of turf to thank her for the instruction of the child which had fed them through the winter, and this small token of his gratitude, humble as it was, he hoped she would not refuse.

These schools, scattered through the island in the midst of the desolating Famine, looked to the traveler like some humble violet or flower, springing in the desert or prairie, where a seathing fire had swept over the plain and withered all that was most prominent to the beholder. Never did I see a company of these little ones, at their cheerful work, or have one present me with a specimen of her attainments, but the unassuming hope-cheered look, eloquently said, 'Will you let us live? Will you give us our honest bread, for the willing labour of our hands, and allow us a dwelling-place among the nations of the earth?' Here in these pretty towns along the coast of Antrim had the poor-laws manifested their handy-work. The advice of Daniel O'Connell concerning them, was: 'If you begin to build poor-houses, you had better at once make one grand roof over the whole island, for in due time the whole country will need a shelter under it.'[21]

This precaution was not altogether a random one, for already had many of the industrious respectable tradesmen and widows who were keeping lodging-houses been compelled to give up their business – the taxes had come in and taken all within doors, which would sell at auction, for the poor-rates.[22] I was directed to a respectable house to procure lodgings for a few days. The disheartened widow said, 'Two days ago I could have given you a well-furnished bedroom and parlour, but now I have neither table, chair, nor carpet on the floors; the money was demanded for a new tax just levied. I could not raise it, my furniture was taken, and I have no means to fetch it back, or to get bread.' She could not expect respectable lodgers to stop with her, and saw nothing but hunger or the poor-house for herself and children. Telling her if she would give me a place to lie down I would stop and give the usual price, she gladly accepted it, and the money paid her for this was all the means she had to get *one* meal for herself and three children, while I was in the house. This was a person of good reputation, kept a tidy, well-furnished lodging-house; and before the extra taxes had been laid on, had been able to put by a little money, but it had all been demanded the past year and the means taken away to procure any more. This was the condition of the entire country.

While riding upon the car the driver pointed to a peculiar dwelling, with a sign for refreshment, saying, 'The woman here is a lucky one, for she pays no rent; if you wish I will stop and let you go in.' The entrance was through a door, into a cave, which narrowed as it extended back till it came to a point, and was very much in the shape of a harrow. A person could stand upright at the mouth, but must stoop, and then crawl if he proceeded. The old woman lit up her torch and crept on, insisting that I should follow. The passage was so long, dark and narrow, that paying the old woman her expected sixpence, I got excused. She had an old bed, lying by the side of one wall of the cave, a little table on the other, on which she kept cakes and 'the drap of whiskey' for the traveller; and she told us merrily that no landlord had disturbed her, and she had got the comfortable 'bit' for many a twelve-month. Happy old woman! It is hoped that when her grey hairs shall be removed to a still darker cave, the inheritance will fall to some other houseless head, who, like her, shall enjoy unmolested and unenvied this happy den, which like comfort few of the poor outcasts of Ireland can ever hope to attain.

Some of the most romantic spots are scattered upon this coast, which is for many a mile enlivened by white rocks and small white pebbles near the sea, so that the whole is so inviting, taking sea, rocks, beautiful road and in many places backed by the rich woodland, that I left the carriage, and loitered among the varying beauties of running brooks, murmuring cascades, neat cottages and pretty churches, and deep green glens. My imagination was inclining to drink in the spirit of the simple little boy who accompanied me. When looking down from an eminence, on the path where we were walking, I saw a crumbling stone cabin deep below me, in so narrow a defile that its opposite walls nearly extended to the perpendicular hills on each side; and inquiring of the child who could ever build there, expecting to live in it, he simply replied, 'Oh, lady! that is a fairy's house; the people have put on the roof many a time, but at night the fairies come and take it off. They live in this glen, ma'am'

'Then the fairies do not like roofs to their houses?'

'I s'pose not, ma'am.'

These fairies have doubtless saved many an agent or tithe-gatherer a 'good baitin'', whose cowardly conscience has come by night to rob some corn or hay-stack for his unjust gain. Leaving my little companion, I ascended higher and higher, till at my feet far away stretched the broad sea; and about were sprinkled cabins, looking like the 'shabby gentility' which a decayed person who had fallen from higher life keeps up. I entered one of cleanly appearance, and stumbled upon a most frightful sight. A woman with a child on her lap gave me an indifferent nod of welcome, and pointed to a bed through the door; supposing some starving object lay there, I turned to look, and on a bed lay her husband, his face uncovered, swollen and black, entirely blind, and blood still fresh about his hair and pillow, and he speechless. She was alone with him, her infant the only inmate: the doctor had just left without dressing his face.

The story was, two hours before, going to his labour, a furious bull had broken from his fastenings and was in mad pursuit after a lady, whose screams attracted the poor labourer. He ran with his spade, rushed between the horns of the animal and the lady, but could not save himself from the bull, which trampled him in the dirt, gored his face, broke his upper jaw, and tore apart one nostril. Three of the animal's legs were tied with the rope when he accomplished all this. The story ended by 'Thank God, the lady was saved, and the mad bull shot by the owner', and not one word of complaint about her husband. When I said, 'What a pity that he went near him.'

'But, ma'am, didn't he go to save the lady, and wouldn't she been kilt if he hadn't done it?' So much for being a *lady* in Ireland, and for Irish courage and humanity.

Returning to Belfast, I prepared for Dublin, and again sought out old Cook Street. Some of my pensioners had removed, but none dead. Their rent had been left to be paid weekly for them, and sufficient knitting given for their employ. Another grant was coming for me to be deposited at Belfast, and the expense of transportation to Dublin would be such, that it was placed in the trustworthy hands of Mrs Hewitson, who could get it conveyed to her destitute people at a smaller expense when she should return. This donation, she afterwards said, was eked out for months at the most sparing rate; and the only relief she had in her power during the following winter season.

A box of clothing was in my possession, and with this and a little money I resolved to go to the western coast, in Connaught. I *went*, and Connaught will long live in my memory, for there are still scenes of *suffering,* of *cruelty* and of *patience* which no other people yet have shown to the world. That people who from the time of the invasion have been 'hunted and peeled', treated as the 'offscouring of all things', driven into 'dens and caves of the earth' as the only shelter, now still live, to hold out to the world that lineament of the 'image of God', which *is* and which *must* be the everlasting rebuke of their persecutors; which says in the face and eyes of all mankind, to their spoilers: 'You have hated me, you have robbed me, you have shorn me of my beauty; and *now,* while famine is eating up my strength, gnawing my vitals, you are turning me into the storm, without food, or even sheep-skins or goat-skins for a covering; and then tauntingly saying, "Wherein have we robbed you?"'

I took the train at Dublin for twenty-five miles, then a coach to Tuam, where I tarried one night. This is the residence of Bishop M'Hale, and a somewhat respectable old town; but the picture of sorrow was here too, and the next morning I gladly proceeded to Newport.[23] It rained hard, we

were on an open car, and the wretchedness of the country made it altogether a dismal ride. When we had reached a few miles of the town, a
dissipated, tattered, and repulsive looking man was seated before me on
the car, which was not a little annoying, for he might be a little intoxicat-
ed. 'Has he paid his fare,' I asked the coachman, knowing that if he had,
he had the same right as I had; and still more, it would confirm me in the
opinion that if he had money to pay his ride, he might have money for
drink. We went on, my unpleasant companion never once speaking, till
we reached our stopping-place, the Post-Office, at Newport. Here, at my
old tried friend's, Mrs Arthur, I met with a cordial welcome, and getting
from the car, was still more annoyed to see this out-of-the-way companion reach the door before me, and fall prostrate in the passage; this was
certainly proof that he had been taking whiskey, for he did not look like
one in the last stages of starvation.[24] My severity upon myself was equal
to my surprise when we found that it was exhaustion occasioned by
hunger. When he could speak in a whisper, he begged Mrs Arthur to take
a few sovereigns, which he had sewed up in his ragged coat and send
them to his wife and children, who were suffering for food. He had been
at work in England, and knowing the dreadful state his family were in at
home, had saved the few sovereigns, not willing to break one, and
endeavored to reach home on a few shillings he had, and being so weak
for want of food, he occasionally rode a few miles when it rained, and
had not eaten *once* in two days. 'Send them *quick*,' he said, 'I shall not
live to reach home.' O, *shame! shame* on my wicked suspicions; how
should I be thus deceived? I *could not*, I *would not* forgive myself. His
story was a true one, and by proper care he lived to follow his sovereigns
home.

The astonishing suffering and self-denial of that people for their
friends is almost heart-rending. It is *expected* that mothers will suffer,
and even die for their famishing little ones, if needful; but to see children
suffer for one another was magnanimity above all. Two little orphan
boys, one about nine and the other five, called at the door of a rich
widow of my acquaintance and asked for food. The woman had consumed all her bread at breakfast but a small piece, and giving this to the
eldest, she said, 'You must divide this with your little brother; I have no
more.' She looked after them unperceived, and saw them stop, when the
eldest said, 'Here, Johnny, you are littler than I, and cannot bear the
hunger so well, and you shall have it all.' They were both houseless
orphans and starving with hunger.

I found here, at Newport, misery without a mask; the door and window of the kind Mrs Arthur wore a spectacle of distress indescribable;
naked, cold and dying, standing like petrified statues at the window, or

imploring, for God's sake, a little food, till I almost wished that I might flee into the wilderness, far, far from the abode of any living creature.[25]

Mrs Arthur said: 'I have one case to place before you, and will leave all the rest to your own discretion. I have fed a little boy, once a day, whose parents and brothers and sisters are dead, with the exception of one little sister. The boy is seven years old, the sister five. They were told they must make application to the poor-house, at Castlebar, which was ten Irish miles away.' One cold rainy day in November, this boy took his little sister by the hand, and faint with hunger set off for Castlebar. And now, reader, if you will, follow these little *bare-footed, bare-headed* Connaught orphans through a muddy road of ten miles, on a rainy day, without food, and see them at the work-house, late at night. The doors are closed – at last, they succeed in being heard. The girl is received, the boy sent away – no room for him. He made his way back to Newport the next morning, and had lived by crawling into any place he could at night, and once a day called at the door of my friend who fed him.[26]

He soon came a fine-looking boy, with unusually matured judgment. The servant was paid for taking him into an outhouse and scrubbing him thoroughly, &c. A nice black suit of clothes was found in the American box, with a cap suited to his head; and when he was suitably prepared by the servant, the clothes were put on. He had not, probably, been washed for six months and his clothes were indescribable; his skin, which had been kept from wind and sun by the coat which had so long been gathering, was white, and so changed was he wholly and entirely, that I paused to look at him; and tied about his neck a pretty silk handkerchief, to finish the whole. 'What do you say now, my boy? I shall burn your old clothes, and you never shall see them again.' A moment's hesitation – he looked up, I supposed to thank me, when to my surprise, he burst into an agony of loud weeping. 'What can be the matter?'

He answered, 'Now I shall sure die with the hunger; if they see me with nice clothes on, they will say I tell lies, that I have a mother that minds me; and lady, you won't burn them old clothes' (turning about to gather them up); and if I had not sternly commanded him to drop them, he would have clasped them close, as his best and dearest friends.

In truth, this was a new development of mind I had never seen before, clinging with a firm grasp to a bundle of filthy, forbidding garments, as the only craft by which to save his life; choosing uncleanliness to decency, at an age too when all the young emotions of pride generally spring up in fondness for new and pretty garments. The silk handkerchief seemed almost to frighten him. Was it the principle of association, which older people experience when they cling to objects which have been their companions in trial, or those places where they have seen their dearest comforts depart? He would not have consented to have left those old clothes behind, but by a promise which he could hardly believe; that he should be fed every day through the winter. He was taken immediately to a school where the children were fed once a day and instructed for a penny a week; this penny, the teacher said, should not be exacted, as he had been clothed by me.[27] I saw the boy through the winter; three months after his clothes were tidy and had not been torn, and he was improving.

His fears respecting the 'hungry' were not groundless: no stranger would have believed that he needed charity when decently clad.

From Newport, I went to Achill Sound. Here was enough to excite the pity and energy of all such as possessed them. This wild dreary sea-coast at any time presents little except its salubrity of air, and grandeur of storms and tempests, tempered with the beauty of its varied clouds when lighted by the sun, to make it the most inviting spot. But now the work of death was going on; and, notwithstanding the exertions of Mr Savage, with the aid of the Central Committee in Dublin, and government relief beside, at times it seemed to mock all effort.[28] Mr Savage seemed to be in the position of the 'ass colt' in Scripture, tied where two ways meet.[29] He had the island of Achill on one side across the Sound, and a vast bog and mountainous waste on the other, with scarcely an inhabitant for many a mile (but the colony of Mr Nangle) which could subsist only but by charity.[30] The groups which surrounded the house, from the dawn of day till dark, called forth the incessant labours of many hands, both male and female, to appease the pitiful requests multiplying around them. Oh! the scenes of that dreadful winter! Who shall depict them, and who that saw them can ever forget? I have looked out at the door of that house, and seen from three to five, six and seven hundred hovering about the windows and in the corners, not one woman or child having a shoe upon their feet, or a covering upon the head, with ghastly, yes, ghostly countenances of hunger and despair, that mock all description. One fact among the many is recorded, which transpired a few weeks before related to me by Mrs Savage, which had novelties peculiar to itself.

ABRAHAM AND SARA[31]

Mrs Savage saw standing at her door, among the crowd, while the relief was giving out, a feeble old woman, bare-footed, and her feet and legs swollen so that they assumed a transparency which always indicated that death had begun its fatal ravages. She was nearly a hundred years of age; her becoming bearing and cleanly appearance, united with her age, caused Mrs S to inquire particularly who she was.

'Why are you here – do you belong in this parish? You are a stranger!'

'I am, in troth, a stranger. My name is Sara, and I have now come into the parish to stop, in a little cabin convenient to ye, and sure ye won't refuse the poor owld body a bit of the relief.'

Abraham, her husband, was sitting upon a form, among the crowd, waiting an answer to Sara's request.

They were fed, but Sara could not be restored. She often called on days when the relief was not given out, and was once told that she was troublesome; she acknowledged it in the most simple manner, and in a few days ceased coming.

Not long after, Abraham called to say that Sara was ill and had been obliged to leave the cabin where she had been stopping, and he had made her shelter under a bank, in the bog, by the strand. She was no longer able to walk about, and daily Abraham brought a little saucepan, suspended by a cord for a handle, to get the broth, which Mrs S provided for his beloved Sara. He said he had made her as comfortable as his 'owld' hands could, but the breath would 'soon be cowld in her', for she could scarcely 'lift the hand to raise the broth to the lip'. This bed was made in the bog, within a few yards of the sea, but sheltered from its spray by a bank, under which a narrow place had been dug by Abraham, which partly covered Sara. Heath was put down for her bed, and pieces of turf for her pillow; a wall of turf a few inches high extended round, making the shape of a bed, against the side of which was a fire of turf, made to warm the broth; and this was Abraham and Sara's house. Abraham's part was wholly unsheltered. For days she was nursed in the most careful manner; her cloak was wrapped snugly about her, the heath under her was smoothed, and her broth carried by Abraham; and he even washed her garments in the sea, 'for Sara', he said, 'loves to be clean'. In spite of all his care the life of Sara was fast ebbing; and Mary A, who had seen before the bed where she lay, called one evening and found her much altered. She raised her up, gave her a little milk, which she could scarcely swallow. 'I am departing,' she whispered, 'and will ye give my blessin' to the mistress?' She had come into the parish, she said, to die, because 'she knew the mistress would put a coffin on her owld body'.

While Mary was here, Abraham hastened to Mrs S to procure some necessaries for the night; then returning, he sat by the side of Sara till she died. He was sitting alone, by her lifeless body, when Mary returned in the morning. The mistress was soon there. She had ordered a coffin, and brought a sheet to wrap around her body, and a handkerchief to put about her head. Mary washed and combed her, and found in her pocket a piece of white soap, carefully wrapped in a linen rag, and a clean comb, which were all that appertained to Sara of this world's wealth, except the miserable garments she had upon her. When the body was shrouded, it was placed in her coffin of white boards; a boatman and Mary lifted her into a boat; Abraham and the mistress seated themselves in it, and were rowed to land, and put the remains of Sara in an out-house belonging to Mr Savage for the night, and a comfortable place was provided for Abraham to lie down. Early in the morning Abraham was found sitting on the cart, which bore Sara from the boat, with his grey head leaning against the locked door, weeping. He had waited till all was still, and then crept to the spot which inclosed the remains of her he loved, to weep alone, in the stillness of night. Not one that saw him but wept too.

This simple-hearted man, like the patriarch whose name he bore, was a stranger and sojourner; like him, he had come to mourn for Sara, and he had come too to ask a burial-place for his dead, though he could not, like him, offer a sum of money. He could not take his choice in the sepulchres; no field of Ephron, nor the trees within, were made sure to him, but in a lone bog, where those who had died by famine and pestilence were buried like dogs, unshrouded and uncoffined, he was grateful to find a place to bury his 'dead out of his sight'.[32] The corpse was borne away by a few boatmen across the channel; and Sara was conveyed to her long home. I saw Abraham early in December 1847, and the bed which he made for Sara on that bleak sea-shore. The turf wall was still unbroken; the smoke, where the fire had been made, had left its blackness, and a piece of turf, partly consumed, was lying by this hearth; the heath-bed had not been stirred, and I begged Mrs S to keep it from the inroad of cattle. A wall of stone should be built around that dwelling, and the traveller pointed to it, as a relic of the greatest interest – *a relic of Ireland's woes!*

It is said that Sara, in her father's house, was 'fair to look upon', and enjoyed in plenty the good things of this life; and, says Mrs S, 'when first I saw her the sun was shining in full strength upon her marble face; and so swollen its wrinkles were smoothed; her countenance was mild, her manner modest and pleasing, and she was an object of much admiration'. She lay in that lowly bed in storm and sunshine, by night and by day, till the 'good God', as she expressed it, should 'plaise to take her away'. Yet lowly as was her couch, lonely as was her wake, unostentatious as was her burial, few, in her condition, were honoured with so good a one.

In the same vicinity was the bed of a little orphan girl, who had crept into a hole in the bank and died one night, with no one to spread her heath-bed, or to close her eyes, or wash and fit her for the grave. She died unheeded, the dogs lacerated the body, gnawed the bones, and strewed them about the bog.

DEATH AND BURIAL OF ABRAHAM

Abraham called one day in December at the house of Mr Savage, and sorrow and hunger had greatly changed his looks. His garments which had been kept tidy by Sara, were now going to decay. He stood silently at the door, with a subdued look, and a little brown bag and staff in his hand. I saw him there, and among the throng marked his shades of sorrow, and inquired who he was. 'It is Abraham, the old hands that made Sara's bed,' was the answer.

Abraham knew and felt the change in himself, and seeking an opportunity, asked for a piece of soap, touching his collar, which Sara had always kept clean, saying, 'I do not like the feel of it'. Food and a little money were given him. He went away, and on his boggy path to his humble home he fell down and broke his arm; he lingered on a few days in destitution and pain, and the next that we heard of him, two men who were walking toward sunset on Sabbath day met his daughter – who had a shelter in the mountain where she had kept her father – with Abraham upon her back, with his arms about her neck, a loathsome corpse which she had kept in her cabin for days, and was going alone with a spade in her hand the distance of an Irish mile to bury him. They took the corpse and accompanied her, and put him into the ground as he was, neither with a coffin nor by the side of Sara whom he had loved and cherished so well.

Thus died Sara and Abraham, and thus they were buried, and let their epitaph be: 'Lovely and pleasant in their lives, though in death they were divided.'

DRINKING HABITS

Let the reader's mind be a little relieved by a subject *different,* though as painful in a *moral* sense as famine is in a *natural* one. I allude to the *fearful, sinful* use of all kinds of intoxicating drinks in Ireland in the time of the Famine. Much noise has been made the last nine or ten years respecting the great temperance reform in that country.[33] But who have been reformed? Travel the length and breadth of the island, even in the midst of desolation and death, and in how many families when a piece of flesh meat can be afforded upon the dinner-table would the tea-kettle for hot whiskey be wanting at the close of dinner? The more costly wines, too, were on the tables of the nobility, and not always wanting among the gentry. The clergy of all denominations in that country are sad examples to the flock. Father Mathew is praised by some of these Bible ministers, because he kept the 'lower order' from fighting at fairs; but the very fact that the vulgar were reclaimed was a stigma upon temperance in their enlightened opinions. Four years and four months residence in Ireland, changing from place to place, and meeting with many ministers of all denominations, not a solitary case do I recollect of finding a minister of the Established, Presbyterian or Methodist church, who did not plead for the moderate use of this fatal poison. I met with one Baptist minister, one Unitarian and a few priests, who abstained entirely.

The Famine, if possible, urged many of the lovers of the 'good creature', to greater diligence in the practice 'to keep themselves up', as they said, in these dreadful times. They preached sermons on charity, they urged the people to greater-self-denial, they talked of the great sin of improvidence, of which Ireland is emphatically guilty; but few, very few, it is to be feared, touched one of these burdens so much as with one of their fingers. There were noble cases of hard labour, and even curtailing of expenses, by some of the clergy; even labour was protracted till it ended in death by some, but these were isolated cases indeed.

An able writer, who wrote the pamphlet on *Irish Improvidence,* placed the subject in the most fearful light when he said: 'Next to the absurdity of Cork and Limerick exporting cargoes of Irish grain for sale, and at the same time receiving cargoes of American grain to be given away at the cost of the English people, may be ranked the folly – if it may not properly be called by some worse name – of seeing hundreds dying for want of food, at the same time permitting the conversion of as much grain as would feed the whole of those dying of starvation, and many more, into a fiery liquid, which it is well known, even to the distillers themselves, never saved a single life or improved a single character, never prevented a single crime, or elevated the character of a single family by its use.'[34]

Reader, ponder this well – enough grain, converted into a poison for body and soul, as would have fed all that starving multitude. While the clergy were preaching, committees were in conclave to stimulate to charity and devise the most effectual methods to draw upon the purses of people abroad.[35]

And what shall be said of the pitiful landlords, who were still drinking their wine, pouring their doleful complaints into government's ears, that no rents were paid; and many saying, as one of these wine-bibbers did, that his lazy tenants would not work for pay, for he had offered that morning some men work who were hungry, and would pay them at night, and they walked away without accepting it. 'How much pay did you offer?' he was asked. 'A pound of Indian meal.' (Indian meal was then a penny a pound.) 'Would you, sir, work for that, and wait till night for the meal, when you were then suffering?' Much better try to procure it before night in some easier way.

But these afflicted landlords, the same writer remarks, when exporting to the continent vast quantities of grain which their poor starving tenants had laboured to procure, and were not allowed to eat a morsel of this food; but buy it from others or starve. Neither can it be doubted, nor should it be concealed, that not a few of these landlords, while their grain was selling at a good price abroad, shared the benefit of many an Indian meal donation for horses, hogs, fowls and servants. The guilty are left to make the application, none others are implicated.

I would not say that every man who takes a glass of spirits, as he says moderately, is guilty of downright dishonesty, or not to be trusted with the property of others; but it may properly be said that such are in the path to the hotbed where every evil work is cultivated; and, therefore more to be scrupled than those who from conscience would 'cut off a right arm or pluck out a right eye' rather than give offence.[36]

Had all the professed Christians in Ireland entirely excluded alcoholic drinks from their tables and houses, thousands might now be living who have been starved.

I was once in a miserable part of the country where death was doing a fearful work, and was stopping in a house ranked among the respectable, when a company of ministers who had been attending a public meeting in the town were assembled for dinner. The dinner was what is generally provided for ministers – the richest and best. Wine and brandy were accompaniments. When these heralds of salvation heard a word of remonstrance they put on the religious cant, and cited me immediately and solemnly the Marriage of Cana and the tribunal of Timothy's stomach for my doom; declaring that God sanctioned, yea required it, and ratified it by taking in moderation what their conscience told them was duty.[37] They were pointed directly to the suffering of the people for bread, and the great difficulty of procuring coffins: all this did not move their brandy-seared hearts. When in an hour after dinner the tea was served, as is the custom in Ireland, one of the daughters of the family passing a window, looked down upon the pavement and saw a corpse with a blanket spread over it lying upon the walk beneath the window. It was a mother and infant, dead, and a daughter of sixteen had brought and laid her there, hoping to induce the people to put her in a coffin; and as if she had been listening to the conversation at the dinner of the want of coffins, she had placed her mother under the very window and eye where these wine-bibbing ministers might apply the lesson. All was hushed, the blinds were immediately down, and a few sixpences were quite unostentatiously sent out to the poor girl, as a beginning, to procure a coffin. The lesson ended here.

And I would conclude this episode by saying that at the door of professed Christians of the intelligent class lies the sin of intemperance in that suffering country, and though some of them have preached and laboured hard in those dark days, yet they have not done what they could, and in this they should not be commended, but rebuked most faithfully.

CHAPTER V

'However darkly stained by sin,
He is thy brother yet.'

It was at the house of Mr Savage, at the Sound, where I first met with the Hon. William Butler. He insisted on my going to Erris as a spot of all others the most wretched, offering kindly to pay my passage in an open boat which was to take him there. We went. He observed on the passage that he had always feared the water, and would prefer any death almost to that of drowning. He was drowned the next season while on a visit to the continent.

We reached Belmullet; he secured me a lodging, but the rector called and invited me to spend the time at his house, and I did so.[1] But here was a place which might justly be called the fag-end of misery. It seemed to be a spinning out of all that was fearful in suffering, and whoever turned his eye there needed no other point of observation to see all that famine and pestilence could do. It appeared like a vast crucible where had been concocted all that was odious, all that was suffering; and which had been emptied, leaving the dregs of the mass unfit for any use.

Well did James Tuke say, in his graphic description of Erris, that he had visited the wasted remnants of the once noble Red Man in North America, and the negro-quarter of the degraded and enslaved African; but never had he seen misery so intense, or physical degradation so complete, as among the dwellers in the bog-holes of Erris.

Figure and mien, complexion and attire,
Are leagued to strike dismay.[2]

The few resident landlords in this barony, containing in the year 1846, a population of twenty-eight thousand, were now reduced, by the extreme poverty of the tenantry to a state of almost hopeless desperation.[3] The poor-house was a distance of forty miles to Ballina; and the population since the Famine was reduced to twenty thousand – ten thousand of these on the extreme borders of starvation, crawling about the streets, lying under the windows of such as had a little food in a state of almost nudity.[4] Being situated on the north-west coast of Mayo, it has the Atlantic roaring and dashing upon two sides of it; and where the wretched dwellers of its coasts are hunting for seaweed, sand-eels, &c. to appease their hunger, and where in many cases I truly thought that man had nearly lost the image in which he was created. This coast is noted for shipwrecks; and many of the inhabitants, in former days, have subsisted very comfortably upon the spoils.[5]

A Mrs D called one morning to take a walk with me upon a part of the sea-coast called Cross.[6] Nature here seemed to have put on her wildest dress, for in the whole barony of Erris there is but one tree, and that a stinted one; and this barony extends thirty-five miles.[7] But here our walk seemed to be through something unlike all I had seen. In some places nature appeared like a maniac who, in her ravings, had disheveled her locks and tattered her garments. In others she put on a desponding look, as if almost despairing, yet not unwilling to be restored, if there were any to comfort her; in others, the bold cliffs dashed by the maddening waves seemed like a lion rising from his lair, and going forth in fury for his prey. Three miles presented us with grand, beautiful and painful scenes; the air was salubrious, the sun was bright; the unroofed cabins, silent and dreary, told us that the ejected inmates were wandering shelterless or dead, many of whom were buried under the ruins, who were found starved in a putrid state; and having no coffins, the stones of the cabins were tumbled upon them.

Mrs D is one of those sensitive beings who is capable of enjoying the beauties of nature, and capable too of suffering most keenly. She had tasted deeply of sorrow – was a new-made widow; her mother had died but a few months previous; an adopted child, a lovely niece of ten years old, had died a few weeks before. As we neared the burying-ground she pointed to the spot, saying, 'There I put her, my fair blossom; and there, by her side, I put her uncle' [meaning her husband] 'five weeks after. But you must excuse me from taking you there, for I could not venture myself where they lie, because they will give me no welcome, nor speak a kind word, as they used to do.' We passed over sand-banks and ditches to the cottage where her father and mother had lived and died, leaving two sisters and two brothers on the paternal estate. The cottage had no wicket-gate, no flowers nor shrubs; but standing upon the margin of the lake, it seemed modestly to say, 'Walk in, my comforts shall be equal to all I have promised.' The interior was neat. Here were the remains of an ancient family who had lived to enjoy, who could walk or ride, could entertain guests in true Irish hospitality for many a century back. But death had removed the head of the family; famine had wasted the tenantry; the fields were neglected. 'And here,' said the sister who kept the cottage, 'we are sitting as you see, with little to cheer us, and less to hope for the future.'

We visited the churchyard, which my companion thought she could not see – a brother offered to be her companion – and we found it upon a rising hillock by the sea-side; it was a Protestant one, and a snug church had stood near, but the landholder, Mr Bingham, had caused it to be taken down and another built in a town or village called Bingham's Town. Here was another specimen of the peculiar graveyards on the sea-coast of Ireland. The better classes have a monument of rough stones put over the whole surface of the grave, elevated a few feet and cemented with mortar. The poorer classes must be content to lie under a simple covering of rough stones, without being elevated or cemented. We wait-ed a few moments till the sister, who sat down upon the grave of the little one, had indulged her grief for the two departed, and I only heard her say, 'Ah! and you will not speak to me'. An ancient abbey was near, said to be a thousand years old; and so closely had the Catholics buried their dead there that it appeared at a little distance like one vast pile of stones tumbled together.[8] The Protestants and Romanists do not choose to place their dead in contact; and these two were distinct. But they, also, had their respectable monuments, for we saw, in a nearer approach, that this graveyard had elevated cemented tombstones; the ground was high, and no walls but the roaring old sea upon one side which sometimes boldly reaches out and snatches a sleeper for his bed. The scattered bones that lay about told that it must long have been the 'place of skulls'. The last year had made great accessions to the pile, which could easily be known by their freshness, and ropes of straw and undried grass brought here by relatives to put over the uncoffined bodies of their friends.

Here were deposited five or six sailors, belonging to a vessel from Greenock which was wrecked on this coast the preceding spring. The bodies washed ashore, and a brother of the lady with me dug a pit and put them in, spreading over their faces the skirt of one of their overcoats, 'to screen,' as he said, 'the cruel clay from their eyes'. These poor sailors, unknown and unwept, were buried by the hand of a stranger on a foreign shore; but somewhere they might have had mothers who waited and asked in vain for the absent ship.

As these sailors have no monument to tell their parentage, let it be recorded here, that in the spring of 1847 a vessel was wrecked on the desolate coast of Erris, and every soul on board was lost.[9] The vessel sailed from Greenock, in Scotland. While sitting in the cottage in the evening, the lady who accompanied me brought a lid of a box which was taken from among the wreck of that lost ship, and on it was written: Soda Biscuits, by —, Corner of Beekman and Cliff Street, New York. The name was so defaced it could not be made out. This added new interest to the shipwreck, when meeting an inscription from the street where I had lived, and the shop in which I had traded, and was told that the vessel was freighted with provisions for the starving of Ireland.[10] This was a mistake.

In the morning, when the sun was rising, we ascended a hill among the desolate cabins where once was the song of health, and where far off in the west the sea stretched wide and the variegated clouds, gilded with the morning sun, were dipping apparently in its waters. 'This', said a daughter of the family, 'was once a pretty and a grand spot. Here, two years ago, these desolate fields were cultivated, and content and cheerfulness were in every cabin. Now, from morning to night they wander in search of a turnip, or go to the sea for sea-weed to boil, and often have we found a corpse at the door, that the brother you see might put a board on 'em. We have often seen an ass passing our window carrying a corpse, wound about with some old remnant of a blanket or sheet; and thus, flung across its back, a father or mother, wife or husband was carried to the grave. Sometimes, when the corpse was a little child, or it might be more than one, they were put into a couple of baskets, and thus balanced upon the sides of the ass, this melancholy hearse proceeded on without a friend to follow it, but the one who was guiding the beast.' These burials tell more of the paralysing effects of famine than anything else can do; for the Irish in all ages have been celebrated for their attention to the interment of their dead, sparing no expense.

When I stood in the burying-ground in that parish, I saw the brown silken hair of a young girl waving gently through a little cleft of stones, that lay loosely upon her young breast.[11] They had not room to put her beneath the surface but slightly, and a little green grass was pulled and spread over, and then covered with stones. I never shall forget it.

> The blast of the desert comes,
> Her loose hair flew on the wind.

In some parts the soil was manured with the slain. When the Famine first commenced efforts were made to procure coffins; but the distress became so great to the living that every penny that could be procured must be given for food; and the famished relatives, at last, were grateful if some hand stronger than theirs would dig the pit and put down the uncoffined body.

One Sabbath, when I was in Erris, the day was so stormy that the church service was suspended. A barefooted woman, who one year before had called to sell milk and kept a fine dairy, came into the house where I was, and calling me by name, said: 'Will ye give me something to buy a coffin to put on my husband. He died yesterday on me, and it would be a pity to put him in the ground without a board, and he is so swelled, ma'am, not a ha'porth of his legs or belly but is ready to burst, and but a five-pence-halfpenny could I gather, and the little boys are ashamed to go out and ask the charity for him.'[12]

This is an illustration not only of the state into which famine has thrown the country, but the apathy of feeling which the most tender-hearted people on the globe manifested – a woman compelled to go out in a most perilous storm, upon a wild sea-coast, unprotected by clothes, and without a morsel of food for twenty-four hours, to procure a coffin for her husband who had died by starvation!

THE SOLDIERS OF BELMULLET

Among the marvels and dreadfuls of Erris, the Queen's soldiers certainly deserve a place in history.[13] Government in her mercy had deposited in a shop some tons of Indian meal, to be sold or given out, as the Commissariat should direct, for the benefit of the people. This meal was in *status quo*, and hunger was making fearful inroads. One hundred and fifty-one soldiers, *cap-à-pie,* were marching before and around this shop with bayonets erect, from early dawn till late in dusky eve, to guard this meal. They certainly made a warlike bloody-looking array when con-trasted with the haggard, meagre, squalid skeletons that were grouped in starving multitudes about them, who, if the whole ten thousand starving ones in the barony had been disposed to rise *en masse*, scarcely had strength to have broken open a door of the shop or to have knocked down a soldier. But here they were, glistening in bright armour, and the people dying with hunger about it.

These soldiers were alive to their duty on all and every occasion. One Sabbath morning when the church prayers were in full progress, they marched up under arms, with fife and drum playing merrily the good old tune of 'Rory O'More'. The modest rector suspended operations, the congregation in breathless silence, most of them arose from their seats; the army entered, doffed their caps, planted their arms, and quietly, if not decently, took their seats and sat till prayers and sermon were ended; as soon as 'Old Hundred' closed the worship these soldiers resumed their arms, and the musicians, upon the threshold of the door, struck up 'The Girl I Left Behind Me' and the congregation, a little confused, walked out. I never heard it applauded nor ever heard it censured but by one. To say the least of the morality of Erris, their drinking and card-playing and dancing habits would well comport with the army or navy. But they were quite in advance of anything I had seen in any part of Ireland. Here I saw the cobweb covering flung about fallen man to hide his deformity torn aside, and scarcely a vestige was there of beauty, amiability or even decency left.

The hotel-keeper was in the habit of collecting a few shillings from lodgers and travellers and distributing them in pennies to the starving, in the morning. These recipients were as ravenous as hungry lions and tigers, as void of reason, and more disgusting to the sight. If man is to be guided by reason, then when reason is extinc, upon what can he fall back? If the instinct that is planted in man is the image of God in which He is made, then where this God is extinguished there can be nothing but a wreck – a mass of neither man nor brute; for if he has lost the image of God and has not the instinct of animals, he stands out an unnatural growth to be wondered at rather than admired. I could scarcely believe that these creatures were my fellow-beings. Never had I seen slaves so degraded; and here I learnt that there are many pages in the volume of slavery and that every branch of it proceeds from one and the same root, though it assumes different shapes. These poor creatures are in as virtual bondage to their landlords and superiors as is possible for mind or body to be. They cannot work unless they bid them; they cannot eat unless they feed them; and they cannot get away unless they help them.

From Belmullet, Rosport was my destiny, a distance of twelve miles – a romantic place on the sea-coast where resided three families of comparative comfort; but their comforts were threatened most fearfully by the dreadful scourge. Fever was everywhere, and hunger indeed had filled a graveyard, which lay at the foot of a mountain, so full that scarcely any distinction could be seen of graves, but now and then a stick at the head or foot of one. By the road-side a family of four or five had made a temporary shelter, waiting for a son to die, whom they had brought some miles across the mountains that he might be buried in a graveyard where the dogs would not find him, as there was a wall about this. He died of consumption, and the family was fed while there and then went away when they had buried their boy. The family of Samuel Bourne was the most comfortable, but they had a burden like an incubus with the mass of starving creatures.[14] Mr Carey, the Coast Guard, was kind, and his wife and daughters patterns of industry and attention to the poor; but with limited means, what could they do to stay the plague?[15] Everything that could be eaten was sought out and devoured, and the most hazardous attempts were made to appease hunger by the people.

This coast has some of the greatest objects of curiosity; and so long have the inhabitants been accustomed to look at them that they walk fearlessly upon the dangerous precipices, and even descend them to the sea, in search of eggs which the sea-gulls deposit there in the sides of the cliffs.[16] Two women presumptuously descended one of these cliffs, not far from Mr Carey's, in search of sloke, which is gathered from the sea.[17] They, in their hunger, ventured to stop till the tide washed in and swept them away. Two men were dashed from a fearful height and dreadfully mangled. One was killed instantly, the other lingered a few weeks and died. They were both in search of eggs to appease hunger. They seemed to face danger in a most deliberate manner and go where none but the goat or eagle would venture.

In this parish I found a specimen of that foolish pride and inability of a class of genteel Irish women to do anything when difficulties present themselves. It was a young lady who lived back two miles upon the mountain, who belonged to one of the faded Irish 'respectables'. She was educated in the popular genteel superficial style, and the family had some of them died, and all broken down: she, with her brother-in-law from Dublin, was staying in a thatched cottage, which had yet the remains of taste and struggling gentility. Two of the peasant women had seen Mr Bourne and me going that way and by a shorter path had hastened and given the Miss notice, so that when we entered, the cottage was in trim and she in due order to receive us. But that pitiful effort was to me painful to witness, having been told that she suffered hunger, and knew no possible way of escape, yet she assumed a magnanimity of spirit and complained not, only expressed much pity for the poor tenants on the land about her and begged us if possible that we would send some relief. Her table was spread with the fashionable ornaments which adorn the drawing-rooms of the rich; and she, with a light scarf hung carelessly about her shoulders, genteel in form and pretty in feature, was already looking from eyes that were putting on the Famine stare. 'What can be done with that helpless, proud, interesting girl?' said Mr Bourne as we passed away. 'She must die in all her pride if some relief is not speedily found! She cannot work, she would not go to the work-house, and there, upon that desolate mountain, she will probably pine away unheeded!' I have not heard what became of this pretty girl of the mountain since. She was covered with the light of beauty, but her heart was the house of pride.

Another interesting character, the antipodes of the mountain girl, resided in the family of Mr Bourne. Nature had endowed her with good sense, education had enlarged her intellect, and travelling had given her that case of manner and address that made her accessible to all without stooping from that dignity which properly repels all uncourteous familiarity. She had passed through great reverses: had been to India – there had a handsome legacy bequeathed; was shipwrecked and lost all; went to South and North America. Her health was destroyed, but her heart subdued and brought into sweet submission to Christ, and she resolved to spend the remainder of her days in doing good to others, however humble their station might be. She had heard of this family, stationed on this desolate spot, who had interesting sons and daughters who wished for instruction. There she went and determined to die and be buried there, secluded from the world. She had written her travels but had placed her manuscripts in hands which were not to publish them till after her death. On that bleak coast she had found where a company of seventeen ship-wrecked sailors had been buried in a mound, and she had requested to lie near their resting-place. She took me to walk, and showed me the forbidding-looking spot. I could scarcely think her sincere, but she assured me that it was a lovely spot to her. She was then perhaps not yet fifty, and why she should think of soon dying and lying there I could not tell. But the intelligent and accomplished Miss Wilson died in a few months after, in the full hope of a happy immortality, and was buried with the ship-wrecked sailors on that rocky coast.

She sleeps in unenvied repose, and I would not wake her.

Here in a humble cabin the kind Miss Carey commenced a little school, to do what she could to keep alive the scattered lambs of that desolate parish in order that she might give them, through some relief society, a little food once a day and teach them to read. Her cabin was soon filled, and without the promise of any reward she laboured on, happy to see the avidity with which these poor children received instruction, and for a year she continued her labour of love with but little remuneration and at last, with much regret, was obliged to return them to their mountain home – perhaps to perish. It was affecting everywhere in the Famine to witness the pale, emaciated children, walking barefoot for miles to school, and study and work till three o'clock, for the scanty meal of stirabout or piece of bread. Dr Edgar had established an industrial school among the tenantry of Samuel Bourne, but when I visited it no other instruction had been given but knitting and sewing. It was at Samuel Bourne's that I met with James Tuke, whose faithful researches and candid recitals of the state of Erris and Connaught have lived and will live in spite of all opposition. I rode with him from Rosport to Ballina, and many a poor suffering one received not only a kind word but a shilling or half-crown as we passed along. His friendship for Ireland overlooked all accidental discrepancies in that misjudged people, and from effects he went to causes, and placed the defects at the door of the lawful owner. My stay in the pretty town of Ballina was a short one, and again reached the dismal Belmullet. Drinking and its sad concomitants were everywhere manifest; not among the 'vulgar lower order' but the respectable class'. The sad fate of a Protestant curate, who was in the asylum, is well known, as well as that of the hotel-keeper, who died shortly after my visit there.[18]

A fresh curate had been stationed in Belmullet, and his prudent sober course indicated good.[19] Three miles from the town lived a single lady, who went by the name of the Queen of Erris on account of some clever doings in a court; and one sunny morning I took a walk to her dwelling near the sea. A sight which had never before fallen to my lot to witness was here in progress. Two well-dressed men mounted on fine horses, furnished with pistols, accompanied by a footman, passed and turned into a miserable hamlet, and instantly all was in motion; every man, woman and child who had strength to walk was out. Soon I perceived the footman driving cows and sheep into the main road, while the armed gentry kept all opposition at bay by showing that death was in their pistols if any showed resistance. It was a most affecting sight. Some were clasping their hands, dropping upon their knees, and earnestly imploring the good God to save them the last cow, calf or sheep for their hungry little ones; some were standing in mute despair as they saw their only hope departing, while others followed in mournful procession as the cattle and sheep were all gathered from every field in the parish and congregated at the foot of a hill, where the brisk 'drivers' had collected them to take them, in a flock to the town. My visit to the Queen was postponed. I followed in that procession; a long hill was before us, the sun was shining upon the clearest sky and lighted up a company which ill contrasted with that of Jacob when he went out to meet his angry brother Esau. The flocks and herds might be as beautiful; but the warlike drivers and ragged, hungry, imploring oppressed ones that followed could hardly claim a standing with Jacob and his family.[20] The hill was ascended, and the poor people halted and looking a sad adieu turned back; and a few exclaimed, 'We're lawst, not a ha'porth have the blackguards left to a divil of us.' Others spoke not, and a few were weeping. Death must now be their destiny.

All returned but one boy, whose age was about fourteen years. He stood as if in a struggle of feeling, till the people had gone from his sight and the 'drivers' were descending the hill on the other side. Instantly he rushed between the 'drivers' and flock, and before the mouth of these loaded pistols he ran among the cattle, screaming, and put the whole flock in confusion, running hither and thither, the astonished drivers threatening death. The boy heeding nothing but the main point, scattered and routed the whole flock; the people heard the noise and ran; the drivers, whether in astonishment or whether willing to show lenity (let their own hearts judge) rode away, the inhabitants exulted and the flock were soon in the enclosures of the owners. But that noble-minded heroic boy was the wonder; facing danger alone and saving for a whole parish what a whole parish had not dared to attempt! His name should never be for gotten, and a pension for life is his due.

A letter is here inserted, which will show faintly the manner of dis tributing donations and the habits of the people.

Belmullet, *October 30th*, 1847.[21]

My Dear Sir: Please prepare yourself. I am about applying some of those 'offen sive points' in my character which I so eminently possess and which may require not only your true charity, but untiring patience, to plod through. I have been rid ing and walking through desolate Erris, and in worse than despair, if possible have sat down, asking – what am I to do? What can I do?

Every effort of the friends of Ireland is baffled by the demoralizing effect that feeding a starving peasantry without labor has produced. And now the sound again is echoing and re-echoing, that on the 1st of November, 1847, the boiler upon mountain and in glen would be foaming and splashing with Indian meal while the various idlers shall have nothing to do but fight their way over necks of old women and starved children, missiles of policemen, elbows and fists of aspi rants, to secure the lucky hodge-podge into can and noggin, pot and bucket; and trail over ditch and through bog, from a quarter of a mile to five, as his hap may be; then to sit down in his mud-built cabin, sup and gulp down the boon, lie down upon his straw till the hour of nine or ten will again summon him to the next warlike encounter.

Indeed, sir, your friend who was last here said he could think of nothing bet ter than to take up a turf cabin with its inmates and appurtenances, and set it down in England.[22] I can outdo him in invention. I would take some half-dozen of your George Thompsons – if so many truly independent members you have – and would transport them through the waste lands of Erris, and seat them snugly around a boiler under full play.[23] They should sit unobserved, and see the whole working of the machinery. The array of rags – each equipped with his canteen to hold his precious gift, should approach; the ghastly features, staring eyes, bony fingers, slender legs; in fact, ghosts and hobgoblins, hags and imps, should draw near, the fighting and tearing, tumbling and scratching should commence and go on till the boiler was emptied, and these *facsimiles* of fighting dogs, tigers and wolves, had well cleared the premises.

I then would invite them to a seat in Samuel Stock's, Samuel Bourne's, and James O'Donnell's parlours.[24] Then let them patiently watch from ten to twelve, from twelve to two, and perchance from two till four, and witness the intensity of action in making out lines, and diagrams and figures to show in plain black and white to government that Pat Flannagan, Samuel Murphy, Biddy Aigin and Molly Sullivan had each his and her pound of meal made into a stirabout on the 3rd of November, Anno Domini 1847. And let it be understood that these Pat Flannagans, Aigins, and Murphys had only to spend the day in the terrific con tests before described to earn this pound of meal, and then betake themselves to mountains and dens, turf hovels, and mud hovels, to crawl in and then and there sup up this life-giving, life-inspiring stimulus. They should further be told that these Stocks, Bournes, O'Donnells, &c. had the privilege of handing over these nightly made-out documents to officers, paid from six to ten, from ten to twenty shillings per day, that they might have the promise of a six months' nightly campaign, should papers be found to be true and legible, as aforetime.

This is but a short preface to the story. My heart sickens at looking over the utter wasting of all that was once cheerful, interesting, and kind in these peasantry. Hunger and idleness have left them a prey to every immorality; and if they do not soon practice every vice attendant on such a state of things, it will be because they have not the power. Many are now maniacs, some desperate and some idiots. Human nature is coming forth in every deformity that she can put, while in the flesh; and should I stay in Ireland six months longer, I shall not be astonished at seeing any deeds of wickedness performed, even by those who one year ago might apparently have been as free from guilt as any among us. I have not been able yet, with all my republican training, to lose the old-school principle of man's total lost state.[25] I have never yet seen him without the restraints of custom or religion anything but a demon in embryo, if not in full maturity; doing not only what he can, but sighing and longing to do more. The floodgates in Ireland are certainly set open, and the torrent has already made fearful ravages.

From Clare and Tipperary what do we hear? One post after another runs to tell that not only deeds of darkness are done, but deeds of daylight desperation, sufficient to startle the firmest. What Moses shall stand up to plead with God? What Phineas shall rush in to stay the plague?[26] Where are your men of moral, yes, of spiritual might? You have them; then bring them out! I look across that narrow channel. I see the graves of martyrs. I see the graves of men whose daring minds stood forth in a majesty of greatness to speak for truth and justice; and though they may long since have taken flight, where are their mantles? Where is your George Thompson? He who shook the United States from Maine to Georgia in pleading long and loud for the down-trodden black man? Can he not, will he not lift his voice for poor Ireland? She who stands shivering, sinking on the Isthmus, between two worlds, apparently not fit for either. Will he not reach forth a kindly hand and try to snatch this once interesting and lovely, though now forlorn and forsaken creature, from her fearful position? Must she, shall she die? Will proud England lose so bright a gem as Ireland might have been in her crown? Will she lose her, when the distaff and the spade, the plow and the fishing net, might again make her mountains and her valleys rejoice; when the song of the husbandman, and the laugh of the milkmaid might make her green isle the home of thousands, who are now sinking and dying in wasting despair?

Do you say she is intriguing, she is indolent and treacherous? Try her once more; put instruments of working warfare into her hands; hold up the soul-stirring stimulus of remuneration to her; give her no time for meditating plunder and bloodshed; give her no inducement to be reckless of a life that exists only to suffer. Feed her not in idleness nor taunt her with her nakedness and poverty, till her wasted, palsied limbs have been washed and clothed, till her empty stomach has been filled, and filled too with food of her own earning, when she shall have strength to do it. Give her a little spot on the loved isle she can call her own, where she can 'sit under her own vine and fig-tree, and none to make her afraid', and force her not to flee to a distant clime to purchase that bread that would be sweeter on her own native soil.

Do you say you cannot feed and pay four millions of these your subjects? Then call on your transatlantic sister to give you food for them. The earth is the Lord's and the fullness thereof; and though she has a right to say she will not send Ireland food to keep them strong in idleness, she has no right to say she will not send them food to give them strength for labour. She has not a heart to say it; foul as her hands may be with slavery, yet she will feed the hungry with a cheerful hand. If she has not done her duty there is room for repentance, yes, effectual repentance. Her fields, the past season, have been waving with rich corn, and her storehouses are filling with the golden harvest. You have given her gold in profusion for the produce of her soil. The blast of the potato has been to her the blossoming and ripening of her pastures – her waving fields of pulse and corn. The husbandman has been stimulated to plow up fresh lands so that he might fill his granaries abundantly with the rich harvest, because free trade has opened your ports and you will demand more of his corn; and why should he not send over a few sheaves as a thank-offering to God for all this bounty? America will do it if required; but an inquiry has come across the ocean. Is it right to feed a country to encourage idleness? Will not the evil be much greater than the good? Answer, you who are statesmen – you who are Christians; answer, you who can. Look at the peasantry of Ireland three years ago, and look at them now! Even their enemies must acknowledge that they are a tractable race, to have developed so much intrigue and cunning under the training of the last two years. Shall I scold, shall I preach, shall I entreat any more? What is woman's legislating amid the din of so many wise magicians, soothsayers and astrologers as have set up for Ireland the last two years. Prophets and priests have so far failed; but certainly there must be a true chord to strike somewhere; for what is now wrong, when traced to its source, may disclose the hidden cause of the evil, and put the willing investigator into a position to work an amendment.

You, sir, who know Erris, tell, if you can, how the landlords can support the poor by taxation, to give them food, when the few resident landlords are nothing, and worse than nothing, for they are paupers in the full sense of the word. What can Samuel Bourne, James O'Donnell and such like men do in their present position? If they have done wrong, and do it no more, the torrent is so strong that they cannot withstand it. I must, and will plead, though I plead in vain, that something may be done to give them work. I have just received a letter from the curate of Bingham's Town saying that he could set all his poor parish, both the women and children, to work, and find a market for their knitting and cloth, if he could command a few pounds to purchase the materials. He is young and indefatigable, kind-hearted and poor, and no proselyte.[27] Mrs Stock has done well in her industrial department.[28] The Hon. William Butler has purchased cloth of her for a coat to wear himself, which the poor women spun, and gave a good price for it.

I pray you, sir, if this malignant letter do not terrify you, write and say what must be done.

A Nicholson.

A week had I been watching a passage to the Sound, and November 9th, 1847, at six o'clock on Monday morning I stepped into a filthy-looking boat, with filthy-looking men jabbering Irish, and sat down on a pile of wet straw, for the rain and sea were still pouring and splashing upon us; and there soaked and drenched, amid rain, wave and tempest, I sat till nearly sunset when the storm ceased, the clouds made an opening for the sun, the air became sultry, and the sea like a molten looking-glass. 'How long have you sailed this boat around this fearful coast?' the captain was asked. 'Twelve years, and not an accident has once happened to me.' The boatmen were obliged to row us in with oars, for not a motion was upon the sea, nor a breeze in the air. Strange and sudden change! The poor fishermen at the Sound had loosened their boats from the fastenings and gone out with their nets upon the calm waters.

My wet clothes were not adjusted, when in awful majesty the Almighty seemed riding upon the whirlwind and storm. The rushing of the tempest lashed the affrighted sea to a fury, the waves in fearful roar dashed over the lofty pier, the blackened clouds were tossing and rolling like a scroll together, and the earth seemed moved as if at the coming of Christ. I actually sat down in a window that overlooked the Sound, and waited in glad suspense the approach of that cloud which should bear the chariot wheels of the Saviour to judgment. Slates were hurled from the roof, windows were broken, doors burst open, and the confused crash so astonished all that none attempted to speak.[29] So black were the clouds that night scarcely was perceived, and had the graves opened, and the sea given up her dead, the living would not have known it, for the breath of the Almighty had not kindled the grand conflagration. Still past midnight the wind and the sea kept up the sublime roaring.

But where were the poor fishermen and the captain who had never met an accident? He was wrecked. The morning dawned, the sun looked out upon a molten sea again, whose placid face seemed to say, 'I am satisfied'. But the stillness of the sea was soon broken by the wail of widows and orphans who were lamenting in loud cries the loss of those they loved. Nineteen of these fishermen, the 'stoutest and best', said Mr Savage, are swallowed in the deep.[30] Honest and industrious, they had stood waiting in fearful suspense, in hunger, and looking in despair upon the tumultuous waves that morning, saying, 'If the good God don't still the storm we're all destrawed'. He had stilled it, and nineteen were lost. Three among the hapless crew struggled with the fearful tempest, and reached the shore, crawled up the cliffs, and were found upon the mountains dead, on the way to their cabins.

On the 28th of November, a fisherman's widow called in who had been twenty miles, to 'prove', as she said, her husband, who had been washed ashore and buried without a coffin; she bought a white coffin and took it to the spot with her own hands, she dug him from his grave, and proved him by a leather button she had sewed upon some part of his clothes.

December 3rd. Another night of darkness and terrible storm. The lightning threw a blue lustre upon everything, the affrighted daughters turned pale, the mother sat in a dark corner, now and then giving a stifled groan, shrinking before the voice of Jehovah when he thundered in the heavens. The next morning while the tempest was still high, a sorrowing old mother and young wife had come, bearing on a cart the body of the son who was drowned on the 9th. The white coffin besmeared with tar stood upon the pier; the mother, wife and sisters were beside it, mingling their loud lamentations with the storm. 'He was as fine a young lad as ever put the oar across the curragh, and had the larnin' intirely,' said the old mother.

The scenes on this coast that dreadful winter are scenes of awful remembrance, and one bright spot alone cheered the sadness. It had been the practice of the mother and daughters to assemble in a retired room in the evening for reading the Scriptures and prayer. One evening a daughter of the family came from the kitchen with the strange glad message, that one of the labouring men had requested that the lady should ('if it wouldn't be too much') come down to the kitchen and read to them there. Joyfully we all went, and found there a company of more than twenty, all quietly seated on forms; the kitchen in the best order, and a bright fire upon the hearth. They all rose as we entered, and one said, 'We wouldn't be bold, lady, but maybe ye wouldn't refuse to raid a little to us.' Testaments were procured, candles lighted and these simple-hearted rustics in their turn read with us, making comments as we passed, till the scene from the interesting became affecting. We prayed together, and when we rose from our knees, one said, 'We never heard so much of the good Christ before.' They all thanked me and gave me hearty blessings, and said good night, calling after me, and 'may the good God give ye the long life, and happy death'. Every night, when it was possible to do so, the kitchen was put in order, and a messenger sent to ask if the lady was ready. I saw one of these men twenty miles from there, standing by his cart, when he spoke (for I did not know him): 'God save ye, lady, we're lonesome without ye entirely, we don't have the raidin, and maybe ye'll come again.'

I passed the Christmas and New Year's Day in Achill in the colony of Mr Nangle, and to the honour of the inhabitants would say they did not send me to Molly Vesey's to lodge; but more than one family offered to entertain me.[31] Mr Nangle I heard preach again, and as he figured considerably in the first volume of my work, it may be said here that he refused any reconciliation, did not speak though a good opportunity presented; and when he was expostulated with by a superintendent of his schools, who informed him that I had visited numbers of them and put clothes upon some of the most destitute, he coolly replied, 'If she can do any good I am glad of it.'

He had eleven schools scattered through that region, reading the Scriptures, and learning Irish; but all through these parts might be seen the fallacy of distributing a little over a great surface.[32] The scanty allowance given to children once a day, and much of this bad food, kept them in lingering want, and many died at last. So with workmen. Mr Nangle had many men working in his bogs, near Mr Savage, and so scantily were they paid – sometimes but three pence and three pence-halfpenny a day – that some at least would have died but for the charity of Mrs Savage. These men had families to feed and must work till Saturday, then go nine miles into the colony to procure the Indian meal for the five days' work. This he truly called giving his men 'employ'.

Another sad evil prevalent in nearly all the relief shops was damaged Indian meal. And here without any personality, leaving the application where it belongs, having a knowledge of the nature of this article, it is placed on record that the unground corn that was sent from America and bought by the Government of England, and carried round the coast and then ground in the mills, which did not take off the hull, much of it having been damaged on the water, became wholly unfit for use and was a most dangerous article for any stomach. Many of the shops I found where this material was foaming and sputtering in kettles over the fire, as if a handful of soda had been flung in, and sending forth an odor really unpleasant; and when any expostulation was made, the answer was, 'They're quite glad to get it', or 'We use such as is put into our hands – the government must see to that'. Such meal a good American farmer would not give to his swine unless for physic, and when the half-starved poor, who had been kept all their life on potatoes, took this sour, mouldy, harsh food, dysentery must be the result. One of the Dublin Relief Committee stated that the government had kindly offered to save them the trouble of carriage by taking the American donations, as they arrived, and giving them an equivalent of that which was already on the coast, which they had purchased: this equivalent was the corn above-mentioned, and the American donations were in the best possible order, and the very article to which the poor were entitled.

Let the policemen speak if they will speak, and testify if many an injured ton of meal has not been flung into the sea in the night from ports in Ireland, which was sent for the poor, and by neglect spoiled, while the objects for whom it was intended died without relief. The novel prudence, too, which prevailed nearly everywhere, was keeping the provisions for next week while the people were dying this, lest they should come short of funds to buy more, or no more would be given them.

The author of the *Irish Crisis*, January 1848, gives a clear statement of many things relating to Grants, Public Works and many other valuable statistics, and upon the whole it presents a fair picture for future generations to read of the nice management and kindly feelings of all parties and 'that among upward of two thousand local officers to whom advances were made under this act, there is not one to which, so far as government is informed, any suspicion of embezzlement attaches'.[33] It further states that the fasts set apart in London were kept with great solemnity, and that never in that city was there a winter of so little gaiety. But he has not told posterity, and probably he did not know that the winters of 1847 and 1848 in Dublin were winters of great hilarity among the gentry. The latter season, particularly, seemed to be a kind of jubilee for songs and dances. The Queen appointed fasts on both these winters, the people went to church, and said they had all gone astray like lost sheep and there was no soundness in them, and some who heard believed that this was all true; but it may be scrupled whether many priests 'wept between the porch and the altar', or that many Jeremiahs' eyes ran down with water, 'for the slain of the daughters of the people'.[34] That the people of England felt more deeply, and acted more consistently than did the people of Ireland, cannot be disputed. Ireland felt when her peace was disturbed and her ease was molested, and she cried loudly for help in this 'God's famine' as she impiously called it; but ate her good dinners and drank her good wine as long as she could find means to do so – famine or no famine; her landlords strained for the last penny of rent, and sent their tenants houseless into the storm when they could pay no longer.

This, her sirs, her lords, and her esquires did. 'No suspicion of embezzlement attached!' when a company of more than two thousand were intrusted with money at discretion, they must indeed have been a rare lump of honesty if some few glasses of wine had not been taken out of it to drink the Queen's health on their days of festivals, or a pound now and then to pay off some vexatious debt, &c. And who shall tell government of that? Shall the United Fraternity themselves do it? Shall the poor, who are powerless and unheeded, tell it? Or shall 'Common Fame', that random talking tell-tale, fly through the kingdom and declare hat Mr —, 'head and ears in debt', suddenly came out 'clear as a horn', hat Mr Somebody was fitting up his house, and where did he get his money? And that the cattle and horses of Farmer G — were getting fat and thriving astonishingly, &c.

It was my fortune to be placed in a position among all classes, acting isolated as I did, to see the inner court of some of these temples (not of the Committees) – with these my business ended when at Dublin. But I had boxes of clothing, and am obliged to acknowledge what common report says here, that the people of the higher classes in general showed a meanness bordering on dishonesty. When they saw a goodly garment, they not only appeared to covet, but they actually bartered, as though in a shop of secondhand articles, to get it as cheap as possible; and most, if not all of such, would have taken these articles without any equivalent, though they knew they were the property of the poor. Instead of saying, 'These garments are not fit for the cabin people, I will pay the full worth and let them have something that will do them good', they managed most adroitly to secure them for the smallest amount. These were people too who were not in want. The poor were shamefully defrauded, where they had no redress and none to lift the voice in their favour.

Among the suffering it was not so. Whenever I visited a neighbourhood or a school, and clothed a naked child, or assisted a destitute family, those who were not relieved, never, in my presence or hearing, manifested the least jealousy, but on the contrary, blessed God that He had sent relief to any one. This so affected me, in schools where I went, that a garment for a naked child was not presented in the school-room. I could not well endure the ghastly smile of approbation that some child sitting near would give who was nearly as destitute as the one that had been clothed. In one of Mr Nangle's schools the teacher was requested to select the children most in want, and let me know that I need not go into the room with new garments for a part to the exclusion of others. These little suffering ones had not yet learnt to covet or envy – always oppressed, they bowed their necks patiently to the yoke.

CHAPTER VI

'There is no god, the oppressors say,
To mete us out chastisement.'

POOR-HOUSE, TURNIPS AND BLACK BREAD

These splendid monuments of Ireland's poverty number no less than one hundred and thirty, and some contain a thousand, and some two thousand, and in cases of emergency they can heap a few hundreds more. Before the Famine they were many of them quite interesting objects for a stranger to visit, generally kept clean, not crowded, and the food sufficient. But when famine advanced, when funds decreased, when the doors were besieged by imploring applicants, who wanted a place to die that they might be buried in a coffin, they were little else than charnel houses, while the living, shivering skeletons that squatted upon the floors, or stood with arms folded against the wall, half-clad, with hair uncombed, hands and face unwashed, added a horror if not terror to the sight.[1]

Westport Union had long been celebrated for its management, its want of comfort in fire, food, lodging and room; but stay and die, or go out and die, was the choice.[2] Making suitable allowances for a rainy day – the house undergoing some changes when I visited it – there then appeared little capital left for comfort, had the day been sunny and the house without any unusual upturnings. The 'yaller Indian', here, was the dreadful thing that they told me, 'swells us and takes the life of us'; and as it was there cooked, it may be scrupled whether any officer in the establishment would select it for his food, though he assured the inmates 'he could eat it, and it was quite good enough for a king'. These officers and guardians, many of them, were men who had lived in ease, never accustomed to industry or self-denial, having the poor as vassals under them; and when the potato blight took away all the means of getting rent, what with the increased taxations and the drainings by a troop of beggars at the door, they found themselves approaching a difficult crisis, and to prop up every tottering wall new expedients must be tried. Many of them sought posts of office under government, and were placed in the work-houses to superintend funds and food; and it will not be slander to say that the ears of government have not been so fortunate with regard to the 'slip-shod' honesty of some of these gentry, as in the two thousand which the writer of the *Crisis* mentions.

When the poor complained, they were told that funds were low and stinted allowances must be dealt out. Nor did the mischief end here; in proportion as the houses were crowded within, so were the purses drained without; and beside, in proportion to the purloining of funds, so was the stinting of food and the extra drains upon the struggling trades-man and farmer.

An observer, who had no interest in the nation but philanthropy, going over Ireland, after travelling many a weary mile over bog and waste where nothing but a scattering hamlet of loose stone, mud or turf greets him, when he suddenly turns some corner, or ascends some hill, and sees in the distance, upon a pleasant elevation, a building of vast dimensions, tasteful in architecture, surrounded with walls, like the castle or mansion of some lord, if he knew not Ireland's history must suppose that some chief held his proud dominion over the surrounding country and that his power must be so absolute that life and death hung on his lip; and should he enter the gate and find about its walls a company of ragged and tattered beings of all ages, from the man of grey hairs to the lad in his teens, sit-ting upon the ground, breaking stones with might and main, and piling them in heaps; should he proceed to a contiguous yard, if the day be not rainy, and find some hundreds of the 'weaker vessels' standing in groups or squatting upon their heels, with naked arms and feet; should he go over the long halls, and in some inclosure find a group of pale sickly looking children cowering about a vast iron guard, to keep the scanty fire that might be struggling for life in the grate from doing harm; should he stop at the dinner hour, and see these hundreds, yes thousands, marching in file to the tables, where was spread the yellow stirabout, in tins and pans, measured and meted by ounces and pounds, suited to age and condition; and should he tarry till twilight drew her curtain and see, in due order, these men, women and children led to their stalls for the night, where are pallets of straw in long rooms (they are sorted and ranged according to sex) to lie down together, with neither light of the sun, moon or candle, till the morning dawn, and call them again to their gruel or stirabout to resume afresh the routine of the preceding day – would not this unin-formed stranger find all his opinions confirmed, that this must be the property of a monarch who has gathered these heterogeneous nonde-scripts from the pirates, highway robbers and pickpockets of his subjects, and had inclosed them here, awaiting the fit out for transportation?[3]

But listen! This honest inquirer is aroused by being kindly informed that this great mammoth establishment, with all its complicated paraph-ernalia of boilers, soup-pots, tins, pans, stools, forms, tables and pallets, together with heavy-paid overseers, officers, matrons, and cooks, are all the work of Christian benevolence! And that the building itself cost more than would a comfortable cottage and plot of ground sufficient to give each of the families here enclosed a good support. And further, so unbounded is the owner's benevolence, that over the Green Isle are scattered one hundred and twenty-nine more like palaces, rearing their proud turrets to the skies, furnished within with like apparatus, for tens of thousands, so that every Paddy, from Donegal to Kerry, and from Wicklow to Mayo, may here find a stool, a tin of stirabout, and pallet, on the simple condition of oathing that he owns not either 'hide or hoof', screed or scrawl, mattock or spade, pot or churn, duck-pond, manure-heap or potato-plot, on the ground that reared him, and simply put his seal to this by pulling the roof from his own cabin.[4]

Should the inquirer be at a loss to conjecture how, when and where his wide-spread philanthropy had a beginning, he is cited back to the good old days of Elizabeth and James, when the zealous Christian plunderer, Cromwell, prepared the way to parcel out the island and entail it forever to a happy few; who found a race of people who would dig their ditches, build their walls, lay out their parks and ponds for a penny or two a day, and above all, could be made patiently to feed on a single root and live in mud cabins or by the side of a rock, or burrow in sandbanks, who would go at their command, and come at their bidding; and beside, for the unleased patch of ground, where they grew the root on which they subsisted, they paid such a rent as enabled the masters of the soil to live and fare sumptuously at home, to hunt the hare and deer over the mountain and glen, with lady, dog and gun, or to travel in distant lands.[5] With all these appliances they had lived on, sending care to the winds, till, from generation to generation they found these 'hewers of wood and drawers of water' had become so multifarious that, like Pharaoh's frogs, they encompassed the whole land, covering bog and ditch, crying, '*give, give*', till dinned and harassed with the undying clamour, they were moved to provide food and shelter in palaces of stone and mortar, where all care of food, raiment and lodging is at an end, and they have only to eat when they are fed, lie down when bidden, rise and put on their clothes when the morning gives them light, and once a week say their prayers in the church or chapel, as their conscience dictated, without leaving the proud roof where they are fed and housed![6]

These palaces certainly in this respect stand pre-eminent over every other portion of the earth, and tell the true story of Ireland's strange management more than volumes of essays would do. To pauperize men, women and children, in sight of and walking over a rich uncultivated soil, as in Ireland, and shut them up, with no other crimes than that of

compulsory poverty, where they are fed, clothed and lodged at the governor's option, inclosed with bolts and bars, like felons, with no more freedom than state prisoners have, is certainly a strange comment on liberty,
a strange comment on the family relationship, which prohibits all intercourse between parents and children except a few hasty moments one
day in seven. The work-houses in Ireland are many of them well managed on the principles as they are established; but, as an overseer in one
of the best-conducted ones said: 'I have been here many years, and have
seen the workings and effects of a poor-house, and can only say – the
best that can be said of them – they are prisons under a different name,
calculated to produce a principle of idleness, and to degrade, never to
elevate, to deaden in the human heart that rational self-respect which
individual support generates, and which should be kept up; and may I
never be doomed to die in a poor-house.'

Nor is this all. The unreclaimed bogs and waste hunting grounds tell
that in no country are poor-houses such an anomaly as in Ireland; and the
Irishman who is willing to work, and is employed there, has no moral
right to be either grateful or satisfied that he has exchanged even a mud
cabin of liberty for a palace walled and locked, where his food is measured and doled, where his family are strangers to him, and all the social
interchanges of life are taken from him wholly. Though a man may be 'a
man for a'that', yet he cannot feel himself one; nor does he seldom if
ever, regain that standard of manly independence which belongs to man,
whatever his future lot may be. [7]

TURNIPS

As turnips made a prominent feature in the absence of their predecessors
the potatoes during the Famine, they should not be overlooked in the
annals of that history. They were to the starving ones supposed to be a
'God-send', and were eaten with great avidity, both cooked and raw.
Many of the cabiners could get but little fire, and they cooked only the
tops, while the bottoms were taken raw. Those who had no shelter to
cook under could not well eat the tops, though they often tried to do so. It
has been ascertained that turnips contain but from ten to fifteen parts of
nutriment to a hundred parts, thence the quantity necessary to nourish the
body must require bulk to a great amount. This root, when boiled, has
ever been considered as safe a vegetable for the invalid as any in the
vocabulary of esculents; and even the fevered invalid, when prohibited
all other vegetables, has been allowed to partake of this, not because of
its nutrition but because of the absence of it, not having sufficient to

injure the weakest body. When it was found that turnips could be so easily grown, and that no blast had as yet injured them, they were hailed with great joy by the peasants and by the people.

But the starving ones soon found they were unsatisfactory, for when they had eaten much more in bulk than of the potato they were still craving, and the result was, where for weeks they lived wholly on them, their stomachs were so swollen, especially children's, that it was a pitiable sight to see them. No one thought it was the turnip but I found in every place on the coast where they were fed on them the same results, and as far as I could ascertain, such died in a few weeks; and the rational conclusion must be that a single root, so innutritious and so watery as the white turnips are, cannot sustain a healthy state of the system nor life itself for any considerable time. When going through the Barony of Erris, the appearance of these turnip-eaters became quite a dread. Invariably the same results appeared wherever used, and they became more to be dreaded, as it was feared the farmer would make them a substitute for the potato, and the ingenious landlord would find a happy expedient for his purse if his tenants could live on the turnip as well as the potato. Like cattle, these poor creatures seemed to be driven from one herb and root to another, using nettles, turnip-tops, chickweed in their turn, and dying at last on these miserable substitutes. Many a child sitting in a muddy cabin has been interrogated what she or he had eaten; 'nothing but the turnip, ma'am', sometimes the turnip-top; and being asked when this was procured, sometimes the answer would be, 'yesterday, lady', or 'when we can get them, ma'am'.

BLACK BREAD

We turn from the turnip and see what virtue there is in black bread; and my only regret is that my powers of description are so faint, that I cannot describe one-half of what might be told of that novel article used for many a month in the county of Mayo. The relief officers there were under govenment pay, and, as they asserted, under government orders; but it is much to be doubted whether the government, had they been served with a loaf of that bread, would have ordered it for either man or beast. The first that greeted my wondering eyes was in a poor village between Achill and Newport where, while stopping to feed the horse, a company of children who had been at school, and received a few ounces of this daily, came in with the boon in their hands. The woman of the house reached a piece to me, asking if I ever saw the like. Indeed, I never had, and had never tasted the like. Supposing it must have been accidental, and that no other of the kind had ever been made, I said, 'This is not such bread as the children usually eat.' She answered, 'They have had it for some weeks.' It was sour, black and of the consistency of liver; but thinking that the baker had been mostly to blame, this bread did not make such an impression on me as that which I saw for weeks afterwards.

A few days after this, a gentleman at whose house I stopped brought into the room a loaf of the genuine 'black bread'. 'Here,' said he, 'is the reward of a day's labour of a poor man, who has been sitting on the ground this cold day to break stones.' Not one present could have told what it was till taking it in the hand; and even then it was quite doubtful whether men would provide such a material to reward a labouring man for a day's work; but it was indeed so. The man who had come into possession of this boon was one among many, some of whom had walked three, four and even five miles, and had laboured through a cold day in March without eating, and this bread weighed a pound. But the material and the colour! The material could not have been analyzed but by a chemist, but the colour was precisely that of dry turf, so much so that when a piece was placed upon a table by the side of a bit of turf, no eye could detect the difference, and it was very difficult to do so when taking it in hand.

The next day, calling on a gentleman of respectability and a friend to his country, he inquired if in my excursions I had met with the bread that the relief officers were giving the poor, adding, 'I will procure you a piece.'. He then sent to the shop where it was kept and bought a loaf; it was common unbolted flour-bread of a middling quality. He sent it back; they denied having or selling any other kind to the poor, or ever having done so. 'Go,' said the gentlemen, 'into the school where the bread is distributed, and then the facts will be palpable.' I went. A school of one hundred and forty or one hundred and fifty girls were in waiting for this bread, which had been sent for to the shop. It came, was cut in slices, and having been baked that morning the effluvia was fresh, and though standing at the extremity of a long room, with the street door open, the nausea became so offensive that after taking a slice for a pattern, and having ascertained from the teacher that this was the daily bread which she had been cutting for weeks, I hastened home with the prize, placed the bread upon paper where good air could reach it; the disagreeable smell gradually subsided, but the bread retained all its appearance for weeks, never becoming sour, but small spots of a greenish colour like mould here and there dotted upon it. These spots were not abundant: the remainder appeared precisely like turf-mould, and was judged to be so.

Where these relief officers made out this article was not satisfactorily explained. '*They* did as they were bidden.' Report said that some twenty-nine years before, the government had deposited in that region some continental material for bread, which had become damaged, and then could not be sold. But twenty-nine years it had withstood the ravages of rats, mice and vermin, and had now come out an eatable commodity for charity. And here it was scattered daily through mountain and glen; and for this equivalent the poor man must give up his land, take off the roof of his cabin with his own hand – for, as the government has not required this, the driver, like a slave one ever faithful to his master's interest and good name, tells the starving cabiner if he will not ascend the roof of his hut and unthatch it, and tumble down the stones with his own hand, that he shall neither have the pound of meal or black bread. Then this driver screens himself behind the flimsy covering that the cabiner did it with his own hands, and the landlord gravely tells you that it was done without his orders, and probably without his knowledge. Slave-owners do precisely in the same way. They employ a faithful driver, pay him bountifully, and his duty is to get the most work done in the least time and in the best way. If a delinquent be flogged to death, the owner is always away from home or somehow engaged – entirely ignorant of the matter. But mark! However often these cruelties may be repeated, the driver maintains his post and his salary. Are the public to be so duped in either case, that the slaveholder and landlord are not satisfied with this flogging and this pulling down of houses? Why, then, are they ever repeated?

The age of black bread and pulling down houses certainly has fallen peculiarly under the reign of the Queen and her agent John Russell; yet it might be wholly unjust to impute either to their orders or even consent.[8] The black bread was a cheap substitute for good flour or meal; and if meddlesome people had stayed at home, minding their own concerns, who would ever have thought of complaining about bread? The poor starving ones had reached that point that they would swallow anything in the shape of food that could have been swallowed, without uttering a murmur.

A few pieces of this bread were put in a letter directed to a friend in London, that the Committee there, acting for the poor in Ireland, might have a sight. The letter was carried to the postmaster and an explanation given him of the precious gift contained in it, and the object of so doing, &c.; that it was to let the people of England see if they acknowledged this article as a provision of theirs for the poor. The letter never reached its destination; the postmaster was interrogated by the writer. He affirmed that he had seen no such letter, nor heard one word about it, when lo! this forgetful postmaster was one of the said relief officers who managed the black bread! 'Whoso readeth let him understand.'

Whether the poor lived or whether they died on this bread, or by this bread, I do not pretend to say, only that death was doing its work by hunger, fever and dysentery continually.

CHAPTER VII

'Earth, of man the bounteous mother,
Feeds him still with corn and vine:
He who best would aid a brother,
Shares with him these gifts divine.'

Newport and its vicinity presented a variety of exciting scenes. Here in this pretty town families of tolerable comfort declined step by step, till many who would have outlived the common changes of life could not maintain their standing in this hour of trial. A former rector by the name of Wilson died in the summer of 1847, leaving a widow and four children on a pretty spot, where they had resided for years, and gathered the comforts of life about them.[1] Here I was invited to spend a few weeks, and would with gratitude record the many favours shown me there; and with deep sorrow would add that I saw step by step all taken for taxes and rent; everything that had life out of doors that could be sold at auction, was sold; then everything of furniture, till beds and tables left the little cottage, and the mother was put in jail and is now looking through its grates, while her children are struggling for bread. Sir Richard O'Donnell is the landlord in possession of most of the land there, and his 'driver', like others akin to him, does strange things to the tenants quite unknown to the landlord, who has been called humane.[2]

But this fearless 'driver' throws, or causes to be thrown down, cabin after cabin, and sometimes whole villages, of which it is said the landlord was entirely ignorant; but the pitiless storm heeded not that, and the poor starved exiles pleading that the cabin might be left a little longer, have no pity, their pot and even the cloak, which is the peasant woman's all by night and by day, has often been torn from her emaciated limbs and sold at auction. Perhaps in no instance does the oppression of the poor and the sighing of the needy come before the mind so vividly as when going over the places made desolate by the Famine; to see the tumbled cabins, with the poor hapless inmates who had for years sat around their turf fire, and ate their potato together, now lingering and oft'times wailing in despair, their ragged barefooted little ones clinging about them, one on the back of the weeping mother, and the father looking in silent despair, while a part of them are scraping among the rubbish to gather some little relic of mutual attachment (for the poor, reader, have their tender remembrances); then, in a flock, take their solitary, their pathless way to seek some rock or ditch to encamp supperless for the night, without either covering for the head or the feet, with not the remnant of a blanket to spread over them in the ditch, where they must crawl. Are these solitary cases? Happy would it be were it so, but village upon village, and company after company have I seen; and one magistrate who was travelling informed me that at nightfall the preceding day he found a company who had gathered a few sticks and fastened them into the ditch, and spread over what miserable rags they could collect (for the rain was fast pouring); and under these more than two hundred men, women and children were to crawl for the night. He alighted from his car, and counted more than two hundred. They had all that day been driven out, and not one pound of any kind of food was in the whole encampment!

When I went over desolate Erris, and saw the demolished cabins belonging to J. Walshe, I begged to know if all had died from that hamlet.[3] 'Worse than died,' was the answer. 'For if they are alive, they are in sandbanks on the bleak sea-shore, or crowded into some miserable cabin for a night or two, waiting for death; they are lingering out the last hours of suffering.' Oh! ye poor, ye miserable oppressors! What will ye do when the day of God's wrath shall come? Have ye ever thought what rock and mountain ye can call upon to screen your naked heads, who would not here give the poor and hungry a shelter? When 'the elements shall melt with fervent heat'; then shall the blaze of these ruins scorch and scathe you; yea, burn you up, if you do not now make haste to repent. Ye lords, when the Lord of lords, and God of gods, shall gird on his sword; then shall these poor be a swift witness against you. The widow and the fatherless ye have delighted to oppress because they could not resist you, and yet you dare to call yourselves by the name of Him, whose mission was mercy, and who marks diligently the ways of him who delights in unjust gain, and is deaf to the cries of the widow and fatherless.[4] Often, when looking at these wandering exiles, woeful as is their case, yet my heart has said how much more woeful is the case of him who drove you into the storm. Well might James say, 'Go to, ye rich men, weep and howl'; and well did Christ pray – 'Father forgive them, for they know not what they do'.[5]

Contrasted with these were a few of better stamp, whose hearts had not become entirely seared by the love of gain: Mr Pounden and his wife, who died by their excessive labours among the poor. He was rector in Westport, and his money and time were faithfully employed in saving and not destroying the poor.[6] His name is now in sweet remembrance by those whom he succoured in their time of need. It was pleasant, too, to see the labourers whom Sir Richard employed in the cultivation of flax in the summer and autumn of 1847.[7] Among the thousands which were happily at work were many women, and their cheerful responses testified how they prized the boon to be allowed to labour, when they could earn but a few pence a day. This work ended, and with it many of the poor were left hopeless, and probably before another spring opened they were sent out into the storm by the driver of this same Sir, who saw them work so willingly.

Mr Gildea, too, had a fine establishment for spinning and weaving.[8] Here are employed about seven hundred, mostly women, spinning and hand-skutching and their earnings were three shillings and three shillings and sixpence per week. The yarn was spun by hand, and the weaving by a spring shuttle. The table-linen and sheeting would compete with any manufactory in any country. Yet this valuable establishment was doing its last work for want of encouragement – want of funds; and machinery is doing the work faster and selling cheaper, though the material is not so durable. What can the poor labourer do – willing to work at any price, and begging to do so, yet cannot be allowed the privilege. Mr Gildea kept a number employed, and employed to a good purpose, many of whom may at last starve for food.

The state of the Famine here might be illustrated by a few facts which came under my observation. The chapel bell tolled one morning early, when a respectable young woman was brought into the yard for interment. No bells tolled for the starving, they must have the 'burial of an ass', or none at all. A young lad improved this opportunity while the gate was open, and carried in a large sack on his back, which contained two brothers, one seventeen, the other a little boy, who had died by starvation. In one corner he dug, with his own emaciated feeble hands, a grave, and put them in, uncoffined, and covered them, while the clods were falling upon the coffin of the respectable young woman. I never witnessed a more stirring, striking contrast between civilized and savage life – Christianity and heathenism, wealth and poverty – than in this instance. It said so much for the mockery of death, with all its trappings and ceremonies, the mockery of pompous funerals and their black retinue. This poor boy unheeded had stayed in the dark cabin with those dead brothers, not even getting admittance into the gate till some respectable one should want a burial; then he might follow this procession at a suitable distance, with two dead brothers upon his back, and put them in with his own hands, with none to compassionate him!

A cabin was seen closed one day a little out of the town when a man had the curiosity to open it, and in a dark corner he found a family of the father, mother and two children, lying in close compact. The father was considerably decomposed; the mother, it appeared, had died last and probably fastened the door, which was always the custom when all hope was extinguished, to get into the darkest corner and die where passers-by could not see them.[9] Such family scenes were quite common, and the cabin was generally pulled down upon them for a grave. The man called, begging me to look in. I did not, and could not endure, as the Famine progressed, such sights, as well as at the first. They were too real, and these realities became a dread. In all my former walks over the island, by day or night, no shrinking or fear of danger ever retarded in the least my progress, but now the horror of meeting living, walking ghosts, or stumbling upon the dead in my path at night, inclined me to keep within when necessity did not call.

The entire face of the country was changed, for though poverty always was brooding her dismal wings over that island, yet now she had sharpened her teeth, and in many parts desperation was driving the people to deeds which had long slept, or which never before had been transacted. A class of persons, driven to madness by idleness and hunger, were prowling at night through some parts of the country, calling themselves Molly Maguires.[10] These go from house to house, in disguise, demanding money, and if denied they card the refuser till the skin becomes lacerated. This scratching is performed sometimes with a card and sometimes with the whin-bush, which is full of small thorns. But these thorns, when applied to the skin, take leave of the bush, and remain there, so that the sufferer must often continue days before he can rid himself of these troublesome comrades. Many of these marauders have been apprehended, yet the practice did not cease because they were encouraged by the country people, who had cattle in the pounds which had been seized for taxes, and these expert gentry, for a small reward, liberated and restored the animals to the original owners. A good supper of the best bread, butter, milk and fowls which the farmer could supply, ended the evening's jollity. White-boys, Peep-o'-day Boys, Lady Clares and Molly Maguires are hereditary entailments, having existed ever since parcelling out the land so unjustly, as a regard of plunder, was done to a few. Uncultivated as the mind of the Irish peasantry may be, it is not inactive, the pool is not stagnant. Life of some kind will sparkle up; and truly, if every oppression was justifiable in making wise men 'mad' it is in Ireland. When the cup is full it will flow over, and the saying that Ireland 'must have a rebellion every forty or fifty years' has a law of nature for its foundation. The grand river that supplies the mighty Niagara, flows quietly on for many a mile, till it reaches a certain point, when it takes a rapidity, gathering force as it proceeds till it meets the fearful precipice down which it has roared and tumbled for ages, and down which it will roar and tumble till nature herself shall be dissolved.

The so-called Rebellion of 1848, which sadly sealed the fate of Mitchel and O'Brien, was precisely this law.[11] They had waited and suffered, suffered and waited, till they reached the awful chasm – the Famine. They had seen it swallow its thousands, and they saw and felt that this chasm might have been closed. They looked on, they agitated, till their philanthropic love of country and deep sense of justice rushed into a temporary madness, rashness and an insanity which hurled them headlong into their present abyss. The Tipperary men, who congregated on that hill with their flocks and herds, gave a rational reply to the priest, who exhorted them to disperse: rational for uncultivated barbarians, as their enemies call them.

The priest pointed them to the absurdity, the rashness of rising against so formidable an enemy as England and her soldiers stationed in the country. 'Better suffer than fight, and fight for nothing, too.' They added, 'It isn't the likes of us, yer Riverence, that looks for the right, or the Repale, but the long winter of the Famine will be on us, and we shall die with hunger; the blackguard taxes will take all the cattle, and we took 'em here, plaise your Riverence, to ate and let the soldiers shoot us, and that will be quick death for us; better than the long hunger, your Riverence – better than the hunger.' Now, that was certainly, for barbarians, quite a civilized if not philosophical answer, and quite in keeping with Irish coolness in difficulty and danger. It was something like a company from a district in the south of Ireland, in the time of the first winter of the Famine. They had given up all hope of life, and consented to go in company to the poor-house, and die there, that they might be buried in coffins. Such a haggard array of misery had never been seen before in one body, and the soldiers were ordered to be on the spot at the work-house to keep all in safety. These despairing creatures paused before the red coats and guns, and implored them to shoot them down and end their long misery at once. This was no false bravado. They were sincere and not one among them, it is believed, would have shrunk in the face of that death.

This rebellion, it should be told, was not that ungrateful affair as has been represented. It was not agitated, or scarcely known, among the thousands who had been charitably fed in the Famine. It originated among the higher classes of well-fed politicians, who were too enlightened not to know the causes of their country's sufferings, and too humane to look on with indifference. They were seconded by a lower class of men, who had not as yet felt the whole force of the Famine in their own stomachs, but knew it must speedily come upon them. 'Give us death by the bullet,' they said, 'and not the starvation.' All this should be taken into consideration; and beside, this rebellion had nothing to do with the sectarian spirit of the country. Protestants were at the head of it, and many of the Catholics chimed in, but the priests, as a body, stood aloof and expostulated with their people to do the same. The O'Connells were loud against it, in word and action; and had the Catholics as a body united their forces, Ireland would have been one vast field of blood.

CROY LODGE AND BALLINA

Through the romantic snow-topped mountains of Doughhill, a son of Mrs Wilson conducted me on her car to Ballycroy, or Croy Lodge, the cottage on a most wild coast where Maxwell wrote his *Wild Sports of the West*.[12] We wound among mountains of the most lofty kind; and hanging over the sea, reflecting their snowy sides from its molten surface, with a bright morning sun shining upon them, they were strangely beautiful. The panorama was exceedingly interesting, and the more so that the peasants appeared better fed than any I had met in the country.[13] The relief-officers here might be more attentive, seeing that this destitute spot, so inclosed, could yield no possible relief.

Stopping to feed the pony, a woman entered, whom we had passed an hour before, with a little girl peeping out from under a cloak upon her back. She told us she had been at Mulranny the day before, in hopes of getting a little meal, and was disappointed; it was not the day that the relief was given out. They were penniless, and had not eaten since the day before, and the walk was nine miles. Having in my reticule a sweet biscuit, it was given to the pretty and clean, hungry child.[14] She took it, and gave me a 'God bless ye, lady', but could not be prevailed to eat it; she wrapped it in her pinafore most carefully, looked up to her mother and smiled, but would not break it. 'How is this?' I asked the mother, 'she must be hungry.'

'She is indeed hungry, but she never saw such a thing before, and she cannot think of parting with it, hungry as she must be.'

Such self-denial in a child was quite beyond my comprehension, but so inured are these people to want, that their endurance and self-control are almost beyond belief. Giving her a piece of bread, she ate it with the greatest zest – she had seen bread before.

We took her upon the car, and for three miles she rode under my cloak, with her biscuit snugly wrapped in her apron, holding it most carefully between her hands; and when we set her down, at the turn of the road and I saw her little bare feet running away, and heard her last word of 'bless ye, lady', with the precious treasure safely secured, I prayed the Savior that he would take that little lamb of his flock, and shelter her in his bosom from the bleak winds of adversity that are so keenly blowing and withering the cheek of many a fair blossom in that stricken country. Some days after the mother found me, and said the biscuit was preserved, to remember the nice lady! How little does it take to make such poor happy!

The country was bleak and barren, and a cordial welcome to Croy Lodge after dark was a pleasant salutation. Here, shut in from wind and cold by a bright turf fire, clean cloth and good dinner, had there been none starving without, the evening would have been a pleasant one. Ballycroy had suffered much, but it was not Belmullet. That ghastly look and frightful stare had not eaten out all the appearance of life and hope which many manifested. A visit to the national school gave not a very favourable impression of the state of the children; nearly a hundred pale-faced and bare-footed little ones were crowded into a cold room, squatting upon their feet, cowering closely together, waiting for ten ounces of bread, which was all their support, but now and then a straggling turnip-top. The teacher, with a salary of £12 a year, could not be expected to be of the nicer sort nor of the highest attainments in education. The improvement of the children would not in some time fit them for a class in college.

From this university I went to a hunting-lodge kept by Mr Wilson, accompanied by the kind teacher who insisted that a watch-dog, kept by the gentleman for the purpose of guarding the premises, would 'ate me' if I went alone. Assuring him that the dogs in Ireland had always treated me with great urbanity, and that I feared no harm, he would not allow it; the 'blackguard', he added, 'will rend ye'; and he kindly conducted me to the door. The dog growled; speaking kindly to him, he led me through the hall and when I was seated, doglike, he put his amicable nose upon my lap. The master approvingly said, 'That dog, madam, is very cross and even dangerous to any ragged person or beggar that approaches the premises; but when one decently clothed enters, he welcomes them as he has done you.'. So much for the training of dogs, and their aptness in acquiring the spirit of their masters.

Never before in Ireland had so good an opportunity been presented me of becoming acquainted with the trade of a real sportsman, its merits and demerits, as now; and knowing that the occupation had been in the country quite a celebrated one, I hoped here to learn its real advantages.

Mr Wilson was keeping the lodge for Mr Vernon of Clontarf Castle, near Dublin, to hunt and fowl as he best could. 'I am dying,' he said, 'with rheumatic pains, brought on by wading through the bogs in pursuit of the hare and wild fowl.' He had a noble company of dogs, terriers and pointers, and was surrounded with all the respectable insignia of a hunter of olden time. 'It is a frivolous employment,' he observed, 'and I have long been sick of gaming.' The room was hung round with all sorts of game which is taken by these gentry; and his little daughter of four years of age brought me a book containing pictures of hares, foxes, fowls and dogs, and quite scientifically explained the manner of taking them, the tact of the scenters and the duty of the pointers, so that I was initiated into the first principles of this fashionable trade. She could read intelligibly, and when I committed an error in the pronunciation or understanding of the maneuvres of leaping ditches and following dogs, she set me right, wondering at my dullness, and sometimes rebuking it.

This child had superior talents, and had the mother who cultivated them the spirit of Timothy's mother and grandmother, she might and would be capable of much use in her age.[15] Her father said she had a great taste for the tactics of hunting and fowling, and had acquired her knowledge of reading so young by the fondness of studying the pictures and spelling out the names of the game. Perverted knowledge! And when carried to the extent that some who call themselves ladies in Ireland have done, and practised with that zest that many have manifested, it becomes a romantic mania, quite in keeping with the mountain squaw of the American forest, whose undaunted process and athletic exercises give her a manliness of look and manner which would not disgrace a Spartan.

An opportunity of improving upon the lessons my young teacher had given me, afterward offered itself in the person of a lady, whose talents at this pursuit had been cultivated to a high extent. She would on a cold morning jump upon her favourite hunting-horse, caparisoned in true hunter's style, her ready attendants, hounds, pointers and terriers in advance or pursuit, and gallop at full speed, till some scenter should get upon the track; then hedge and ditch, valley and hill, were scarcely heeded. The sure-footed horse knew his duty, and no circuitous route was taken; if a hedge intervened, it was leaped or broken through; if bog or slough sunk him mid-deep, her cap and feather were soon seen tossing high and dry above all mire and danger, pursuing still faster as excitement grew warmer, till the lucky dogs gave signal that the object was secured. Then the delight, the ecstasy, of seeing the palpitating victim in its agonies, in the power of her faithful pets; and thus the live-long day the sport continued. At night she returned, with the dogs, game and companion of her chase, who was sometimes her father, who had delighted from her childhood to cultivate this fondness in his daughter. Sometimes it might be a brother, and sometimes a generous party would compose the company. But the coming home, the sit-down for the recital of the pleasures of the day – if the victim were a hare, this was a valuable equivalent. The manner of its flight, its narrow escapes, its terror, was so delightful to witness when the dogs were close upon it, and then the dying. All would be minutely described, the dogs would be gathered and caressed, each by his pet name. A good dinner around the family table was served to each, and two or three of the largest always slept in a bed with some members of the family. The most exquisite tenderness was manifested lest the dear creatures should suffer cold or hunger. Yet this tender-hearted Miss, who could not suffer an unkind word to fall upon the ear of her favourite pointer, would go into raptures of delight at the agonies of the timid hare. Her features seemed to have acquired a sharpness, her expression a wildness, her skin a brownness, and her whole appearance was like a true hunter, living and enjoying the constant pursuit.

There is a kind of enchantment, a witchery, hung around an open-air exercise like this, which the more it is practised the more it is loved, till all that tends to elevate the mind and cultivate the best principles of the heart are effaced; and it is quite doubtful whether the subject of this false pursuit can ever become truly and substantially a valuable member of society.

But Croy Lodge must not be forgotten. In and around it, upon the exciting sea-shore, was much that would have given delight, had all been as plentiful about every hearth and table as was around the one at which I was sitting. The first Sabbath after my arrival, a written invitation from an officer of the coast guard was sent us to attend church service across the strand in his watch-house. An open boat conveyed the family and myself to the thatched station-house, where in tasteful array were arranged officers, and all the instruments for killing, hanging in glistening order upon the walls, while in the midst of this embryo battle-field the young curate from Belmullet read his prayers and sermon in a most becoming manner; and we returned in company with Mr Hamilton, the coast-guard officer, who closed the evening by reading and prayer.[16] A Sabbath of singular mixture – boating, prayers, and warlike paraphernalia, all in the same breath; by ministers, officers, and hunters, all believing and practising these different professions. Religion is strangely stirred up in Ireland: it makes a kind of hodge-podge in everything, and is marked with little or no distinction in anything.

Monday, a visit to Doona across the strand introduced me to some curiosities. The tide was ebbing, and for a quarter of a mile before reaching the castle we were to visit we saw stumps of large trees, which centuries ago must have been a rich grove, though not a tree at present is anywhere on the coast, and the sea now occupies the entire lawn, where these once stood.[17] The family residing near the castle are of respectable lineage, by the name of Daly, and in true Irish ancient style set before us meat, bread and potatoes – the last the greatest compliment that could be paid to a guest. The castle, Maxwell says, was built by Granuaile; but not so, its whole structure is so different, its walls so much thicker than any in the days of Gráinne's reign, that its date must have been centuries before.[18] Its history has an incident which will render it a lasting name.

Not a century ago, the christening of a farmer's child was in progress one night in a house near by. The waiting-boy was sent to get a fresh supply of turf; he dropped his torch of dogwood among the dry heap which was piled in the castle, which so heated the walls that they crackled and tumbled, and in their fall set fire to a multitude of casks of contraband spirits. The explosion so frightened the jolly inmates that they fled in dreadful terror from the ruins, and they now stand as that night's festival left them, giving the solitary advantage of showing the thickness of the walls and the curious construction of a building, whose true origin has not been certainly defined. Once, it was a spot of proud grandeur: now a heap of desolation marks the whole for many a mile, where gardens and groves once were planted.

Wednesday morning, at five, I took a car for Bangor, met the mail-coach, and went through a cold, dreary country for twenty miles to Crossmolina. A little cultivation and a few trees tell the traveller that the town is near. Six miles further we reached the hospitable house of Peter Kelly, mentioned in these pages – and surely no character is better deserved than is his for that excellent trait; and the kindness I received under his roof never can be forgotten.[19] Such families should live in the records of history as pleasant mementoes for the grateful, and examples for the parsimonious, that if such can be taught, they may have the benefit of using hospitality without grudging. The cheerful sacrifices made in the house, that I might not only stay but be made comfortable, were so in contrast with the pinching and squeezing which often is met in families of the would-be-thought hospitable, that surely it might be said that he descended from a generous stock, as instinct not cultivation seemed entirely the spring of action in him.

The remembrance of Ballina is sweet and pleasant to the soul. That 'Codnach of gentle flood', the sweet river Moy, that flows quietly and richly through the green meadows there, must leave pleasant associations in the minds of all lovers of nature who have wandered upon its banks. Though it was in the dark days of the Famine, in the dreary month of February, that I entered Ballina, yet everything looked as if men and women of good taste and good feeling dwelt there. It was here that the indefatigable Kinkead laboured and died, in the year 1847.[20] His simple tablet hangs in the church where he preached; but he needed no marble monument, for his name will be held in everlasting remembrance. He was eyes to the blind, and the cause he knew not he sought out. Free from sectarianism, he relieved all in his power, and spoke kindly to the bowed down; he wiped the tear from the eye of the widow and fatherless, and brought joy and gladness into the abodes of those who were forgotten by their neighbours. He had a co-worker in his labours of love, who died a little before the Famine, in the person of Captain Short. He had been a naval officer; but by the grace of God had become a follower of the meek and lowly Jesus, and devoted his time, talents and wealth to the cause of God and his fellow-creatures. In their lives, these two, like Jonathan and David, were united; and in their deaths they were not long divided. Mr Kinkead, who was but thirty-five, left a widow and son and daughter. The widow is worthy to bear his name. She too, like him, is found among the poor, promoting their temporal and spiritual good in every possible way. In her are united much that makes woman appear in that dignified light, that tells for what she is intended and what she might be if kept from the trammels of a false education, and early brought into the covenant of grace.

I met the widow of Captain Short in the wilds of Erris, and her name and remembrance were pleasant to my heart. In her house in Ballina I passed happy hours. She entered feelingly into my object in visiting Ireland, and it is but just to say that though not one pound was then at my command to give in charity, yet had thousands been in my possession to bestow, I could not have wished more kindness than was manifested to me then. Their courtesy seemed to be of the genuine kind flowing from the heart. The town has a population of ten thousand inhabitants, Episcopalians, Baptists, Presbyterians, Methodists and Roman Catholics – the latter claiming the majority. The ladies here were much interested for the poor; a society for spinning and knitting was in operation, and the eagerness of the women to procure work was affectingly manifested on the day of meeting, when crowds would be waiting in the hall, some falling upon their knees, begging for spinning to be given them, when the most that spinners could earn would be eightpence a week.[21] Those who prepared the flax by hackling could earn from eighteen pence to two shillings a week. So far have manufactures cheapened this work that the ladies who give it lose at that low price. The distress of Ballina was increasing, the poor-law system is impoverishing all the middle classes who must become paupers, if not beggars, unless their taxes are reduced. No complaint was made in this place of the partiality or neglect of relieving officers; all seemed to bless the hand that fed them, and however rebellious the Connaught people may be, no indications were here given of insurrection.

The Baptist minister, who is a missionary, stationed there with his praiseworthy wife and children, has been an instrument of doing much good.[22] Without being a proselyter, he had gathered a church counting nearly a hundred, chiefly from the Romish population. His humble chapel stands open, the seats free; and passers-by often step in from curiosity and stay from inclination, till their hearts become impressed with the truth, and they are finally led to unite in building up a church which they once supposed was heresy. The character of this missionary may be told in a few words which a lady in the Protestant church uttered, in answer to – 'Who is the most active labourer in town among the poor?'

'Mr Hamilton does the most good with the least noise, of any man among us.'

A respectable banking-house is established in the town, at the head of which is an Englishman; his active wife is an Irish lady. They are friends to Ireland, and not blind to the causes of its evils.

It has been remarked, that most of the English who reside in Ireland become quite attached to both country and people, prejudices being blunted by nearer acquaintance. The six weeks of pleasant acquaintance there cultivated must be exchanged for different scenes. This old seat of kings, with its raths, stones of memorial, green meadows, gently flowing Moyne and abbeys, but above all the people, courteous in manner, and kind in action, must be left forever.

The last day of February 1848 will be remembered as one that took me reluctantly away from a town and people peculiarly endeared to my heart. I was not coldly hurried away to a coach alone, leaving the family in bed who had taken their farewell the evening before. Miss O'Dowda, Miss Fox and two little daughters of Peter Kelly accompanied me, and as the high-mettled horse galloped and hurried us away, I looked a sad and tearful adieu.[23] The sun was bright, the meadows on the banks of the Moyne were green, and the ride full of interest. The same sun was shining, the same river flowing – but where were the proud kings with their shields of gold and warlike bearing that once held their sway over this pretty landscape? Dead, dead! Some moss-covered stone in a crumbling castle or abbey tells their demise, and the children of the mountains heedlessly trample on the monument.

The children, yes, the children of Ireland, cling to my heart beyond and over all else, and when fond remembrance turns to Ballina, the courteous, well-disciplined, affectionate children of Peter Kelly sometimes make me regret that I ever had seen them, because I shall see them no more. The Irish, both in high life and low, are a pattern to all Christian nations in the early training of their children. No visitor has cause to dread the clamour in a house, or the confusion and breaking up of all that is comfortable and quiet at table in an Irish family. They are not first at table – first and best served, monopolizing all attention to their own pampered palates, selecting the most palatable food, &c. – but seldom are they present with guests, and if so, their demeanour in most cases is an honour to the governess and mother who has disciplined them.

We soon found ourselves on the borders of the celebrated Pontoon Lakes; but who shall describe them? 'Why,' said one in Ballina, 'among all the tourists who have visited Ireland, have none more particularly described these lakes, and the whole scenery?' For this plain reason, description must here fail. There is so much in such varied confusion and beauty that nothing is particularly marked; the eye is lost in the view as a whole. Before the Famine, I was whirled one cold day over the one-arched bridge by a surly coachman, who, in answer to my inquiries of the picturesque scenery, said that 'it was a divil of a starved rocky place', and he was 'glad when he saw the end on't'. The lakes on this sunny day had the finest opportunity to set off their transparency; and for many miles they glistened, widening and narrowing, bordered by all manner of fantastic rocks and heath till we reached the Pontoon Bridge which passes over a narrow neck connecting the two lakes. These lakes are called Cullen and Conn. The current flows different ways in the course of the day, as Lough Cullen has no vent but to discharge its overflowing waters into the larger lake. Lord Lucan has built a hotel, police barracks and a few cottages under the wooded rocks which overlook Lough Cullen; but all seem quite deserted under Cummer mountain, having only a caretaker to tell its pedigree. The rocks are thrown together upon one side, in masses, as if ready to fall asunder; some lying at the foot of cliffs, as if precipitated from them, and one of immense weight is poised upon a summit, by a small point, which to the passer-by appears as if jostling ready to fall; and we were told that a skein of silk could be drawn between the two rocks. We took the road from the lower lake to the left, and followed the tortuous ravine till we reached a small one-arched bridge, opposite which is a most picturesque barren island, covered with heath, and a black rock, which contrast beautifully with the blue water of the lake. The wooded hillocks, bordering the lakes with varied foot-paths, give the visitor all the advantages of pleasant views from their elevation upon the bold expanse and the rocky shore upon the other side.[24]

In its moss-covered rocks and richly wooded hills Pontoon resembles Glengarriff, but it wants the curling smoke between the rocks, and the tree-tops ascending from turf cabins, and here and there a flaxen-headed urchin upon the top of the thatch to make the whole picture. We wound along, meeting now and then a sudden peep, through trees, on the path which leads three miles farther to the once tasteful domain of Mr Anderson, which afterward I visited with Mrs Bourke, and found the mansion desolate, the walks grown up with weeds; and all the ancient grandeur which once was here displayed, reminds one of the old blasted fortunes of a hunter who had exhausted his wine-casks, drunk the last health, and sounded the last horn over these broad lakes, and now tattered and slip-shod, was recounting his hunting valour in some shebeen house, where whiskey, pipes and song enliven the present, and put out all light of the past. The declining sun warned my friends that they must return, leaving me to walk or sit upon a stone while waiting for the coach that was to take me to Castlebar. I saw the last wave of the hands of the kind young ladies and flirting of the handkerchiefs of the little Kellys as they whirled around the point which took me from their sight. It was not a mawkish sentimentality that made me feel like giving up the coming lonely hours to an indulgence of weeping. I was alone, in a land of strangers, amid Famine, pestilence and death, going I scarcely knew where, and could not expect to find another Ballina before me; and the last few weeks served to heighten the contrast of what had been suffered, and what must rationally be expected to await me. The coach came and shut me in, and no more was seen till Castlebar was reached. Here was a town that had tasted deeply the cup of woe; she had a splendid poorhouse, and it lacked no inmates, yet the streets were filled with beggars.[25] Many beautiful seats of respectable families are about the town, some in tolerable vigour, and some giving the last look upon former grandeur. Some interesting facts are recorded of this old assize town. Many trees have borne on their limbs the bodies of miserable culprits; and now the more genteel drop effects the same work in a different way.[26]

March 14th. Criminal cases were going forward now in court, and the attorneys, Dublin-like, had come prepared with wigs and gowns for the first time, a practice heretofore not in vogue in Connaught. The ladies in Castlebar were curious to behold this novel sight, but custom had prohibited them hitherto from appearing in these places. Two prisoners were to be tried for murder; and wishing to know how Ireland, which has been somewhat celebrated for trials of this kind, managed such cases, in company with a young lady of the family, I went. We found a favourable position in the gallery, where we could see the court and prisoners. The case was this: a publican had become offended with a neighbour, and determined to be revenged by giving him a good beating. Not wishing to do it himself, he called in two men, gave them an abundance of whiskey, and for a few shillings they agreed to do it well. The man was waylaid at nightfall and the beating went on. Many joined in the affray, some to rescue, and some to assist. The man was killed. The evidence went to prove that one of the two gave a heavier blow, and he must have finished the work, consequently he was guilty. The attorney, Bourke, made a most able defence, and though a Roman Catholic, he dwelt most solemnly on the last grand Assize, when that court as well as the prisoners at the bar must be judged by an impartial judge, and condemned or acquitted, as their real state should be found.[27] The judge was celebrated for clemency, and gave a plain impressive charge, that if the least doubt remained on their minds they must lean to the side of mercy.

What must have been the conflicting emotions of the miserable men, when that jury retired? They both stood coolly, as is the peculiar habit of that impetuous, hasty people in the face of danger or death; and the jury soon returned with a verdict of guilty for one. What a fallible tribunal is man! How could a jury decide, in a riot like that, who was the murderer, and how could they decide that either intended murder? It appeared a haphazard jump to get rid of the case. In the evening I was in the company of three of the jury, and spoke of the responsibility of being a juror, where life and death are concerned. One most exultingly responded that he liked the responsibility well, and should be glad to have it in his power to hang every murderer he could catch; they deserved no mercy, and he would never show any. A second one confirmed it, and all manifested that lightness that was horrid for men who had just condemned a fellow-creature to the gallows. It is hoped these jurymen were not a common specimen of the class in Ireland; if so, life must hang more on the prejudices and retaliating propensities of a jury than on the evidence or merits of the case. The poor man was reprieved and transported for life. The inhabitants had strenuously exerted themselves in his behalf, knowing that the publican was the instigator, and whiskey the instrument of the murders. This good creature certainly has some marks in his forehead that look like the 'beast'.

Patrick's Day was opened with a little apprehension on the part of the people throughout the country. 'Conciliation Hall' had given an invitation to all parts for the people to assemble that day, and send a united and earnest appeal to government for a redress of grievances and Repeal of the Union, holding up France as an encouragement for action.[28] The deplorable state of the country, the loss of confidence in landlords and the abatement of the influence of the priests, left something to fear, that when so many should be assembled the irascible temper of the nation would be stirred up to dangerous acts. In Castlebar, the people collected had Mass; the priests exhorted them to be quiet, and in the evening the principal houses were illuminated. Boys assembled, lit up a tar-barrel, drew it through the streets, shouting, 'Hurra for the Republic', while men walked soberly on, more as if following a hearse than if stimulating their countrymen to deeds of valour or rejoicing at conquest. The mirth of the land has emphatically ceased, the spirit is broken; every effort at convivility appears as if making a last struggle for life. The shamrock was sprinkled here and there upon a hat, but, like its wearer, seemed drooping, as being conscious that its bloom was scathed and its beauty dying forever. The deep disease in this body politic has never been thoroughly probed, and the evil lies where probably it has been least suspected. The habits of the higher classes for centuries have had little tendency to enlighten or moralize the lower order, and yet, when all is taken into consideration, drinking habits included, the scale must preponderate in favour of the latter.

Some respectable families in and about Castlebar were doing to their utmost for the poor. Mr Stoney, the rector, was employing many of them in spinning, but so isolated were these efforts that little could be done to stay the plague.[29] Two miles from Castlebar I spent a Sabbath in the family of the widow Fitzgerald, relict of a British officer, who was an English lady from the Isle of Wight, much attached to Ireland. Though the mother of a numerous family, she draws, paints and plays on the piano, as in the days of her youth. Her spacious drawing-rooms are hung around with elegant specimens of her taste in painting; and, then seventy-three years of age, she appeared to have lost none of the vigour of intellect which she must have possessed in her youth. A son-in-law, meek believer, the Protestant curate of the parish, was residing with her and the whole constituted a family of love and peace, and of the kindest feeling toward the poor.[30]

An unexpected invitation to visit the parish of Partry, by the active Catholic curate who resided there was accepted.[31] 'You will find him', Protestant gentleman remarked, 'an active, honourable man among the poor, and one who has done much good.' The country about him scarcely had a parallel, even in Skibbereen.[32] Eleven miles from Castlebar opened a bright spot of taste – a glebe-house and tidy new chapel – which this indefatigable curate had built, in spite of all poverty.[33] In the chapel were a few half-dead children huddled upon the floor, some around the altar with their writing-books upon the steps for desks, without table or benches. These the curate had gathered among the starving, for the sake of the black bread, which kept them barely alive. The neighbourhood abound in novelties, strange and romantic, but most of them must be passed over to leave room for details of the people.

This indefatigable man had caused a fever shed to be erected on a bog bordering upon the Lake of Mask, where pure air is circulating, and a snug cottage stands near in which the matron who keeps the hospital resides. Thirty invalids were here, mostly sick from the effects of hunger, with swollen legs, many of them past all hope. Far away from any inhabitant, this hospital, cottage and their inmates stood, struggling to keep up the dying flame of life, only to suffer fresh and hopeless troubles. Solitary as this region everywhere is, it was once celebrated ground. That

day's excursion to me was full of strange scenes and strange anecdotes.
Here stood the stone raised in memory of the death of John, the priest
killer; here is the site of an ancient abbey, but twelve feet wide; here, on
the borders of the lake, is an anvil belonging to a forge, which is of such
weight that it has never been raised from the bed into which it has sunk,
and where it is supposed to have lain for centuries. An iron-ore bed is
near the spot, as useless as all materials for improvement are in Ireland.

This parish borders on the famous Joyce country and is replete with
interest, where in days of yore robbers and murderers sported at will. A
noted robber by the name of Mitchell was taken in a house pointed out,
now in a crumbling state, but then occupied by a landlord who entertained the mountain robber, and had even bargained away his daughter to
his desperado. A handsome reward was offered to secure this fearful
prowler, and the landlord, in spite of family relation or treaty, determined
to make sure the prize. One night when Mitchell, overcome with a mountain excursion of plunder, had gone to sleep with his pistols near him, the
landlord wetted the pans, went out and took in the magistrates to
Mitchell's bed, who was still asleep but soon awaked, seized his pistols –
they refused to act. He was secured, bound and finally executed.

On the route this day, among all the rarities, was the christening of an
infant in a miserable dark cabin by this priest, which he assured me was
the only birth he had known for months. May I never seen the like again!
The dark mud cabin, the straw on which the mother lay, the haggard
countenances of the starving group, the wooden bowl of 'holy water', the
plate of salt, the mummery of the priest while he was putting the salt of
grace to its lips, the blowing with his breath to infuse the regenerating
spirit into the soul – were such a trifling, fearful combination of nonsense
and profanity to my dark mind that it was quite difficult to keep a usual
degree of sobriety. But the priest escaped with no other lecture than an
exclamation of nonsense, when we were out of the cabin.

To do these poor priests justice, they have laboured long and hard
since the Famine, and have suffered intensely. They have the most trying
difficulties to encounter, without the least remuneration. In the best of
times, their stipulated sum is but ten pounds a year, the remainder must
be made up by 'hook and by crook'. Weddings and christenings formerly
gave what the generosity of guests could bestow, which was always so
small, that a Protestant lady once, from pure benevolence, attended one
of these cabin-weddings in the poor parts of the country and put four
pounds into the plate as it was passed round. She said the priest was a
peaceable citizen, very poor and very kind, and why should she not give
his, which she could spare, and he needed. In the Famine, night and day,
their services were requisite, no fevers nor loathsome dens, nor even

caves could exonerate them. They must go whenever called, and thi
without any remuneration.

One day's excursion will better illustrate this fact than genera
remarks can. I went to a spot on purpose to see for myself, and that day
asked the priest to show me the most that he could of the realties of the
Famine, and soon I was gratified. The sight was too much, and in a few
hours my way was made back in the rain over the fearful waste alone to
the glebe-house. We were soon met by applicants of all description beg
ging on their knees, clinging fast to the poor man, begging for God'
sake that he would give them letters to the relieving officer for the pound
of meal, asking advice how and what to do when they had pulled down
their cabins and had no shelter. The rain was falling, the roads bad, and
the multitude so increased as we proceeded that it was very difficult to
make our way. He told them they must let me pass decently as a stranger
who had come out to see them through pity, and kindly added, 'You
know I would relieve you, but cannot.' Not one impatient word ever
escaped him through the whole, although their unreasonable importuni
ties were dreadfully tormenting. I had heard so many relieving officer
and distributors scold and threaten, and had struggled so hard myself to
keep patient without always succeeding, that I inquired how he kep
without scolding. His answer was, 'Sure, as I can give them no money,
should give them kind words.' Here were cabins torn down in heaps, and
here were the poor, wretched, starving women and children, crawling
together by the side of ditches, or in some cabin still standing, to ge
shelter from the rain, scattered too, over a wide extent of country. 'Wha
shall I do?' said the despairing priest. 'Let me die rather than witness
daily such scenes as I cannot relieve.'

I left him to go farther into the mountains where some of the dying
had sent for him, and ascended a little eminence alone, and saw the
smoke of the humble abode of the parish priest by the name of Ward, and
all without and within gave proof that if he had lived for gain, he had
missed the road thither.[34] He was a simple-minded priest of the old
school of Ireland, and had added no new-fangled notions of modern
style, and welcomed me to his house like an old patriarch of four thou
sand years ago. The poor found in him friend whose warm heart and
open hand always were ready to give, so long as he had anything to
bestow. Thirteen hundred of his parishioners had died in Partry of the
Famine in twelve months out of a population of six thousand. I returned
home with benediction added to blessing upon my head, for having come
to visit so poor and so neglected a people as his in those desolate moun
tains. The curate did not reach home till late in the evening, drenched
with rain; he had left without shelter a dying man, with his wife and

daughter standing by, and giving them the last sixpence he had returned, for he could do nothing more. At the dawning of day the daughter stood at his window, saying her father was dead, and begged that he would go and do something to assist in putting him away from the dogs!

Thursday, April 13th. A drive to Ballinrobe presented a beautiful variety of scenery. Lake Carra is spread out, dotted with islands and indented by peninsulas, with a long bridge across it called Keel, inferior to none but Pontoon. Three miles from the glebe, and we were in sight of the tall steeple of the chapel, towering presumptuously for so unpopular a religion; for time was when the Romish Church was not allowed steeples of any dimensions, and they now make no great pretensions in the steeple way.

The town of Ballinrobe is somewhat picturesque, and was once the assize town of Mayo; but the judges saw fit to remove it to Castlebar; and report says, that some trifling complaint concerning bakers and cooks was the cause. But the town still boasts a famous poorhouse, well filled, a proud barrack, with a noble supply of the fighting gentry, placed there as we are told to make up for the removal of the assizes. A beautiful river, bordered with trees, winds through the town, occasionally a pretty cottage peeping between them, with two ivy-covered ancient ruins among tombstones and naked skulls, with inscriptions of such ancient date that time had worn them so that they were almost entirely defaced.[35]

An invitation to dine at Dr Rafe's introduced me to a lady in Mrs Rafe who might justly be classed among intellects and attainments of the highest order. I had seen many well-bred ladies in Connaught, but not one who was better acquainted with books, and who could converse on something beyond small talk with greater facility and understanding than Mrs Rafe.

From Ballinrobe the famous Cong was visited, known as containing so many natural curiosities and ancient historical events. The abbey here is one of great interest, large, and designed with exquisite carvings, and beautiful arches of doors and windows.[36] The niches are entirely filled with bones. Here is interred the famous Roderic O'Connor, among the neglected rubbish; and priests and people in one confused mass, mingling their dust among peasants and beggars. But the beauty of Cong is that ordained by nature; the river and green meadow and hillock, where stands a most enchanting lodge backed with wood, which is seen with great advantage from the top of a hill upon the opposite side, which every tourist should be mindful to ascend.

The lake, the town, the church standing in the walls of the old abbey, the river, lodge, and wood in front, a promontory of the brightest green; and, as a finish, the pier, containing some of the choicest stones of the abbey carved with hieroglyphics, give to the whole picture a view beautiful and novel in the extreme. The 'Horse Discovery' is a chasm into which a horse plunged when plowing. The chasm is now descended by artificial stone steps, and standing upon the bottom the water is seen sparkling far back and murmuring at your feet in darkness. Spars are hanging from the roof, and the aperture above is fringed with vines and ivy, giving a sombre look to the whole.

The 'Lady's Buttery' comes next; this is a shelving rock, covered with grass and shrubbery, under which flows the river Cong, also somewhat rapidly, and is lost in the lake some quarter of a mile below.

The 'Pigeon Hole' is the lion of Cong; it is so called because pigeons are wont to make nests in the dome. This hole is descended by forty-two stone steps, quite steep, and at the bottom is the river that runs through the 'Buttery', flowing most cheerfully here, and forming a little eddy in which fish are sporting. These caused great excitement among the troop that had followed us, a legend being told that the fish in this pool had lived there ever since its discovery, without multiplying or decreasing These patriarchs consequently are of very ancient date; and a young lad told us that one of these fathers had been caught and put upon a gridiron to broil, but made his escape into the water, and has now the marks upon his ribs so that from age to age he has been traced; but he can never be caught, nor can any of his comrades be induced to nibble a bait.[37] The fish had not been seen for a long time, and the company and curate were highly rejoiced that these black gentlemen should come out to salute us.

The river, after passing this eddy, flows rapidly through a fearful cavern, arched over with black stones, many of which seem to have tumbled down and lay piled along through the dark chamber. An old woman for many a year had been the keeper of this cavern, and with a bundle of dried rushes lighted she led the visitors on, showing a lofty ceiling of stone, cut in the most fantastical shapes. The fearful slippery passage over slimy and uneven rocks, tumbled and piled together, the music of the water hastening away to hide itself under the earth again. The grand dome of black stone, and the graceful curtains of the ivy hanging and swinging at ease, all lighted up by the glaring torch, made an underground picture sublime, terrific and beautiful in the extreme. This profitable estate is now in possession of the granddaughter of the lately deceased inheritor; and the elasticity of the young damsel testified to her full confidence in her own powers, as well as hopes of a fortune in the end. The environs of Cong contain a quantity of black stone which is much used in building, covering the ground in layers, through the fields about the town.[38]

A dinner was in waiting at Dr Rafe's, and no one could have thought when looking upon the table, that famine was ranging without. On a beautiful site at Ballinrobe this indefatigable priest has leased a piece of thirty acres of land, at one shilling per acre, where he intends building a monastery for nuns and children of the poor.[39] A curious stone stands upon the spot, and no manuscript has yet told its pedigree; but its lofty upright bearing says it is of noble origin.

The industry of this curate appears, if not supernatural, urged on by an irresistible impulse almost unparalleled. Shall it be credited that in thirteen weeks he converted a barren spot into a fine site for a chapel and glebe-house. After demolishing the old chapel, he built and finished them both in excellent taste. The wall, which surrounds a large handsome lawn before the house, is built of stone, which was quarried in one day and the whole completed in three hours. The entire parish were invited to the chapel to hear Mass at nine o'clock; then all were encouraged with having music and amusement to their hearts' content when the work should be finished. Eight hundred assembled. The curate assigned a certain portion to be erected by so many, and thus confusion was prevented – the work went orderly on. And this three hours' labour completed a wall inclosing the chapel and glebe-house, fringed upon the top in front with a peculiar kind of stone from the lake, which is jagged, porous and black, and when struck, gives a sound like iron. The wall is whitewashed, the stones upon the top left black, adding an air of ornament to the whole. A young shrubbery is already looking up in the door-yard, giving to the lately barren waste bog an appearance like a young garden, fresh and green.

These people, called Roman Catholics, certainly must astonish the Orthodox world by their untiring zeal for the good of the church in Ireland. With everything to oppose, they urge on their way; a government church forcing upon them restrictive laws very severe, and a labouring class of real paupers. With these drawbacks they build chapels, finish them well, and 'through evil and through good report', nakedness and famine, they urge their way, erecting chapels in the midst almost of hetacombs of the slain! The curate was asked where he got money for all this. 'Money was not wanted,' was the answer. Seventy carts were in train, drawing the stone when cut from the quarry. The stone was free, labour was free and every parishioner performed his part cheerfully. The little money that was required for the trimmings the bishop supplied. The coarse, trite saying of John Bunyan's imprisonment may be fitly applied to the government church in Ireland. A writer remarks 'that the devil run himself out in his own shoes when he put John Bunyan in jail'.[40]

The curate shall be dismissed after one more allusion to his everawake zeal in all and everything. The poor-house in Ballinrobe did not exactly suit his notions of justice to the inmates. He called upon the

Guardians and apprised them that a fearless, scrutinizing friend to the poor from the United States was visiting all the soup-shops and work-houses in Ireland, and was showing up the dishonesty practised among them by taking notes which were printed for the information of government. Not suspecting that my name had gone before, in the innocence of my heart my way was made thither, and I was happily disappointed at finding the house in such excellent order. Officers and servants were all at their posts, and everything done to make the visit most agreeable; yet, there was such an appearance of affectation in the whole that thoughts did arise whether in reality all was so. The purloining of the public bene-factions since the Famine has given so much cause for suspicion that all whose hands are not thoroughly clean, shrink from observation.

The guardians of the poor in Ireland will have a sad account to render at the last in many cases, it is greatly to be feared. Feeding the poor on two scanty meals of miserable food, when there are funds sufficient, has been the accusation which has proved too true in many parts, and has operated so powerfully upon the inmates, what when once out they have chosen death out-of-doors rather than going in again.

I found some few hungry men on my way, putting a few potatoes in a field, and inquired why they should lose their potatoes and their time in this hopeless undertaking. The answer was, 'Plaise God we'll have the potato again'. The 'potato again', is the last wreck to which they are still clinging.

April 17th. With a sister of Peter Kelly I went to 'Old Head', and was first introduced into one of the dreadful pauper schools where ninety children received a piece of black bread once a day.[41] It was a sad sight, most of them were in a state of rags, barefooted, and squatted on the floor waiting for a few ounces of bread, with but here and there a frag-ment of a book. The clean schoolmaster, on a cold day, was clad in a white vest and linen pantaloons, making the last effort to appear respectable, labouring for the remuneration of a penny a week from each family if by chance the family could furnish it. These ninety all belonged to Mrs Garvey's tenantry, and there were others looking on who had come in likewise, not belonging to her lands, who wishfully stood by without receiving one morsel.[42] I looked till my satiated eyes turned away at a pitiful sight like this. Neither the neat cottage, the old sea, nor my favourite Croagh Patrick could give satisfaction in a wilderness of woe like this. When will these dreadful scenes find an end?

Naught but desolation and death reigned; and the voice of nature, which was always so pleasant on the sea-coast, now united with the whistling of the wind, seemed only to be howling in sad response to the moans and entreaties of the starving around me. The holy well, where the nimitable drawing of the blind girl was taken, is near this place.[43] In years gone by this well was a frequented spot where invalids went to be healed. It is now surrounded by stone, covered with earth, and a path about gives the trodden impress of many a knee where the postulant goes round seven times, repeating a Paternoster at every revolution, and drops a stone which tells that the duty is performed. A hole is shown in a stone where the holy St Patrick knelt till he wore the stone away. A poor peasant girl, in the simplicity of her heart, explained all the ceremonies of the devotees and virtues of the well, regretting that the priests had forbidden the practice now. A company soon entered the churchyard and set down a white coffin, waiting till the widow of the deceased should bring a spade to open the grave; and while the dirt was being taken away she sat down, leaning upon the coffin, setting up the Irish wail in the most pathetic manner. She, by snatches, rehearsed his good qualities then burst into a gush of tears, then commenced in Irish, as the meagre English has no words to express the height of grief, madness or joy.[44] The ground was opened but a few inches when the coffin of another was touched. The graveyards are everywhere filled so near the surface that dogs have access, and some parts of the body are often exposed.

A debate was now in progress respecting good works and the importance of being baptized into the true church. Mrs G., who professed to be a papist, disputed the ground with them, till the contest became so sharp that I retired, for their darkness was painful. It seemed like the valley and shadow of death, temporally and spiritually.[45]

The little town of Louisburgh, two miles from Old Head, had suffered extremely. An active priest and faithful Protestant curate were doing their utmost to mitigate the suffering, which was like throwing dust in the wind; lost, lost forever – the work of death goes on, and what is repaired to-day is broken down to-morrow.[46] Many have fallen under their labours. The graves of the Protestant curate and his wife were pointed out to me in the churchyard, who had fallen since the Famine in the excess of their labour; and the present curate and his praiseworthy wife, unless they have supernatural strength, cannot long keep up the dreadful struggle.[47] He employed as many labourers as he could pay at four pence a day, and at four o'clock these 'lazy' ones would often be waiting at his gate to go to their work. He was one day found dining with the priest, and the thing was so novel that I expressed a pleasant surprise, when he answered, 'I have consulted no one's opinion respecting the propriety of my doing so. I found,' he added, 'on coming here, this man a warm-hearted friend to the poor doing all the good in his power, without any regard to party, and determined to treat him as a neighbour and friend, and have as yet seen no cause to regret it.' This same priest was not able

to walk, having been sick, but he was conveyed in a carriage to Mrs
Garvey's and most courteously thanked me for coming into that miserable neighborhood, and offered to provide some one at his own expense
to convey me into the Killery mountains, to see the inimitable scenery
and the wretched inhabitants that dwell there.

In company with the wife of the curate and the physician, I went
there.[48] The morning was unusually sunny, but the horrors of that day
were inferior to none ever witnessed. The road was rough, and we constantly were meeting pale, meagre-looking men, who were on their way
from the mountains to break stones and pile them mountain-high for the
paltry compensation of a pound of meal a day. These men had put all
their seed into the ground, and if they gave up their cabins they must
leave the crop for the landlord to reap, while they must be in a poor-
house or in the open air. This appeared to be the last bitter drug in Ireland's cup of woe!

'Why,' a poor man was asked, whom we met dragging sea-weed to
put upon his potato field, 'do you do this, when you tell us you expect to
go into the poor-house, and leave your crop to another?'

'I put it on, hoping that God Almighty will send me the work to get a
bit.'

We met flocks of wretched children going to school for the bit of
bread, some crying with hunger, and some begging to get in without the
penny which was required for their tuition. The poor little emaciated
creatures went weeping away, one saying he had been 'looking for the
penny all day yesterday, and could not get it'. The doctor who accompanied us returned to report to the priest the cruelty of the relieving officer
and teacher, but this neither frightened or softened these hard hearts.
These people are shut in by mountains and the sea on one side, and roads
passable only on foot by the other, having no bridges and the paths
entirely lost in some places among the stones. We left our carriage and
walked as we could; and though we met multitudes in the last stages of
suffering, yet not one through that day asked charity, and in one case the
common hospitality showed itself, by offering us milk when we asked
for water. This day I saw enough, and my heart was sick, sick.

The next morning the Protestant curate wished me to go early to the
field and see the willing labourers in his employ. He called one to the
hedge, and asked if he had the potatoes in his pocket which he had gathered some days ago. The man took out a handful of small ones. 'These',
said the curate (the tear starting to his eye), 'are what this man found in
spading up the ground here; and so little have his family to eat at home
that he has carried them in his pocket till he can find some little spot
where he may plant them, lest if he should leave them in the cabin they

would be eaten.' This man had a family of four to support on the four-
pence earned in that field.

One interesting and last excursion ended my painful visit in this
romantic, desolate region. The company was made up of Mrs Garvey, a
cousin of hers of the same name, a widow who possessed land in these
vales and mountains for four miles, and her two sons.[49] The distance was
eight miles, the road narrow, winding, rocky and in some places entirely
lost, excepting the foot-path of the shepherds.[50] Our vehicle was a cart
with a bed in it for the accommodation of the two ladies, who had never,
like me, been jolted on this wise, and were now submitting to all this
hardship for my amusement. With much fixing and re-fixing, ordering
and re-ordering, bed, baskets of lunch, extra cloaks and so on, all adjusted, we were well under way for these 'Alps on Alps'. We had not made
more than two miles of this journey when stones, brooks and no road
said 'Ye can go no further'. We did, by getting out and lifting the cart,
and at length found ourselves in a flat vale with a pretty river flowing
through it.[51] Scattered here and there were the once-comfortable cabins
of the tenants of the last-named Mrs G, now every cabin either deserted
or suffering in silent hopelessness, and all the land lying waste.

The poor cabiners would meet us, and say to their landlady, 'God
bless ye, and once ye didn't see us so, but now we are all destrawed.'
'And how, Mary or Bridget, do you get on? Have you any meal?' And 'I
am sorry that I couldn't send you any more', &c., were the salutations of
this kind landlady, who had not received one pound of rent since the
Famine. I thanked her most gratefully for the favour she bestowed on me
in keeping from my ears those heart-scathing words to the starving poor I
had heard so much from landlords and relieving officers during the
Famine. 'I could not upbraid them,' she answered, 'for until the Famine,
scarcely a pound of rent has been lost by them all; and my only sorrow is,
that I can do nothing to keep them alive, and not lose them from the land.'

Four miles took us to the foot of a pile of Alps, at the bottom of which
was sleeping a sweet lake, cradling in its bosom a little green shrubbery
island, the habitation of wild fowl entirely.[52] The precipitous rocky path
made it impossible to use the cart, and our crushed clumsy feet were now
put in requisition. Though our walk was a rugged one, yet we were not
losers; for Ireland, above all other countries probably, should be visited
in this way, having two superior advantages. First, there is so much of the
romantic reality to be seen everywhere, both in antiquities and nature;
and second, the courtesy of the peasants, which makes every rough place
easy; and if they have not milk to offer you, the purest water that ever
sparkled in fountain or well is springing up everywhere to refresh the
traveller. We had nature to-day in her full dress, and besides the pleasure

of seeing that heartfelt welcome which was manifested toward the 'blessed landlady', I contrasted it with a walk taken one sunny day with a rich landlord, a few months before, whose tenants were all 'lazy dogs': he had tried them twenty-five years and could make nothing out of them, and now they were starving, they were all looking to him, &c. These tenants, when they saw us approaching, walked away without any recognition; or if in close contact they gave a slight touch of the hat, with no welcome, nor 'blessed landlord'.

'Your tenants, sir,' I observed, 'do not appear so hearty and courteous as is customary for the mountain peasants in many places.'

'I told you I could never make anything out of them, and intend clearing the whole land another year and getting in a better set.'

The landlady this day was pointing me from cabin to cabin, where lived an industrious man or tidy woman, and 'I must lose them all'.

Proud mountain rose, in conical form, upon mountain, as if by some volcano they had been shot up perpendicularly; streamlets were trickling from their sides, and the rich heath and sedge covered their surface. These lofty piles give pasturage to cattle, sheep and goats, and we saw the faithful shepherd's dog leaping from rock to rock, gathering the flock to drive them to better forage, and the little shepherd-girl sitting upon a crag to watch the little charge; and under the mountain was nestled the cabin of the herder who for twenty years, he told us, had guarded the flocks upon the tops and sides of these lofty mountains. By the wayside was a large fold into which all the sheep are gathered when the different owners wish to ascertain if any are missing, or when any are wanted for use. The owner and not the shepherd sustains the loss if the number be wanting. The sheep live and thrive upon these rich mountains, summer and winter. The mountain-goat, so peculiarly adapted for climbing the crags, we saw here; his shaggy mane waving in the breeze, as he nibbled the sedge and heath upon the highest peaks.

Our road was upon a fearfully precipitous side of a hill hanging over the lake. We had reascended the cart, and were obliged again to leave it, and the chubby Mrs Garvey, in doing so, like a sack of wool, made a somersault and rolled upon rough stones. Her justifiable shrieks were echoed by our hearty 'O dears!' for we expected to see her mangled arms, body and legs, making their fearful tumble into the lake below. When we saw her peep out from under her mutilated bonnet, and found that life was still in her, though she insisted that she was dead, quite dead! my uncourteous laughing powers had no alternative but to drop into a dead, grave silence, which was more uncourteous still. For united with that natural abstractedness into which my mind always drops when in the midst of nature's grand scenery, my appearance amounted to a state of sullenness. We hobbled down the hill, leading our unfortunate tumbler, right glad that she was not actually broken in pieces by the fall, though certainly she was not benefited by it for the day. We reached a little flat lawn by the side of the lake, took our picnic, and commenced new difficulties: a stream must be crossed – there was neither bridge nor stepping-stone, nor could the cart assist us. We wandered to and fro; at last, taking the clothing from our feet, we waded over slippery stones and gained the shore, not far from the Adelphi Lodge.[53] Its whereabouts we knew by the evergreens that adorned the mountains. We wound round a path which showed us on the right a conical heath mountain, lost in the skies; and no sooner had we passed that than one on the left, as though broken from its side, rose in view.[54] Thus we proceeded, threading our way by the side of a pretty stream, till we saw the cottage built by Lord Sligo, now in possession of the Plunkets – three brothers – who named it Adelphi.

A river winds round the domain which connects the sea on the left with the lake on the right; a mountain of the grandest and boldest stands in front of the cottage, without a tree, presenting a most beautiful picture of light and shade; the sides being spotted with a yellow appearance mixed with the heath and sedge, reconciling the eye to the absence of the tree.[55] At the back of the lodge stands another like mountain, forming, in unison with everything around, a scenery distinct from any other in Ireland. It was once the resort of the gay, where resounded the bugle and hunter's horn: its lakes, its rivers, its mountains, gardens, cascades and walks now appear as if the struggling gardener was trimming here and there a festoon, and fastening a decaying plant anew to some supporting stalk, that he might keep alive a relic or two of its former loveliness. But alas! the beauty of Ireland is departing, her gay ones are becoming sad; the cruel sport of the hunter which once was the delight of the fashionable has ceased, and the timid hare may now trip and leap among the brakes and ferns without starting at the bark of the fearful packhound in pursuit. The setting sun, as it warned us to depart, gave such an enchanting look to the dark mountains hanging over the lake and pretty river, that I could not but:

Cast a longing, lingering look behind.[56]

There was a fearful eight miles in advance. The stream must be waded, the precipitous foot-path hanging over the lake at nightfall was before us; but so completely abstracted had I become that if no company had been there to have urged me forward, the moonlight, if not the morning, might have found me sitting looking alternately at the mountains and lakes. We made our way through the defile, and reaching a little hamlet a solitary man came to meet us and welcomed me in true Irish style to his country, adding, 'in a twelvemonth I hope to be in your country'. A young son had gone two years before, and sent him back £19 for the voyage. 'I am leaving,' said he, 'praise God, a good landlady, who can do no more for us, and we can do nothing for her.'

'This man', said Mrs Garvey, 'is one of my best tenants, and I am lost by parting with him, but cannot ask him to stop.'

This romantic tour ended in the evening and I stopped with the 'good landlady' over the night and arose while all were asleep in the morning, and scoured through the pretty wood that fringed the river and back of the house, and selected the choicest moss-dotted stones, both great and small, for a rockery; and when the labourers had arisen, they assisted in carrying and wheeling them upon the lawn which fronted the cottage and bordered the stream, and around a solitary young fir standing there we placed these stones.[57] The daisy and primrose were in bloom. These were dug and planted in the niches, while the landlady added her skill in setting the young plants, when, in three hours – the same time that the wall of the Partry Priest was in building – there was a rockery of firm finish, blooming with the young flowers of spring. This was my last work in the county of Mayo, and frivolous as it might be, it was so in accordance with the ancient customs of Ireland and my own feelings too that when I turned from it forever, I said, 'Stand there, when the hand that raised you shall be among the dead; and say to the inquiring traveler who may visit this spot, that Asenath Nicholson, of New York, raised these stones as a memento of the suffering country she so much pitied and loved, and as a monument of gratitude to the God who had conducted her safely through all the dangerous scenes encountered while passing over it.'

A branch of the Garvey family lives near Murrisk Abbey, situated on Clew Bay, at the foot of the Croagh Patrick.[58] The house stands near the sea, embosomed in wood, a garden of three acres, with useful horticultural productions at the back of it and the abbey at a little distance. The walls of the abbey are of smooth stone in small blocks; the building contains numerous apartments. A place is reserved for the burying of priests, and a pile of their leg and arm bones are now in a window to leave room for fresh inmates.

The Irish appear to have no regard for their dead when the flesh is consumed, but leave the bones to bleach in the sun and the skulls to be kicked about as footballs in any place. A return through Westport to Castlebar gave a sight of suffering and degradation which could not be heightened. A coach is always the rallying point for beggars; and this morning the Roman Catholic Dean was upon the top, and I went out to take my seat, but was happy to retreat into a shop, for I supposed that all the inmates of the work-house were poured out for want of food and were sent to prey upon the inhabitants.[59] In this dreadful flock there was not one redeeming quality, not one countenance that smiled, nor one voice that uttered a sally of Irish wit – all was piteous entreaty, without deceit; for no proof was needed of sincerity but the look they gave us. I was urged to my seat through the crowd, and no sight like that had ever met my eyes as when that coach whirled from that haggard assemblage.

SOUP-SHOPS

It is well known that among the many devices for the cure of Ireland's Famine, the soup-shops and 'stirabout' establishments ranked among the foremost and the most effectual for some time. These were got up in many places at a great expense, so much so, that had they expected to have fed the nation on beef-bones and yellow Indian for centuries to come they could not have been more durably made and fixed. There was quite a competition to excel in some places, to make not only durable boilers but something that looked a little tasty, and he that got up the best was quite a hero. But the soup-shop of soup-shops, and the boiler of boilers, the one that sung the requiem to all that had gone before was the immortalized one of Soyer, the French soup-maker and savoury inventer for the West End of London.[60] It would seem that the government, on whose shoulders hung this mighty potato-famine, had exhausted all its resources of invention to stay the plague but the one last mentioned, and, driven to their wits end, they happily hit upon this panacea.

Every minutia cannot be given, either of the getting up or the recipe itself, but the sum and substance was simply this – that a French cook from London was sent to Dublin with a recipe of his own concocting, made out of drippings, whether of shinbones or ox-tails was not specified; but this dripping was to be so savoury, and withal so nourishing, that with a trifling sum Paddy could be fed, and fed too so that he could dig drains, cut turf and spade gardens, on an advanced strength, which flung both the potato and yellow Indian entirely in the back-ground. The work commenced: a new and splendid soup-shop in French and West End fashion soon gladdened the eyes of the expecting Irish. 'By dad,' exclaimed one as he passed it, 'and there's the creature that'll do the heart good; not a ha'porth of the blackguards will be fightin' for the yaller Indian when that's in the stomach.'

So great was this work that the city was moved when the sound went forth that the boiler was ready and the soup actually under way. A great and general invitation was given to the lords and nobles, with wives, sons and daughters, to be there and test this never-equalled sustainer of

life and zest of palate. Carriages, horsemen and footmen, lords in velvet
and broadcloth, ladies in poplins, satins, flounces and feathers, bedizened
the train. Nor was this all: when anything great or good is afloat, the
patriotism of Paddy, in high life and low, is aroused, and he waits not for
cloak, shoe or hat – if cloak, shoe and hat be lacking – but is ready on the
spot. And here every beggar, from Liberty to Cook street, from way-side,
hedge and ditch, whose strength was adequate, swelled this living, moving panorama. Wherever a feather waved in the breeze, there a rag flut-
tered in thrilling harmony. The procession entered the hall, where soup-
ladles, plates and spoons were in bright array. Lords and dukes,
duchesses, baronesses, and 'ladies of honour', walked round this fresh-
steaming beverage, each taking a sip, and pronouncing it the finest and
best. The hungry ones heard the verdict, and though some doubting ones
might scoff, yet the multitude went away declaring they believed that the
'blessed soup would put the life in 'em'.

The celebrated patentee received his sovereigns, and returned to his
sauce pots and dripping-pans in the metropolis of John Bull. The recipe
was made over to safe hands, the fire extinguished under the boiler, the
soup-shop closed, and poor Paddy waited long and in vain for the expected draught; nor did he awake from his hopeful anticipations till the
streets of Dublin resounded, by night and by day, with:

Sup it up, sup it up, 'twill cure you of the gout, &c.[61]

The poetry in refinement of style, in orthography or punctuation, did
not equal Cowper's 'John Gilpin', but in aptness of invention, and clear-
ness of description it was not a whit behind, and when the echo was
beginning to swell on the breeze.[62]

Up flew the windows all,[63]

of many a dwelling, whose inmates would shrink from the gaze of the
vulgar, and blush to be found reading by daylight, wit so coarsely
expressed. The soup recipe was not entirely a thing of naught. It brought
to the ballad-maker and ballad-singers ready case for many a week; and
the host of disappointed hungry ones who followed in the train found in
the poetic excitement a momentary pause of pain, which said:

That the cheek may be tinged with a warm sunny smile,
Though the cold heart to ruin runs darkly the while.[64]

I soon left for Cork. A visit to the house of Mr Murry, who, in union
with his fellow-labourer, Jordan, had established a church of the
Independent order, under the auspices of the Irish Evangelical Society.[65]

Their labours are blessed; the Roman Catholics appear to feel that in that little organization good is doing, and often when mention was made of it the answer would be, 'they are a blessed people'. Many expressed a desire that they might build a chapel, and some few had actually contributed a little for that purpose. These men had preached Christ and treated the people kindly, and they met with no serious opposition. They had been impartial in their distributions through the Famine, and had never attempted to proselyte either by a pound of Indian meal, or ten ounces of black bread.

A rainy morning took me from Castlebar, and in a few hours I reached Tuam and first visited the work-house. Eighteen hundred were here doing the same thing – nothing. But one improvement, which is worth naming, distinguished this house. All the cast-off bed-clothes and ticking were converted into garments for the poor, and given them when they left the house. Their rags which they wore in, were all flung aside, and they went decently out. Next I visited the convent and here found half a dozen nuns hiding from the world, and yet completely overwhelmed with it.[66] They had a company of four hundred children, most of them who were starving in the beginning of famine, and have instructed and fed them daily. This was the first school I had visited during the Famine where the children retained that ruddiness of look and buoyancy of manner so prevalent in the Irish peasantry. 'We have tested', said a nun, 'the strength of the Indian meal. These children, through last winter, were fed but once a day on stirabout and treacle, and had as much as they would take; they were from among the most feeble, but soon became strong and active as you now see.' They assembled for dinner, and as had been their custom they clasped their hands and silently stood, while one repeated these words: 'We thank thee, O God, for giving us benefactors, and pray that they may be blessed with long life and a happy death.'

'The good Quakers', said a nun, 'have kept them alive; and the clothes you see on them are sent through that channel, all but the caps, which we provide.' These children were taken from filth and poverty, never knowing the use of the needle or value of a stocking, and now could produce the finest specimens of knotting, both ornamental and useful. And looking upon these happy faces one might feel that Ireland is not wholly lost.

My next visit was in the work-house at the old town of Galway. The distress here had been dreadful, and most of them seemed waiting in silent despair for the last finishing stroke of their misery. One cleanly clad fisherman of whom I made inquiries invited me to visit the fishermen's cottages, which before the Famine were kept tidy, and had the 'comfortable bit' at all times. 'Now, the fisheries are lost, we are poor to keep up the tackle, and are all starving.'[67] I followed him to a row of neat cottages, where the discouraged housekeepers appeared as if they had swept their cottage floors, put on the last piece of turf, and had actually sat down to die. 'Here we are,' said one (as she rose from her stool to salute us), 'sitting in these naked walls, without a mouthful of bread, and don't know what the good God will do for us.' This fisherman then showed me into the monks' school-rooms, who were teaching and feeding a number of boys, and showed me some new fishing nets which the kind Quakers had sent, and he hoped, if they did not all die, that the 'net might sairve 'em'.[68]

The work-house here was on the best plan of any I had seen; the master and matron had been indefatigable in placing everything in its true position, and appeared to feel that their station was a responsible one, and that the poor were a sacred trust, belonging still to the order of human beings. The food was abundant and good, and the parents and children allowed to see and converse together oftener than in other like establishments; and now, in March 1850, the same report is current, that good order and comfort abound there, beyond any other. Everlasting peace rests on the heads of those who do not make merchandise of the poor for gain.

From Galway, Limerick was the next stopping-place, and the poor-house in that place was so crowded, the morning so rainy, and the keepers so busy in gathering the inmates to the stirabout, that but little that was satisfactory could be obtained.

Cork was reached in the evening, with the loss of a trunk by the inattention of the coachman, but in a few days it was restored by the honesty of a passenger. As the comfort of the travelling public depends so much on coachmen, and as passengers beside have a heavy fare to pay, it would be unjust to the public, as an individual, not to give a second testimony to the celebrated Bianconi's cars and car men.[69] I should have been happy to have found that my complaints in the first volume respecting this establishment were not realized as habits, but merely accidental, and that further acquaintance might insure greater esteem; but a second trial told me that thus far severity had not exaggerated. I paid my passage at Limerick for Cork, went to Fermoy without any serious difficulty; here vehicles and horses were changed, my trunk placed beyond my care, new passengers seated till the car was quite overcharged, when the carman said with insolence, as he saw me waiting for a seat, 'Get on and stand up, or else stop till to-morrow, I'll not wait for ye.'

'My passage is paid to Cork, my trunk is beyond my reach, or I would wait,' was the answer.

'Get on quick and stand there, or you're left.' I ascended the seat, and holding by the luggage rode ten miles standing in much peril, while the carman occasionally looked around and made some waggish joke, much to the amusement of decently clad gentlemen, not one of whom offered me a seat.

The reader may justly inquire – is this the Irish politeness, of which so much has been said in these pages? It is not instinctive Irish politeness – this is always pure and always abundant; but it is the habit put on and cultivated by such as, having no claim to family or rank, have, mushroom-like, started suddenly from a manure-heap into a little higher business, and having no education that has in the least disciplined the mind, they at once assume the airs of imperious landlords and keepers of whiskey-shops as the best means of establishing their advanced standing.

The county of Cork is the largest county in Ireland and once had four walled towns – Cork, Youghal, Kinsale and Bandon. It has an extensive sea-coast, and ten good harbours. It is everywhere well watered, and was once supplied with all kinds of game and cattle, wool, and woollen and linen yarn. It, like all Ireland, has been sifted and shaken, divided among septs and kings, and is now resting under the gracious shadow of the Queen Victoria. The population numbered in the year 1841 about 107, 682. The beautiful River Lee, where vessels from the Cove of Cork enter, flows through the city, giving from the hill top and side to the neat trellised cottages that hang there a cheerful aspect of life and commerce which few towns can claim. A sail from Cove Harbour up the Lee to the city cannot be surpassed in beauty on a pleasant evening. The Venetian boatman might here find material enough to add a new stanza to his Gondolier song; and if angels retain any wish for the sin-scathed scenery of earth, they might strike here their golden harps, and sing anew the sweet song:

Peace on earth, and good will to men.

The whole distance is so variedly enchanting that the overcharged eye, as it drops its lingering curtain upon one fairy spot, pauses, in doubt whether its next opening can greet beauties like the last. Cove, now a town containing a population of about 7000, is built upon the sloping side of a hill, in terraces; and at the foot of the hill is a line of houses called the Beach and Crescent.

This beautiful town, now named Queenstown – in honour of the landing of Victoria in the summer of 1849, when Her Majesty placed her foot for the first time on that green isle, and honoured that spot with its first impression – was, half a century ago, but a miserable fishing hamlet, the remains of which are most hideously and squalidly looking out, on the north side, called Old Cove. However squalid the old houses may look, there are more redeeming qualities here than any town in Ireland. It is snugly sheltered from winds by the hill; and this hill is so continually washed with fresh showers from the buckets of heaven that it needs no police regulations to keep the declivity in a condition for the most delicate foot and olfactory nerves to walk without difficult or offence. Then the broad old river spreading out beneath its foot, presenting a harbour of six miles in length and three in breadth dotted with four islands, Spike, Hawlbouline, Rocky and Coney, with two rivers, Ballinacurra and Awnbree, beside many pretty streamlets emptying into it. The harbour is backed by hills of the greenest and richest, and ornamented with five Martello towers, so called from a tower in the Bay of Martello in the island of Corsica.

As nearly all the present names of places in Ireland had an Irish root, and this root has a signification, a knowledge of these places the history in many cases in a clear and useful light. The village and glen of Monkstown stretched along, with the church and old castle, with spire and towers overlooking the whole, first meet the view; then a mile further, Passage, a village extending nearly a mile, with a quay and bathing houses, and taken as a whole is interesting, as busy thoroughfare. Blackrock Castle soon catches the eye, and its situation and happy construction can hardly be improved by imagination. It looks out upon Lake Mahon and the picturesque islands which dot it; and further on upon the right is Mount Patrick, where stands the tower dedicated to Theobald Mathew; and before reaching Cork, embosomed in trees, is the seat of Mr Penrose, called Woodhill, and possesses the undying honour of the spot where the daughter of Curran was married to Captain Henry Sturgeon.[70] It is long since Moore sung in sweet strains the never-to-be-forgotten melody of:

> She is far from the land where her young hero sleeps,
> And lovers are round her sighing;
> But coldly she turns from their gaze and weeps,
> For her heart in his grave is lying.
>
> O! make her a grave where the sunbeams rest,
> When they promise a glorious morrow,
> They'll shine o'er her sleep like a smile from the West,
> From her own lov'd island of sorrow.[71]

Cork stands on a marshy spot; its name in Irish is Corcaig, signifying a moor or marsh, and the city owes its origin to St Fin Bar, who first founded a cathedral in the seventh century near the south branch of the Lee, and from this beginning Corcaig-more or the great Cork arose; and though this city has passed through changes and great sufferings, yet it has for a long time maintained a respectable, if not high standing, for intelligence. Schools are numerous, and some of them of a high order, and the labouring classes are mostly well educated in a plain way. The Roman Catholics give nine thousand children gratuitous instruction in the various schools, and the Protestants have done much, their schools being liberally endowed, and probably it would not be exaggeration to say, that in no city in the kingdom of like population would more people among the poorer classes be found who could read than in Cork.

The convents, too, have done nobly in this respect, educating a multitude of children of the poor without any compensation.[72] J. Windell has justly said 'that the great majority of the working class are all literate, and generally acquainted with the elements of knowledge; the middle classes, in intelligence, and in the acquisition of solid as well as graceful information', are entitled to a very distinguished place'.[73] The Royal Cork Institution has a library of from five to six thousand volumes, the Cork Library has nine thousand volumes, and the Cork Mechanics' Institute has a small one, beside private libraries of considerable note. It may be doubtful whether it can be said that, as in the one in Belfast, there are in it no works of fiction.

The summer of 1848 found the city rallying a little from the fearful effects of the Famine; for in a county so large, embracing so much sea-coast, marshy ground, &c., there must be found many poor in the best times in Ireland. The Friends' Society, connected with the Dublin Central Committee, acted with untiring efficiency; and Theobald Mathew laboured for months in giving out American donations which were intrusted to him.[74] The nuns, too, had children to a great amount, whom they daily fed. The British Association, likewise, were there, but death fearfully went on. Let the walls of that work-house tell the story of the hundreds carried out upon sliding coffins, and buried in pits. Let the cemetery of Theobald Mathew show its ten thousand, which he buried there in huge graves, opening a yawning gulf, and throwing in lime, then adding coffinless bodies daily, till the pit was filled; then opening another, till ten thousand were numbered![75] The rain had washed the loose dirt away in some spots, and parts of the bodies were exposed in a few places. A painful sight!

The Cork Committee acted most efficiently, and the name of Abraham Beale has left there a sweet and lasting remembrance.[76] Beside the city of Cork, the rural districts were in the greatest distress, and this benevolent, indefatigable labourer turned his energies unceasingly to those districts, faithfully discharging his duty till his health failed; and his biographer states, that 'His last act of public duty was the attendance of the Relief Committee, in which he had so assiduously laboured'. Typhus fever took him in a few days to the mansion which, doubtless, was prepared for him. For though he said, 'I have been but an unprofitable servant', yet the living testify that his profiting appeared unto all.[77] He died in August 1847 while the scourge was still raging; and in 1848 his name was fresh on the lips of many in that city, who, with his two bereaved sisters, say they have lost in him a friend and a father.[78] 'The memory of the just is truly blessed.'

Though in the summer of 1848 many were suffering, yet the workhouse was not filled with the dying as before, and the sliding coffin never met my eye.[79] The indefatigable nuns still were overwhelmed with children, many of whom were placed there by Father Mathew and in one contiguous to his chapel were about thirteen hundred, who were fed when food could be obtained.[80] One of the most affecting items of the Famine, if item it may be called, is the multitude of orphans left in that afflicted country, and the saying was becoming quite a common one, when a hungry child was asked where he lived, or where his father and mother were, to answer, 'They died sir [or ma'am], in the stirabout times'. This alluded to the year 1847 particularly, when the stirabout was most in vogue. The 'black bread times' now have an imperishable name in the west of Ireland, and Soyer's soup will not die in the memory of the wags of Dublin, till wars, pestilence and famine shall cease to the ends of the earth.

The environs of Cork had not lost any of their charms by the scourge, and Blarney seemed to have put on new beauties; her old castle and Blarney stone, now supported with two iron grasps, are still looking forth from the shrubbery and trees which wildly surround it, for the good taste of the owner keeps the pruning knife confined to his enchanting gardens and walks, and allows nature here to frolic according to her own vagaries.[81] The sycamore, oak, arbutus, elm, ash, holly, copper-beech and ivy were mingling and co-mingling, without any aristocratic airs of family descent or caste.

A stranger here would wonder what famine could have to do in these pleasant grounds; and while rambling among its moss-covered stones, wild flowers and creeping ivy, its shady seats, alcoves and grottos, we felt that an Italian gardener could scarcely make a spot more enchanting, even though an Italian sky should mingle its blandness.

The company, too, in such places, has much to do in heightening or diminishing the pleasure, and even beauty of such scenes. Mine was a happy lot this day. The young Beales, who were the party, with a London acquaintance, had a natural and cultivated relish for treats like these, and while we were taking our picnic in that grove of delights, gladly would I have forgotten the sorrows of the past and avoided a dread of the future, but could not; for notwithstanding Blarney pleasure grounds we were in woe-stricken Ireland still, and we knew that desponding hearts and hungry stomachs were not far distant. A cheerful walk home led us through Blarney Lane, in the suburbs of Cork, where the neatness of the cottages, with a flower-pot in many a window, had an interest beyond what had been presented in any suburb of Ireland's large towns since the Famine. We took welcome liberties to look occasionally in one, and found all invariable tidy, and what was still more creditable, the women were busy at work. This said that Cork had still a living germ within her, that might and would be resuscitated; for if woman's hands are well employed, however unnoticed her little inventions and doings may be, they at last work out and bring forth untold comforts, which are more valuable because diffused insensibly where most needed.

'The little foxes spoil the vines,' and little things are the foundation of all great ones, and had Ireland, as well as the whole world beside, looked better to this, better effects would have been produced.[82] Cork may boast as many efficient men, and active useful women, probably, as any town in Ireland. It has a Father Mathew and a William Martin to urge by precept and example the importance and benefits of sobriety and industry; it has a Society of Friends, whose religion and discipline encourage no drones, and its intelligence has broken down that caste which so much exists in many parts of the country, and rendered the people of all classes more accessible than in any other city in Ireland.[83] Fifteen weeks stopping there heightened my admiration of the true hospitality and capabilities of inhabitants; and those flowery hill-sides and rose-covered gateways and windows that hung over the Lee, will be held ever in the sweetest remembrance. The little room, where one week of the pleasantest was spent, deserves an acknowledgment which I am not able to give. May that cottage and its inmates long be united as happily and sweetly as their industry and beauty so richly merit.

A short excursion to Castlemartyr, fifteen miles from Cork, took me through a richly cultivated country, where fields of wheat, barley, and oats are ripening for the harvest; but five fields of blasted potatoes that we passed, said that they had not yet recovered courage and strength to look out again upon the world, as in days gone by.

The feelings of the people are so sensitive that they are not willing to speak of the subject when the fields begin to droop, and when mention is made of the appearance of a new failure, everything favourable is brought to bear on the subject; and often one member of a family has been known to keep all knowledge from the others that might have reached him.[84] Castlemartyr was once a parliamentary borough; the castle has long been famous for battles and plunders, and King William's forces, after the Battle of the Boyne, charged a body of three hundred Irish, who fled to the castle, were driven out, the fortress surrendered with the loss of sixty men, and sixteen prisoners taken.[85] The Irish, in 1671, got possession of the town, but were driven out, and the castle since has laid in ivy-covered ruins, being used as a wine-cellar by Lord Shannon. It is surrounded with the loftiest trees, and a lawn of emerald green runs down to a lake upon one side of it. A thousand acres of the most richly cultivated land belong to this domain; canal, three lakes, an extensive deer park, walks and rides, a flower garden of rare beauty, and kitchen garden of great size. Near the castle stands his lordship's house, containing a centre and two wings.[86]

The apparatus for hunting is a great curiosity. Forty-two pleasure-horses for this sport were stabled here in apartments much better than the dwellings of the labouring class, and the richly tipped harness, with their bright stirrups and saddles, were still hanging as mementoes of former greatness and ready for use, should the absentee find it for his benefit to return to his pleasure grounds. The Famine and other embarrassments have compelled him to suspend his hunting pleasures at present; his hounds were dismissed, his horses sold, and his carriages remain in silent waiting.

The town had suffered like all others in the Famine, and the rich widow where I stopped told sad tales of what had passed; but so engrossed was she with the loss of her husband that she could find little space for the woes of others in her heart. She took me upon a desolate sea-coast some ten miles distant, and there was misery ever fresh and ever young. The strange leap from a domain in Ireland to a hut or village of the poor is nowhere so vivid in any county as here. I was glad to leave this spot and return to Cork; but a few short excursions more must finish all. A flower-show was a treat which always brings out all that is beautiful to the eye, so far as fashion is concerned. Here lords and ladies are found, and though they would not like a vulgar stare, yet they would not disapprove of a little admiration given to style and beauty. The show was a splendid one, and gave great credit to the skill of gardeners who are certainly not inferior in taste in Ireland to any in the kingdom. The ladies too, were the ladies of Ireland – fair to look upon.

SPIKE ISLAND

Strangers were not permitted, in the year 1848, to visit the convicts on Spike Island, but fortunately being a few days in the family of Doctor Maurice Power, MP, he was, in consequence of his standing, allowed a peep among them, and had the privilege of taking all who belonged to his family – his wife, daughter and myself were his company.[87] This island is rough in its appearance, containing some one hundred and eighty acres, and has been a fortified island from about 1791-2. Here we found convicts from every part of Ireland who were deemed worthy of an exile from home for the space of seven years. The number of these victims was about eight hundred and forty; some employed in digging out rocks and levelling rough places, some in making mats of cocoa-nut bark, some knitting, and some marching round a circle made up on the pavement for exercise and punishment. A school is kept where for two hours in rotation all who are of suitable age, and cannot read and write, are taught these branches. The teacher remarked, when pointing to three hundred pupils, 'these persons are docile, and I believe honest; their only crime being taking food when starving'.

Some of these young men and boys had thrown a stone into a bread-shop, some had stolen a turnip, and some a sheep; but every one was induced by extreme hunger to do the deed. But we are gravely told in Ireland that property must be protected, though life should be squandered. The teacher added, 'I cannot look on these men and boys as criminals.' A few others had been guilty of manslaughter; and one gentlemanly appearing man had been guilty of embezzling public money – he was overseeing the making of mats. A dexterous pickpocket, not yet fifteen, was present from Dublin, who had, when there, fifty men under pay; and in the presence of us all he showed his propensity, by keeping one hand upon his work and the other apparently carelessly upon the skirt of Doctor Power's coat near the pocket. This sad boy will not be cured by forced abstinence. The keepers informed us that he steals for the pleasure of it – taking what he does not want, such as handkerchiefs and stockings, which he can neither wear nor dispose of.

The lodging-rooms were large, and well ventilated; and the numbers sleep in the same apartment without any guard. The solitary cells were very cold, the walls reeking with wet; but as these are only for the incorrigibles, if none behave unseemly, none need to inhabit them. The room where the unfortunate Mitchel was confined when on his way to Bermuda was shown us; it was larger than any other single room, and had the luxury of a board floor, and would, if nicely fitted up, make a tolerable farm kitchen.[88] But report fell far short of the reality when she said that this traitor was treated more like a gentleman than a felon; occupying a drawing-room, well furnished. The bread was good, made of unbolted wheat meal, and the quantity quite sufficient. Cocoa is given every Sabbath morning, and meat for dinner. Much better in any way were these convicts than any inmates of a work-house in Ireland. We sailed from Spike up the beautiful Corigaline, and its winding course presented us rich beauties of foliage, gentlemen's seats and rose-covered cottages. A clear sun, like that of my native home, shone upon this landscape; and in sight of the river, mid the song of birds, with children sporting about us, in this wooded spot we took a pleasant picnic which was greatly valued by me, because the car men were sitting too, at a little distance, partaking of the same repast, when one sent a civil inquiry to Mrs P to know if the pudding had whiskey in it, as he was a teetotaller, and could not take it if anything of the kind were in it. He was assured it was pure.

The whole to me was quite American, Dr P having graduated in a college there, his wife being a native, and his daughter born there, and had he not been an MP we might have talked republican things.[89] Why is this partiality for country and home so deeply fixed in the human heart? Is it not selfish, and does it not tend to contract, and even sour the mind against what often is more valuable than home produce?

THE MATHEW TOWER

Among the many interesting subjects of people and things in the city of Cork may be included as pre-eminent this beautiful tower, standing upon Mount Patrick, overlooking the pleasant waters of the Lee. It is three miles from Cork on an elevation of eight hundred feet, and was erected by William O'Connor entirely at his own expense. Theobald Mathew visited London in the year 1843, and his generous reception suggested the idea to O'Connor, who was present, to erect a monument in commemoration of the event, and as an honorable memento to future generations of the indefatigable labours of the great Apostle of Temperance.[90] The history of this spot gives to the visitor a double interest, especially so, when he is told that the founder was a tailor, who, through his shears, was enabled to give three thousand guineas for the tower alone.[91]

A few years since, this now blooming garden of trees, shrubs and flowers, was a wilderness of woods, and the soil the most unpromising. O'Connor purchased twenty acres, cut down the trees, leaving a few for ornament, dug up the roots, and made an entirely new soil by materials taken from the mud and gravel of the Lee, at Cork, and planted this new-made land with potatoes, giving employment to a great number of men; and when the harvest was gathered he made the whole of it as an offering of the first fruits to the poor. The Sisters of Mercy shared largely in this donation, as almoners of the gift. He then built a neat cottage, which he inhabited with a sister who has since deceased. A fine gravelly walk conducts the visitor from the gate leading to the cottage through a rich thicket of laurel, arbutus and firs, opening upon a tasteful flower ground, descending from the cottage, which is ascended by fourteen stone steps with iron railings.

On the right and left from the hill two rooms are fitted up in good modern taste for the reception of visitors. In the centre of each stands a table, one containing the periodicals of the day, the other only a large ancient Bible. The walls are adorned with a variety of pictures, some of which are the best specimens of drawing. Two, which are dedicated to the Queen and Prince Albert, and executed entirely with a pen, by McDonnell of Cork, are almost without a parallel.[92] They contain an address by the Mayor, Aldermen and Council of the city of Cork, on the birth of the Prince of Wales in 1841. They are both executed in a manner that entitles them to a standing among the highest ornamental works. A portrait of O'Connor hangs in the same room, with one of Edim Forest, and a few others, of the best model. The left-hand room represents the Queen, with an infant on her lap, and another child standing by her side; another of the Virgin and Child of peculiar beauty; a frame-work containing the baptismal cake of one of the Queen's children, and a vial of caudle. The frame is lined on the back with a piece of satin, embroidered with the crown of the King of Prussia, and is a piece from the vest he wore; the sides are of embroidered satin, like that worn by the Queen, with her crown wrought upon it, and which is worn on the baptismal occasions of her children. A fourth is Louis Philippe receiving the visit of Victoria in France, beside two other pictures not named.[93] In the hall hangs the picture of the testimonial or tower, and opposite is the monument of Scott.

In a little opening at the back of the hall is a glass case, containing a choice collection of shells, and on each side from this are two nicely furnished bed-rooms. These rooms with a kitchen include all the dwelling part. Two wings, with artificial windows, are attached to the cottage; the glass, frame and blind, are such a finished imitation of the reality that one must touch them to be convinced of their mockery. Two winding paths from the cottage lead up the ascent to the monument. A circular stone wall containing a small fountain is the first object. In the centre of this is a curiously-wrought pedestal, surmounted by a large basin, in which is seated a boy, whose business is to spirt water from his mouth through a small tube, when any one is so kind as to open a pipe underground by a key which pipe communicates with one from the top of the tower, which conveys the water from a cistern fixed near the top; near this fountain stands a boy grasping in his hands a snake, which is wound about one leg; but the boy holds him fast in defiance: this is the serpent alcohol. On the right of the boy stands an angel to strengthen him. Theobald Mathew is standing back, and over this group, in a figure larger than life, with his right hand pointing to the fountain, while his left arm rests upon a pedestal.[94] Above all this stands the testimonial, the door facing the west. Two dogs are resting upon a pedestal at the entrance; both are portraits of one dog, who saved the lives of eight men who fell into the Thames. He was elected a member of the Humane Society of London, and now wears a gold collar. Next to the door stand two warriors, one a Roman, the other a British officer, representing the two religions.

Peeping over the wall is the head of a grey horse, and around the tower are various statues. The first is Fidelity, represented by a female with a dog looking up to her face; Faith, with a cross; Hope, with an anchor; Charity, with a child in her arms and Plenty, with a bunch of wheat in her hand.

The tower is circular, though all in one massive pillar, yet it has the appearance of two, one smaller and taller, with the union jack waving from the top. There are two apartments in this tower, the window cases and frames are of fluted oak, surmounted by carved heads, stucco-work is over these, and continued along the ceiling. Inclosed in a glass shade, on a rosewood pedestal, is a model bust of the apostle Mathew, and over this, one of the Right Revd Dr Murphy, Bishop of the Catholic church.[95] A massive chimney-piece has upon it a basso-relievo figure of Father Mathew, holding in one hand Britannia, in the other Erin, the emblems of both countries surrounding them.[96] A large chandelier is suspended from the ceiling, and the upper portions of the windows are of stained glass. This circular room is sixteen feet in diameter.

This description is minutely given because there are pleasant and painful reminiscences of my visit to that spot. Theobald Mathew was there. 'He is now in the land of my fathers.'[97] Friends were there that will meet me no more; and the generous heart was there who fitted this enchanting elysium for the man he so much honoured, and for the happy resort of friends who might honor him too. The cottage, the garden and testimonial are there. The hyacinth, the rose, the holly and fir are still blooming in fragrance and verdure; but, alas! the heart that designed and the hand that completed them are cold in the dust.[98] That relentless scourge, the cholera, which has spared neither age nor station, has laid him low; and who will trim afresh that hill-side and brighten the neat cottage and pretty summer-house, for the happy eye and sweet resting spot of the visitor and stranger? Who will keep open the welcome gate that introduces to shrubbery walks of arbutus and flower-beds; and to the chaste testimonial, which has been and must be the admiration of every eye that has rested upon it? Will it fall into hands that will add fresh garlands to honor the memory of him who erected it? Who will still say to every lover of temperance and beauty, 'Come in freely and banquet on these delights of nature and of art'? Or will contracted minds and penurious hearts close its gates to all but aristocratic passports and shilling fees? Let sacred respect for the honour of the generous departed forbid it; and let love for the benevolent apostle to whom it was dedicated forbid it.

While penning these pages, intelligence of the death of O'Connor was forwarded me by the pen of one who first introduced me to that spot, and this circumstance prompts to the insertion of the following documents, as a tribute of respect due to the deceased, and which to me are doubly valued, because this tribute did not wait till he to whom it was owing should be no more. What a comment on good sense and justice, what a mockery of the dead, to write eulogiums and build costly monuments to him who, while living, was carelessly neglected or wilfully despised! O'Connor's history, as was related by a friend, was simply this: he was the son of a poor widow, belonging to a rural district, and was early sent to Cork where he acquired the trade of a tailor, and by persevering industry, good conduct and economy he became first in the profession of a merchant tailor, and through his shears he amassed a handsome fortune before reaching the meridian of life. With this fortune, let the Mathew Testimonial tell part of the honourable use he made of his money. He had no family, but his attachment to friends was deeply manifest in the love he bore toward the sister who lived with him in the cottage on Mount Patrick. He left it when she was buried, and said he could never tarry in it another night, and observed that it was purely out of respect to strangers that he ever visited it.

The origin of the letters which follow was simply this: when going over these grounds, through the cottage, and through the tower, but one item seemed to be wanting to make the whole complete, that was, a few choice literary books to grace the centre-table of that otherwise well-fitted drawing-room. It was proposed to a few friends, and was done without any intention of display, or wish to have it thus memorialized. A letter was sent me the following day, and an answer returned the next. They both unexpectedly appeared in print in the *Cork Examiner* a few days after, where they doubtless would have slept forever had not the death of O'Connor revived so painfully the visit to that beautiful spot.

If ever vanity, ambition or pride have stimulated me to seek notice or applause from men, these propensities have been so subdued that when contempt has been added to privation I have felt an inward gratitude that since in Ireland so few comparatively hindered my labours by false attentions and fulsome flatteries, which travellers too much seek in foreign lands; and never should any of the neglects or rudeness which have been received been recorded; were it not that the character of the people was the object to find out and show, rather than to draw pity or favour to myself.

THE MATHEW TOWER – MRS NICHOLSON[99]

Last week Mrs Nicholson, now well known by her tour on foot through Ireland, and the very interesting book which she has written descriptive of her wanderings, paid a visit to Mount Patrick. She was accompanied by some friends. She was met by the Very Revd Mr Mathew, Mr O'Connor, the hospitable proprietor, and some other gentlemen. After visiting the Tower, which is now superbly finished and promises to stand in firmness and durability for the next five hundred years, and perambulating the grounds which are laid out in a highly ornamental style, the parties partook of lunch, which consisted principally of fruits and coffee. Mrs Nicholson and the friend who accompanied her, are, besides being strict total abstainers, also vegetarians, disciples of a strict dietetic school in which no animal food is permitted. The object of her visit was then announced; it was to present to Mr O'Connor a small but beautiful select library, in testimony of her ardent respect for the cause and the Apostle of Temperance, and in kindly appreciation of the services and worth of Mr O'Connor, who not only built a testimonial unexampled in the history of such memorials erected by private individuals, but with a hospitality that cannot be over-estimated throws open his grounds daily to the public. Mrs Nicholson presented the following short address:

'These volumes are presented by a few friends of temperance, in grateful acknowledgment of his generosity in throwing open his tasteful and beautiful place to the public, and for the purpose of affording a profitable recreation to its numerous visitors; with a desire that the lovely spot may be ever sacred to that glorious cause, to whose most successful and untiring advocate it has been dedicated, and to the advancement of universal philanthropy.'

Cork, August 28th, 1848.

The reply was as follows:

MADAM, I receive the books with pride and pleasure. The subject of each volume, and the names of the authors, remarkable in our literature for their genius or scientific knowledge, are the best tests of your own pure taste and judgment.

Ten years have elapsed since I found this spot a wilderness; four since a monument, I hope an enduring one, has been erected, to perpetuate in a small degree the true greatness and glory of the Christian benefactor of Ireland. As that monument belongs to him and the public, and as those grounds, which you and others have been pleased to eulogize, are but the abiding place of the Tower of Temperance, so my gates have never been closed, and never shall be, against visitors, whether they be residents of our own favoured but unfortunate land, or citizens of Europe, or of your own great country.

It is a singular spectacle to witness – a lady gently nurtured and brought up, giving up, for a time, home and country and kindred, visiting a land stricken with famine, traversing on foot that land from boundary to boundary, making her way over solitary mountains and treading through remote glens where scarcely the steps of civilization have reached, sharing the scanty potato of the poor but hospitable people, and lying down after a day of toil in the miserable but secure cabin of a Kerry or Connaught peasant. All this is unusual. But above it shines, with a steady light, your sympathy, your benevolence, your gentleness of heart, and your warm appreciation of the virtues, rude but sincere, of a people whose condition it is necessary to improve in order to make them content and happy.

The first step to raise them socially, to create in them self-respect, and elevate their shrewdness into the wisdom of morality, has been taken by the *man* whom you revered so much, and to whom and not to me you have this day paid a grateful and graceful tribute. May he live forever in the memories of his country!

You are about to depart for your own great country because you could not witness again the desolation of another famine.[100] But you will carry back from Ireland the heartfelt sense of her people for past kindness to your Christian countrymen. To them, to the generous people of England, and to the Society of Friends in England, Ireland and America, we are indebted, but utterly unable to discharge the debt.

I beg to subscribe myself,

Your grateful servant,

WILLIAM O'CONNOR

Mount Patrick, August 31st, 1848.

TO WILLIAM O'CONNOR[101]

SIR, The unmerited compliment you publicly bestowed on a stranger, in the last week's *Examiner*, deserves a public acknowledgment, and the more cheerfully given because it affords an opportunity of saying that not to me alone is the honour due of the small bestowment of books upon your table. It says, 'there are hearts in Cork that do appreciate the Mathew Testimonial, as well as the noble generosity of the man who designed it, and though small the offering, it may be the prelude to more liberal demonstrations of a people's gratitude'.

These few volumes, it is hoped, are but the alphabet to a well-chosen library that shall one day grace a room in the Tower, affording the citizen and the stranger a profitable, as well as a pleasant recreation.

And now, sir, allow me to say, that in a four years' tour through this beautiful isle – from the Donegal sea to Cape Clear, from the mountains of Wicklow to the Killery Peaks – I have never seen from the top of mansion or castle a flag so gracefully waving – a flag on which is inscribed so much love of country, so much just appreciation of worth and so much that deserves the appellation of 'Well done', as that which is flying in the breeze from the tower of Mount Patrick; and should my eyes ever again look out upon the proud mountains and waters of my own native land, when memory shall revert to the summer of 1848, the brightest and happiest associations will be the hours passed in the cottage and tower, the garden and walks dedicated to the man who lives for humanity. And though I return to my people with a sorrowing heart, that the tear is still on the long wasted cheek of Erin, yet this shall be my joy, that there live among her country-loving sons hearts that can feel and hands that can act, when worth and virtue make the demand, and to the proud monument of Mount Patrick will I point as a witness to all who may sail up the green banks of the sweet-flowing Lee.

When the hand of Theobald Mathew shall cease to rest on the head of the pledge-taking postulant, and when he shall have been gathered to the dust of his fathers; when the generous heart that devised the lasting memorial shall have stopped its pulsation forever; on every health-blowing breeze that fans the flag of Mount Patrick, shall be whispered – 'Peace to the Apostle of Temperance, who said to the wine-maddened brain of the maniac, peace be still, who wiped the tear from the face of heart-stricken woman, and who lifted up him that was ready to fall'.

And when from heaven's high battlement his gentle spirit shall look down on this Tower, future generations shall rise in succession and call him 'blessed'.

And let their long-sounding echo reverberate over mountain and glen, 'honour and gratitude to *William O'Connor*'.

ASENATH NICHOLSON
Ireland I love thee still.
September 4th, 1848.

CHAPTER VIII

'Oh! could we from death but recover.'

THE GRAVE OF CHARLES WOLFE

It was in the cottage of Dr Power that unexpectedly the sweet strains of the 'Soldier's Grave' were struck by Mrs P, and awakened again those sensations which were stirred, when in the city of New York, a few days before sailing for Ireland, I heard them for the first time; and here was told that the author was sleeping in a humble burying-ground but two miles from the spot.[1]

In two days Mrs P accompanied me to the strangers' churchyard adjoining an old crumbling ivy-covered ruin of a church, where sleep together in a rank grass-grown spot, the sailor and the soldier who dies from home, in this harbour, and where seldom a foot tramples on the wild weed that grows tall in the uneven inclosure where they sleep.[2] Here and there a coarse monument tells that Captain M or Lieutenant G died in this harbour, Anno Domini, ———, but Charles Wolfe was not among them. His was a bed detached, and confined within the wall of one corner of the church, with a humble flat stone over his breast. The roof of the church is gone, and the entrance to his grave, when the sexton is not here to unlock it, is over the wall by climbing a ladder. A look through the key-hole showed that luxuriant weeds and stones from the crumbling wall had well-nigh concealed the epitaph, which told his age and death.

His short story was easily rehearsed; for like all true merit he was unostentatious, and asked not that the world should honour him. His birth-place was Dublin, in 1791, a descendant of the military hero Wolfe, who was slain at Quebec. He was sent to Bath, in England, in 1801, to school, where his mother removed at the death of his father, then to Dr Evans's, then to Winchester, where his amiable disposition made him greatly beloved, and his classical attainments gained him great distinction without flattering his vanity. He never in one instance received a reprimand from a teacher, and his sister adds that to her recollection he never acted contrary to his mother's wishes during his life. He cheerfully gave up the idea of a military profession, which he had imbibed, because he found it was unpleasant to his mother. In 1808 the family returned to Ireland, and in 1809 he entered Dublin College. He soon distinguished himself as a poet; his *Jugurtha Incoraratus* was written in the first year of college, the year when his mother died, an event which left a lasting impression in his heart. He soon after won a prize and became a college tutor, obtained a scholarship, and his talents for prose and verse, as well as oratory, soon manifested themselves.

The poem which gave him such deserved celebrity was published without his knowledge, and it originated in his mind by reading a paragraph, as follows. Sir John Moore had often said, that if he was killed in battle, he wished to be buried where he fell.[3]

'The body was removed at midnight to the citadel of Corunna. A grave was dug for him on the rampart there, by a party of the 9th Regiment, the aide-de-camps attending by turns. No coffin could be procured, and the officers of his staff wrapped the body, dressed as it was, in a military cloak and blankets. The interment was hastened, for about eight in the morning some firing was heard, and the officers feared if a serious attack were made they should be ordered away and not suffered to pay him that last duty. The officers of his army bore him to the grave – the funeral service was read by the chaplain, and the corpse was covered with earth.'

Thus they buried him at dead of night, and –

> But he lay like a warrior taking his rest,
> With his martial cloak about him.[4]

His biographer says, had he written no other poetry this poem would have entitled him to the name of poet of poets. He had one peculiarity: in reading, he analyzed the subject to its origin, and there tarried so long that he seldom perused it to the end; he digested thoroughly what he did read, but seldom read a book through. He was an enthusiastic admirer of the scenery of his own country. Lough Bray, Wicklow and the Dargle have been graphically portrayed by his pen.

He became pious, but humbly laid his attainments at the foot of the cross, and in November 1817 he took an obscure country curacy in the North, where his indefatigable labours and affectionate heart won him the love of all his flock, especially the poor, but who could not appreciate his talents, nor 'enter into the deep feelings of his soul'.[5]

Here he laboured, and here he loved to labour, and would have died among the simple flock he loved for Christ's sake, but his friends removed him to the seaside at Cove.[6] His sermons were but precepts of which he was living example. His sickness and closing scene were replete with all that is lovely in the Christian character. To his relatives who stood round him, he said, 'the peace of God overshadow them, dwell in them, and reign over them'; and to a relative who hung over him, he said, 'Close this eye, the other is closed already – and now farewell.'

Thus this poet and Christian died, and thus is he buried in that lonely deserted place among the dead of almost every clime, who have been huddled and housed here, apart from country and kindred, and where few but strangers' feet ever tread the way to their isolated resting-place.

There was something to me quite forbidding in the associations that hung around the grave of Charles Wolfe, in that deserted corner:

> O, breathe not his name, let him sleep in the shade,
> Where cold and unhonoured his relics are laid;
> Sad, silent and dark be the tears that we shed,
> As the night dew that falls on the grass o'er his head.[7]

The summer of 1848 was pleasant and unusually sunny, and the hopes of the poor peasant revived as he saw the potato looking up again, in freshness and strength; but alas! a few days laid all his prospects in the dust. A brother of Theobald Mathew had planted a field of twenty-seven acres, in almost certain faith that they would not be blasted; for weeks they flourished, and promised to yield an abundant crop.[8] The poor people in the neighbourhood were blessing the good God for the beautiful patch of the 'kind gintleman', and seemed as happy as though they were ripening for their own use. They have been known to go and look into the field and take off their hats, and in humble adoration bless the name of God for his great mercy in sending them the potato again. This was their usual practice when they saw a field looking vigorous. But in one night the spoiler came – this beautiful field in the morning had, in isolated spots, the withering touch of the fatal disease. In a few days the rich extensive crop would not pay the labourer for his toil in gathering it. All was over, and in silent despondency each one submitted to the stroke. The 'still small voice' seemed to say, 'Be still, and know that I am God'.[9] It was something for which man could not reprove his brother, and he dared not reproach his God. 'And what', said an old woman, sitting by her vegetable stall, 'would become of us miserable bodies, if God Almighty had sent the blast on us, and left the potato?'

This was in the autumn of 1845, when but a partial failure took place – the blast had not then fallen on man; but it did fall, and swept them down as grass before the mower's scythe, yet not one of the victims, through long months of starvation, was heard to murmur against God. They thanked His holy name, both when they saw it dried, as by a scorching heat. It was one of the most touching, striking features of the

Famine to see a family looking into a withered patch, which the day before looked promising, and hear the exclamations of wonder and praise, weeping and thanksgiving, mingled together. 'He's sent the blast blessed be His holy name! His blessed will be done – and we'll all die with hunger, and praise God we're all poor sinners,' &c. They literally and practically carried out the principle of one in ancient days, who said 'Though he slay me, yet will I trust in him', for though year after year they saw the root on which they and their fathers had lived melt away yet they would not be persuaded but that the good God would give them the potato again; and in 1846-7-8-9, when each successive year had produced the same if not worse effects, they yet persisted in saving, often times by stealth, some part of a sound potato, to keep it from the hungry mouths of their children that they might put it in the ground, and 'Plaise God will have the potato again' would be the persevering reply to all expostulation.[10] So wedded are they to this root, that notwithstanding many know and deeply feel that it has been their rod of oppression, yet they emphatically 'kiss the rod, and Him that hath appointed it'; and could a decree now go forth that the potato should be restored to its pristine soundness and health, and that the present generation and their posterity forever should feed on this root exclusively and have work six days a week, at four pence or sixpence a-day, there would be a universal jubilee kept through mountain and glen, and bonfires would from hill-top to bog extinguish the light of moon and star for many a joyful night. And let it be expected by those who would do good to Ireland, and elevate her in the scale of being, that it will be many a long year before the sickle will be as joyfully and heartily worked as the spade.

This spade has a thousand associations, entwining in and about the hearts of parent and child, which no other instrument of husbandry can claim; it has cut the turf that lighted up the mud-wall cabin, and boiled the blessed potato; it has dug the pit in front of the cabin for the duck-pond; it has piled the manure-heap at the corner, mountain high; it has planted the ridge which furnished their daily bread; it has made the ditch, and repaired the road; it has stood by the hearth or door through many a dark and stormy night, to guard the little stack for the cow against the tithe gatherer; it has been a fireside and field-companion; and above all, and over all, it has measured and hollowed out many a last sleeping bed for a darling child, a beloved husband or wife, and in the dark days of the Famine it has often been the only companion to accompany the father, mother, husband, wife or child, who has had the corpse of a hunger-stricken relative in a sack or tied to the back, to convey it to the dread uncoffined pit, where are tumbled, in horrid confusion, the starved dead of all ages.[11]

The sickle has not that claim to the affections of what is genteelly called the 'lower order'. It is more aristocratic in its station and occupation. It has been used in the hands of the poor to reap down the fields of the rich for naught; it has cut the wheat and the barley for the tax-gatherer, the landlord and the 'surpliced hireling', who 'reaps where he sowed not', and 'gathers where he has not strewed'.[12]

With all these considerations, it must be expected that this instrument will be approached with caution, if not suspicion; and wonder not if they feel like David, when the armour of Saul was put on him, to go out and meet Goliath: I cannot go with these, for I have not proved them. He who would reform must not only know what is to be done, but how it is best to do it effectually. The Irish will never be laughed or preached out of their relish for the potato, neither should it be attempted; let them love it, let them cultivate it, but let it not be like the grass of the field for the bullock who is adapted entirely to that food, and which has never failed to give him a supply. Teach the Irish by use that they need not relish the potato less, but they may love the bread and other esculents more; that should one fail, they may turn to another with convenience. Give them good healthy food as substitutes, and cast the musty, sour Indian meal with the black bread away. Frighten them not with sickening dangerous food, and tell them it is because they are dainty and savage that they do not relish it. If what is given them be 'good enough for kings', then let kings eat it; for if God has 'made of one blood all the nations of the earth',[13] he may have made the palate, too, somewhat similar. If bread will strengthen John Russell's heart, it will the 'bog-trotter's' also; if a fine-spun broadcloth with gilt buttons becomes the backs of the Queen's ministers, then surely a coarser texture, without patch or rent, would not sit ungracefully on the shoulders of Paddy. Let him, if made in the image of God, be a man too; and let him not be thought presuming, if he be one of the Queen's subjects, should he aspire to mediocrity among the humblest who call themselves so. If the Irish say most heartily, 'Long live the Queen', let the Queen respond heartily, and 'while I live I will do good to my Irish subjects'. If the sixty-two mud-wall huts – to each hundred in the worst parts, and twenty-three in the best, as Mr Bright asserts – look a little untidy in an isle where castles and rich domains dot the green surface, why not substitute the comely cottage? If the manure-heap be unseemly to the eyes and unsavoury to the nose, plant in its stead the vine and the rose – for be assured, in no isle of the sea will they bloom fairer.[14]

England has held this pretty gem of the ocean by the cable of king and queenship for centuries, floating and dashing alternately in the vascillating uncertain waves of hope and desperation, casting in oil when the tempest runs highest, pulling the cord gently and whispering 'Sister', when she finds her loosening her holdings to make for a more open sea; and then promises to repair her breaches, and make her to 'sing as in the days of her youth'. But there she is, rocking and floating still, her wild tresses dishevelled, her head uncovered and her feet still bare. One hundred and thirty years ago she had one hundred and sixty families that had no chimneys in their hovels; now she has sixty-two in one hundred not fit for man to inhabit in one part, and on an average of something like forty-four or forty-five through the whole island, from which the beaver and woodchuck might blush to be found peeping.

Why, in the name of all that is common sense or common decency, if she cannot be remodelled, if she is rooted and grounded in her everlasting filth, her disgusting tatters and frightful rags, is she not cut loose and left to sink or swim, as best she can manage? If she can be transformed into anything like comeliness, why is she hung out a never-fading, never-dying scarecrow to all the world beside? If the last four years have not turned her inside out, and shown her, in the face of heaven, to the nations of the earth, if any deformity remains which is yet to be served up – for one, I pray, 'have me excused'. If England by this time do not know of what sort this her sister island is, if she do not understand either her disease or her cure, all may be given up as lost, for until 'the elements shall melt with fervent heat', the earth disclose her slain and the 'sea give up her dead', can any more that is forbidding, revolting and even terrific be held out to the world than has that island presented for ages gone by. And if she is loved, why not cherish her? If hated, why not wholly cast her off?

To the words of the faithful, fearless, warm-hearted John Bright, let the philanthropist respond: 'Abolition of primogeniture for underived property; registry of property; reduction of the enormous charges for stamps for the sale and purchase of land; security of tenure for the practical labourers of the soil; abolition of the Established Church in Ireland; extension of the suffrage, and reinforcement of the representature in the Imperial Parliament.'[15]

If the aristocracy of the United Kingdom have heaped evils unnumbered upon Ireland, why should not the people of the United Kingdom make ample restitution? 'And let all the people rise, and say in one united doxology, "Amen, so let it be".'

WATER CURE

While lingering in and about Cork, among all its gardens and pleasant walks, a spot two miles from Blarney Castle – well known for the past five years as the Water Cure establishment, kept by Dr Barter – should not be passed over in silence.[16] The Doctor has persevered through and over all prejudices, sufficient to make the place a very desirable one on many accounts. Its location is well chosen, standing on an airy, sightly eminence, looking down upon the rich vales and woods of Blarney, its own backwoods left, with the exception of a few foot-paths and seats, to its natural wildness. Its picturesque bathing-house or cottage, and its cultivated farm, of which the Doctor is the principal manager, make it, taken as a whole, a place of interesting resort. The house for patients is large and pleasant, its inmates made up of such as have hope if not faith, that plunging and dipping, showering and drinking cold water, possesses special, if not super-excellencies in the healing way, when applied scientifically, more than when old Dame Nature, in her homespun manner, tells them to drink when they are thirsty, and wash when they are smutty.

His terms are calculated better for the purses of the higher classes than for the poorer sort: consequently he does not keep a hospital of charity, and those who resort there for a time find good, intelligent company, and when not made into mummies, or ducking and sweating, can walk or ride, read or chat, as they may find it most congenial. The table is abundantly supplied with eatables, so that flesh-eaters as well as anti-flesh-eaters may have all they can rationally ask, the only prohibition being tea and coffee. Many have tested the efficacy and declared it good, and it would seem impossible that a summer could be passed on that mountain, with the pure breezes of Ireland fanning the blood and the sparkling water kissing the skin, and not be cured of whatever disease he had if the disease had not passed the healing art.

The Doctor is a great agriculturist, and if he had the bogs and hunting-grounds made over to him, famine if not pestilence would vanish from that rich soil. He thinks much and talks when disposed, and is physiologist enough to know that flesh and gravies are not the food suited to the system of any invalid; yet with a desire to please, or to retain invalids in his house, he practises these inconsistencies, as he candidly acknowledges them.

A week was pleasantly passed in the house and upon the premises; and were a spot pre-eminently happy for everything needful and social to be chosen, that might be the one to meet all cases. Whoever is devotional may have his Bible and prayers; whoever is merry may have psalms and the piano; whoever wants exercise may find battledores, swings and woody walks; and whoever wants bathing can find bathing-tubs, and cold or warm water.

FRIEND'S FUNERAL

A funeral under any circumstances, or among any people, whether Christian or pagan, has a solemnity which casts a shade, for a moment at least, over all levity. And never probably in war or peace, in pomp or destitution, among civilized or uncivilized, was there a procession bearing to its last home a body from which the soul had fled, which did not produce on the minds of the multitude a check, if not a reflection, that the deep, damp vault where the departed is about to be shut from the light of the world and the converse of his fellow-men, was a mysterious hiding-place into which secret the souls of the living did not wish to enter.

It was about midsummer on a sunny morning, when looking from the door of William Martin in Cork, a procession unexpectedly moved before my vision, and never in the short space of a moment did more painful and pleasant remembrances pass in review.[17] Painful, because were again presented the friends who in my native land, one by one as they departed, rose in succession before me, and because I knew there were sorrowing hearts in that train – and mine well knew the pangs of such; but pleasant, because in the comely throng, who with slow and solemn step measured the distance, the unnatural custom which mock fashion has introduced was not manifest. Woman was in that procession, precisely the procession where she belongs – woman, whose heart emphatically can 'weep with those that weep', woman, who loves to the last, and acts to the last. Why, tell us why, should she not follow to the narrow, dark house the relative she has cherished, or the neighbour she has valued and loved; the friend with whom she may have taken 'sweet counsel, and walked to the house of God in company'? Why should she not go in company now to the house appointed for all living, and where she shall, in her own due time, be transported? Pleasant, too, because the vain trappings of hireling undertakers, nodding plumes, and mourning horses and black hearses were not there. It was simply and truly a friend's funeral.

Not stopping to inquire the name or age of the deceased, or who would accompany me, I crossed the street and joined the procession.[18] Like the burial in the city of Nain eighteen hundred years ago, much people of the city were there.[19] A mile or more through the town gave time for that reflection so suitable and profitable when the soul is necessarily summoned to the face of that 'King of Terrors', and there interrogated as to its present state and future destiny. Slowly and silently the entrance to that inclosure, where the dead were congregated, was opened and passed; and as with the pen of a diamond was that panorama impressed on my eye and heart. It was a square of smooth green, with the exception of the unpretending hillocks, which, without a stone, told that the dead lay there. The whole inclosure was surrounded by trees of rich summer foliage. These, as they waved gracefully over the wall, shed a trembling shadow upon the emerald covering of the beds of the sleeping, and the still house of death was quietly approached, and every member of that Society sat down together to this mourning feast, and there in solemn sweet silence waited to hear what God would say.

The narrow bed was open before them; the plain coffin that inclosed the body of the dead was waiting to enter; an interval of some thirty minutes of solemn silence was broken by a deep-toned measured voice, and never before did the words, 'Blessed are the dead that die in the Lord', so sweetly, so solemnly, so unearthly, fall on my ear – as if standing on the Isle of Patmos, the voice that spake to John seemed to reverberate through that assembly, that to me appeared as if already standing on 'Mount Zion before the Lamb'.[20] The sentences were short and pithy, and from them I ascertained that the departed before us was an aged female, who had fulfilled as a faithful hireling her day and had come to the grave like a shock of corn fully ripe. He praised her not in studied eulogiums; he held her not up between us and the Lamb who redeemed her as a bright pattern for our imitation, but he said deeply and emphatically, 'Yea, they rest from their labours and their works do follow them.' He dwelt a moment on that sweet rest prepared for the people of God, and if any were there who had not entered into it, surely they must then have felt a desire.

He was followed by one who addressed the Majesty of heaven with that adoration which always marks the manner of one whose supplications emanate from the deep working of the Holy Spirit within the soul, and that speaks because it feels, and feels because it has something to feel. It was done – the coffin was carefully let down to its long resting place. Dust to dust met, green sod was fitly placed on her breast nor was the silence in the least broken till all had passed the inclosure.

I would not exchange that hour for a thousand dinner parties of fashionable professors, or pompous burials of the titled great, who have lived but to be honoured, and whose true epitaph could only be:

He lived and died.

The time was drawing nigh when effects must be gathered, and Cork must be left. The season had been spent most pleasantly and profitably, for cultivated minds were ever at hand, and hospitable boards were always made welcome. To designate who was the kindest would be a difficulty wholly uncalled for, as all and every one were more than courteous. Justice compels an acknowledgment of one distinguished favour, which was and is more prized for the manner in which it was done. The Irish, I have before remarked, are in their habit of giving most nobly removed from an ostentatious display, or from a manner which makes the recipient feel that he is so deeply indebted that he can never be discharged.

In the year 1845 I stopped in the house of Mrs Fisher, who generously refused any compensation; when the second visit was made to that city, I again took lodgings with her, determining to pay; but as she was generous in the first instance, I did not inquire terms, lest she might suppose it an indirect suggestion for a second gift.[21] On my departure the bill was called for, fifteen weeks uncontrolled access to drawing-room or parlor, and good lodging. Not a shilling was demanded and not a shilling would she accept. This was hospitality, apparently 'without grudging', and certainly without display.

I sailed from that harbour with a heart full of gratitude to all with whom I had been conversant, and full of sorrow that my eyes would never again see those kind friends who had made my stay so pleasant; and the last farewell of the kind Theobald Mathew and the hospitable, intelligent Beales, who were ready at the packet, was the finishing touch to sensations already too pressing upon me.

The captain had generously given my passage, and ordered the steward to see that all and everything was prepared for my comfort. This, by my own negligence, or in some other way, was not performed, and the night to me was a sad one. When all had stepped on shore, and the ring of the packet bell died on the ear, I sat down upon the side of the vessel, and with feelings much like those when sailing out of New York, a passive, stoical indifference, amounting almost to selfishness, passed over me; and I turned away, and could not or would not look upon the sweet hills that hung over the Lee, and scarcely did I see the wave of the handkerchiefs on that lovely South Terrace, as the steamer sailed, where I had enjoyed so much.

The passage was rough, the wind high, and the night long, cold and dreary. Wrapping my cloak about me, I had reclined under a little awning on the deck, not once asking for a berth in the cabin, and not till a stranger aroused me, and said, 'It is both imprudent and late to be stopping here', did my stupor leave me in the least. Then it was too late to find a bed, and the remainder of the night was passed as uncomfortably as it commenced.

It was not wholly the parting with kind friends, or shutting my eyes forever on waters, flowers, rich valleys and hills that so unnerved me; but it was Ireland, that land of song and of sorrow, that I was leaving forever. It was Ireland, where I had been so strangely sent, so strangely preserved, and to which I was so strangely linked by sights of suffering and unparalleled woe. It was Ireland that was still drinking that fathomless cup of misery extreme, whose bottom has yet never been sounded, and whose brim is still running over, welling up and oozing out, in spite of long and deep draughts continually tasted. The visitor among strangers who is receiving tokens of kindness and presents of remembrance in the routine of other engagements may not examine and appreciate all in possession till the hurry is past, the visit ended; and then coolly and calmly the parcel is opened, and every memento, however valuable or trifling, has a just estimate, if judgment be competent to the task. My parcel was left untouched that night; passive, enduring, as if covered suddenly by an avalanche, which only left room for breathing, with no room for struggling, was all that could effectually be done.

The morning found me in Dublin; and here new trials were in waiting. My trunk, containing nearly all that was valuable in wearing apparel, was left in the care of the poor woman where I had lodged through the winter. She had before been intrusted with it, and her honesty had never been doubted. Her husband had become intemperate, and she had been placed in this great house by the landlady to keep it and wait on lodgers, who paid her what they saw fit. The lodgers had left, all but one, and she had no resources; her children, three in number, were crying for bread. She went to the trunk, took a dress, and carried it to one of the nuisances – a pawnbroker's – and procured bread. She took a second and third, until the trunk was emptied of garments to the number of fourteen, together with a few valuable books and other etceteras, among which was a silver teaspoon, which had seen nearly half a century and had been the admiration of many a Connaught and Kerry wight when sitting with them around the basket of potatoes. This, which was carried in my pocket, wrapped in clean paper, served for knife and fork, tea-cup, plate, and saucer, during every tour over mountain and bog. Blessed companion – it had become part and parcel of myself. Beside it was a true born American, and had an indenture made by an agonized child when in the act of taking medicine. Sacred relic!

Bridget met me at the door – the usual gladness and hearty salutation were wanting. 'How are you, Bridget, and how are the children?' was answered by, 'Bad enough, God knows, and bad luck to you.'

'What luck to me?'

'Your clothes are gone, and I couldn't help it.' Not in the least suspecting her integrity, the natural inquiry was, 'Has the house been robbed?' Frankly, she replied, 'No, but I have taken them. My children were starving with hunger. I found the trunk open, which a painter who went into the chamber opened, as I supposed. You had long been gone, it was uncertain when you would return, and I might and should redeem them in a few weeks, and they are all in the pawn.' The cause and effect were both before me in a true light, and the question is left to mothers, how they might have acted in a case like this. She had heard me say that life was more valuable than property, and when that was in peril, property became the moral right of him who had tried every expedient to save life, but especially when the taking of it did not threaten the same condition of that in which he was placed. She had said, 'I will never see my children die for bread. I will work, I will beg, and when neither will do, I would go and stand on that bridge [which was under the window] and if asking would not do, I would seize the first that my hands could wrench from any one passing.'

She had flung me back on my principles by acting up to hers, and what could be said? She could have been transported; and the whole city, who knew the affair, and had never been hungry, neither entered into her starving case nor pitied me for my foolish forbearance. The rich landlady who had recommended her to me coolly said she would put her out of the house, and she did so; and I found poor Bridget in a miserable hovel, with no means of support, and regretted that the landlady had ever known the circumstance. All the garments but one were found, but many of them too mildewed to be worth redeeming; the missing one was the best, and doubtless was taken by the painter. But the spoon – ah, the lucky spoon! It is now in a closet where I am sitting in London, doubly, yes, trebly valued for its extensive travels and fortunate escapes. I look at it, and think of the peasant children and the potato, and poor Bridget and the pawnbroker.

The reader is left to name this tale *Lights* or *Shades* of Ireland, as best suits his principles; for myself, in my heart, I could not pronounce the woman a thief, and would as soon have trusted her in all common cases after this as before, and am glad that her children did not starve when my garments were lying useless.

The time for a little review of the past, and preparation for the future, had now come. Ireland had been explored, and England was in prospect. The Americans had written that the last donation was on the ocean, and probably no more would be sent.[22] Why should my stay be protracted for the inward voice was continually urging, 'I have finished the work that thou gavest me to do'? Far, far be it from me to say that this work was well finished; many, many mistakes might be corrected, but this I would candidly and humbly say: they were not wilful, but ignorant or misjudging ones. So faithful was conscience in her scrutinizing, that hours, yes days, when sitting alone in a chamber at Richard Webb's, preparing for London, she would ask, and earnestly too, had I done what I could?[23] Had I not sometimes consulted my own case? Had I laboured to the extent, with hands, feet, money, tongue, pen and influence to do, by little or by great means, what my Master had required? Had I not sometimes, when condemning the whiskey-drinking and wine-bibbing of the clergy and gentry, spent a penny on some little relish to take with my bread, when that penny would have given a poor labouring man a pound of meal, and my bread could have been taken without it? Had I not burned a candle an hour, when neither reading or working, or put an additional piece of turf on the grate, when the poor, sick, dying cabiners had not either? Had I not paid a shilling for riding when my feet were able for the journey? But above all, that trunk of clothes! When packing it to leave, the question was suggested – is not this laying up treasures on earth? And should 'moth corrupt', or 'thieves break through and steal', my hoarding would be justly rebuked.[24] I had often thought, as the last alternative, of selling everything for bread to give the starving that could possibly be spared, without leaving myself in a suffering state. This had not been done, the clothes were hoarded, and the virtual thieves – the pawnbrokers – had taken if not stolen them.

This was followed by the startling passage, 'If thine own conscience condemn thee, God is greater than thy conscience, and knoweth all things.'[25] Oh! what searching of heart is there contained in the Holy Scriptures. Then again – had I by precept and example presented Christ, and so walked in Him that all who saw me took knowledge that I had learned of Him? Had the words of eternal life been read and explained in every place where God gave me ability and opportunity, as might have been? Had I been as faithful in rebuking the sins of the great, where opportunity presented, as I had those of the mean and despised? Had a gift ever blinded my eyes to lead me unjustly to favour the giver, and had the kindly heartfelt welcomes of the poor been as grateful in some lowly mud cabin, and the humble invitation to a dinner of potatoes as flattering as the polished salutations of the rich, with the proffered arm of the master of the feast to sit down to a sumptuous table with honourable invited guests? Had I rejoiced with 'exceeding great joy', when my name had been cast out as evil, when reviled, and all manner of evil falsely said against me? Had that legacy of long standing and sure title been as salutary and as gratefully received, as would have been a bequest from the government for sacrifices made for the poor? All this and more sunk deep, and remained long, when conscience arraigned me for rendering the stewardship of that four years' labour. 'What hast thou done with thy Lord's money?' Ah! what indeed? Has a portion been given to 'seven, and also to eight'? Has the bread been cast upon the waters; and shall I find it after many days? To the cross I flee, there let me hide – simply, simply, solely there I cling.[26]

Turning from myself and the retrospect of the past four years, the coming out from Cork, at the last and almost finishing touch of the whole presented Theobald Mathew with the impression made on my mind when he stood on the dock, by the packet, on the Lee, as the vessel sailed away. His countenance is a marked one, and would be distinguished as such in a crowd of strangers. But grief and blasted hopes have so scathed his warm heart that though he retains that benignity of expression so peculiarly his own, yet the pencil of sorrow has so shaded it, continued anxiety has so paralyzed that hope which ever is, and ever must be the wellspring of the soul, that there seems a trembling doubting in every feature whether to settle into a desponding passiveness, or struggle to maintain that wonted complacency which has seemed an innate and inseparable part of his whole constitution.[27] The scourge that has laid waste his people has withered, has scathed his very soul. He stood 'between the living and the dead', like a Phineas, till the plague was measurably stayed, when, in letting go his strained grasp, he found, he felt that his own hand had been weakened, and though he complained not, he saw, he knew that many who had cried 'Hosanna', if they did not say crucify him, crucify him, would turn away and walk no more with him.[28] The palsy that shook his body was a faint shadow of the palsy that withered the springs of his heart and dried up the life-blood of his soul. Great as was his goodness, and good as was his greatness, they neither of them had power to sustain a fabric whose framework was gentleness and confiding love.

When the blast swept over him and he felt his feet sliding, he reached out his believing hand to the supports he thought near him – they were gone! It was then that the 'iron entered into his soul', it was then that he found that love dies with money, and popularity thrives best when its hand is fullest and needs it the least; it was then that he found experimentally that benevolence must be content with its own reward till the 'time of the restitution of all things', when every man shall be rewarded according to his works; and that though he might have given 'all his goods to feed the poor', his recompense in return from his fellow man might only be, 'Who hath required this at your hands?' When a man is in trouble and his feet are fast sliding, the prompt inquiry is, 'What brought him here? Has he been industrious, has he been honest, has he been temperate?' But when he is in prosperity, and the tide of fortune flows smoothly, who inquires whether he honestly, industriously or soberly acquired this prosperity? Who stands aloof from sharing his honours, which flow from his abundance, lest these honours come from an abundance too unjustly acquired? Has he robbed the poor and despoiled the widow and fatherless to fill his granaries and decorate his halls? Who has any right to investigate that? Let every man mind his own business, is the rebuke.

Theobald Mathew was in debt – how came he there?[29] Why everybody knew it was not to aggrandize himself; but he is in debt – he must have been imprudent if not dishonest! True, he was, as the world calls it, in debt, but virtually he owes no man anything – the world never has, the world never will, the world never can repay him. His debt is giving to the poor, when the poor were dying, what he then thought was justly his own, and justly tangible; and that depravity is to be pitied that imputes blame to generosity like this – a generosity which seeks not its own, but the good of those who are ready to perish.[30] He loved his country, he loved his fellow-man of every clime, and his whole life has been spent in seeking their good. When he saw the world had misunderstood him, then he suffered unutterable things; and the shock that both body and mind sustained has left an impress that throws a constraint upon that full freedom which his real friends have been wont to exercise toward him. So abstracted does his mind at times appear that it is sometimes difficult to know either what chord to touch or what time to strike it, lest the unostentatious sensibilities of his heart should be awakened afresh to painful sensations.[31]

God preserve him, as well as all others, who live for the world and its benefit. The current of man's heart must run in a different channel before it can render at all times even blessing for blessing, and better is he treated than was his Master, if the question do not apply to him also, 'Many good works have I shown you; for which of these works do you stone me?' The last famine has drawn out the true character of the people there, in a light most favourable to be understood; it has shown what is in man by a dissection of almost every part of his system and they never can hide again as they have done, and the great pity is that amid so much upturning there has been so little cleansing. True, the pool has not yet become quiescent, nor the sediment had time to settle; and when it shall, many that were filthy will be filthy still, and those that were righteous will be righteous still.

Though truth must and will triumph, judgment sometimes long delays, and the accusations against the nation of that island have a foundation in truth, yet the perverted judgment of men have so misapplied them that at present the force they contain falls almost powerless. That there is injustice there cannot be denied, and this injustice has often been exercised by those who would have been least suspected. The Famine, in spite of all evasions, has told some singular tales of this. The liberality of all nations has been most shamefully abused there, but the poor were not in the fault, and yet the poor must and do suffer all the sad consequences; for now, while the wail of woe and death is still going up in many parts, the response is neither money nor bread, but 'they have been ungrateful, they have been dishonest, and we are tired of hearing of Ireland'.

Were I to speak from honest conviction of what passed there, in much of the distributions belonging to government and much from other places that went through paid hands, had it been cast into the sea, the fishes might have been better benefited than were the starving; but to private donors, and to the churches of England and the labouring classes, who intrusted their offerings to isolated churches and isolated almoners of their gifts, without fee or reward, let it be said, their donations in most cases were well applied and greatly blessed. I have known and record it with pleasure, that when a church there, from one here, was presented with money, clothing or food, the minister of that church would divide it among such men and women as cheerfully sought out and supplied the most needy with the utmost integrity. Many felt, apparently, that it was the Lord's money in very deed, and belonged to the Lord's poor, and that they must render a strict account of their stewardship; and had one half even that the government sent been withheld, and the other half intrusted to such hands as managed with like discretion and honesty, many more lives would have been saved and less complaint of ingratitude been made.

It must be seen that the work was a most arduous and difficult one, and it takes much less time and trouble to sit quietly at home and dictate how it should be done, or complain when it is finished how badly it was executed, than it would to have gone in person and performed the task. It was a hurried work – the four millions of starving men, women, and children were calling for food to-day, they were calling in earnest, they could not wait days, and possibly weeks, till the honesty of a landlord, or the integrity of a rector should go through the trial of a jury; they could not stand round the doors of a church or chapel waiting the decision of bishops and clergymen, priests and monks whether the bread taken in commemoration of the Lord's death were transformed into a part or whole of his real body or not before they could have a piece of it; consequently, what was to be done must be done quickly, and in the kindly feelings which promptly lighted up, the givers would naturally and properly throw promiscuously whatever relief could be gathered by any hands that would offer.

The government of England might possibly have dozed a little too long, regardless of what these her thriving landlords in that green isle were doing; they might not have precisely understood how they were feeding, housing, and paying their serfs that were squatting 'lazily' upon their soil; they might not have applied the laws of mind precisely to this point, that these laws possess the unvarying principle of fixing deeply and firmly in the heart of the oppressor a hatred toward the being that he has unjustly coerced, and the very degradation to which he has reduced him becomes the very cause of his aversion toward him. Therefore such landlords, when famine pressed sorely upon their unpaid tenants, would necessarily by this law pity least, and neglect most, those who by accidental circumstances might be in greatest want.

Those full-fed, government-paid clergymen, who had learned the law of love through her own bread and wine exclusively, and whose jaundiced eyes saw dark and foul spots on all her surplices but her own, would be quick to discern that the 'curse causeless does not come'; and that as the Roman Catholics embodied the majority of the sufferers in Ireland, and the Roman Catholics were mostly fed on potatoes, and as God had blasted these potatoes, therefore they ought in humble acquiescence to say 'amen!' while the smoke of this torment was ascending if not be willing co-workers with God in the infliction of the punishment. When such did give what was intrusted to their hands it was not always given 'with cheerfulness', or without what they thought a merited rebuke. 'Don't you see now,' said a pert wife of a curate of this class, 'don't you see what your idolatry has brought upon you?' Handing a starving woman tauntingly a little food – 'you've been told that something dreadful would come upon you long before, but you would not believe. Now are you ready to come out of that church?'[32]

'How', said a bystander, 'could you speak so unkindly to that poor starving suppliant at your door; should you like the same treatment under the same circumstances?'

'I should deserve it; and beside, how could I see her die under those awful delusions? Would it not be better to show her Christ, and try to direct her to Him?'

'Christ! how can she understand anything of Him, while in that church?'

This is not a facsimile of all in the government church, neither is it an isolated case. Another instance only shall be named, and it is named as an illustration of the spirit that was too much in exercise there, and how it acted upon the sufferers.

A poor man with a numerous family applied to a rector of the Established Church for a portion of the donations committed to his care for the parish. 'Where do you go to church?' was the question.

'I am a Catholic,' the man answered.

'Ah, yes, give your soul to the priest, and come here for me to feed your body; go back, and get your bread where you get your teaching.'

'This will learn 'em,' said the exulting sexton of the church who related the incident, 'this will learn 'em where they are.'[33]

The poor man went away without relief, though he belonged to the parish, and had a claim. Turning them over to the priests was the worst part of the spirit; for the priests, in the first place, were not a government-paid people, and in the next, they had at that time no donations intrusted to them; and to tantalize a hungry man with that retort was like hanging him in gibbets, and then telling him to eat bread.

Such treatment was calculated not only to drive the poor to all sorts of intrigue, but to make them hate still more a religion that they always supposed to be false. The question which the Quaker put to the rector could well apply here, when he remarked that no good would be done to the Papists in Ireland while they rejected the Bible. 'What good, friend, has thy Bible done thee?' Ah, true; what good does it do any who practice not its spirit? It is not intended to imply, by these statements, that the clergy of the Established Church in Ireland during the Famine were all bigots, or all hard-hearted, and without any true Christianity; but it is intended to say, that the spirit of bigotry and partiality was there, and wherever manifested, whether by that religious party or any other, and a most unfavourable effect both on the bodies and minds of the suffering. The government could not control that, any more than a crazy inebriate can help doing what he is tempted to do. But the inebriate, when he is sober, should keep so and not put himself in the power of an enemy that can injure him so much; and if the experience of two or three centuries in Ireland have not proved that carnal weapons are not needed in a church, and that Christ, who should be the head of it has no occasion for them, surely they must be dull learners.

The Christian may despair of conquest when kindness and love have no effect, and in the Famine, when these were exercised, they were felt and acknowledged. Let any stranger, in the year 1850, go into every parish in that country, and make investigation of the true state of feeling, as it would naturally flow out without any design; and if that stranger made no party allusions that should awaken jealousy, he would hear lavish blessings bestowed on dissenters of every grade, where these dissenters had manifested a kindly feeling. 'And there's the rector that would do the heart good', 'There's the blessed minister, that's worth the day's walk to hear his discourse', 'And would ye see the lady that's the blessin' to the poor?' &c. Do you say this is selfishness? It is a just appreciation of right and wrong; and where right is not exercised why should it be acknowledged? What gospel requires that a man should say of an unjust neighbour that he walks uprightly, lest some evil-eyed partisan should judge him by his own narrow spirit? And blinded as the world is by sin, and perverted as education may be, there are things done which will bear looking in the face without blushing; there are things done so well that an enemy, however skillful, could not improve them; and there are fallen men and women in the lower ranks of life, without any refinement of education, that can appreciate these well done things and even do them too; and with all the zigzag movements in the Famine there were some redeeming qualities, there were some things carried on and carried through, which were not accused of sectarianism, for the simplest reason – none was manifest.

The Society of Friends justly merit this acknowledgment, and they have it most heartily from every portion of Ireland. Not belonging to that Society, my opportunity of testing the true feelings of the poor was a good one, and when in a school or soup-shop the question was put – 'Who feeds you?' or, 'Who sends you these clothes?' – the answer was: 'The good Quakers, lady, and it's they that have the religion entirely.' One young man seriously inquired of me what sort of people they might be, and if their religion were like any other, and where they got such a good one. 'By dad, don't you think it's the best in the world?' It certainly produces good works among the poor of Ireland, was the reply. 'And where may they say their prayers? I wish I could hear 'em; or, don't they say prayers?' He pressed so closely, that vague answers would not avail. The foundation of a faith which was so different from what he had seen in any people, as he said, 'intirely', he determined to make out; and finally inquired if they suffered persons of other faith to see them worship, and added, 'I should like to see it.' He was directed to a meeting in Dublin which was open on that day, and after getting all preliminaries as to how he must behave, he ventured in.

The meeting was a silent one; he saw no altars, he heard no prayers, and his astonishment at their worship was equal to his admiration of their goodness.

'And wasn't it quare they didn't spake?'

'They were waiting in silence till they should have something given them to speak.'

This increased the difficulty and he went away perfectly confounded, wishing he could know something more about them, 'for they must be a blessed people'.

This simple-minded lad lived in a remote part of Ireland, had never been in a city before; and he said that he had seen these good people in the mountains giving alms, and 'didn't they spake so kindly', he added.

'I intended to see 'em if I could find where they stopped.' Simple-minded youth, what could he do more?

Whilst writing this, a report has been sent me of the Birr Mission, at Parsonstown in Ireland, under the superintendence of Mr Carlisle, and I happily find by the following extract this fresh proof of the effect of kindness on the hearts of the most bigoted.[34] The Report states:

The medical coadjutor of the Mission, noticed in our last Report as having been sent to us from Edinburgh, continues his labours most assiduously and most usefully. Nothing has done so much toward removing the prejudices of Roman Catholics against us – even those who formerly were most opposed and most bigoted – as his kind, unwearied, and skillful attention to the sick poor. It has already opened the way for the word of God to many families from which it formerly was debarred; and we observe that the prejudices of a class of society above the poor, with whom he has no direct intercourse in the way of his profession, are giving way before this kind and conciliatory approach to the population generally.

Were there space in these pages, like instances might be multiplied, and two which come under my notice were so in point, that they are entitled to a record in a better place.

A few miles north of Dublin, in the winter of 1847 and 1848, a minister of the Independent church was sick for weeks, and his life seemed suspended in doubt for some days. One Sabbath, in a chapel, after the morning service was finished, the priest called the attention of the people to his case, and added, 'If he dies, God will take from us one of the best men in the country, and who will fill his place? All we can do is to pray for him, and surely you will all do that.' Voices were loud in responding, 'yes, yes'; and they tarried another hour and went through their prayers for the sick. Now, as inefficient as these prayers might be, they were the legitimate offspring of kindness and goodwill which this minister had practised, till he had not only removed prejudice but had substituted like feelings of kindness.

The second case was that of a good woman who belonged to the Methodist denomination. She had been a pattern of good works in her neighbourhood, without regard to party; and the poor loved her as their long-tried friend. She died. The priest of the parish was noted for his peace-making spirit and liberality. The Sabbath after this good woman's death, he concluded the exercises of the day by naming the circumstance, and saying, 'When God takes such good ones from the earth as this woman was, the living have not only cause to mourn, but to tremble, lest that his anger has gone out against the inhabitants, and He will not suffer such righteous ones to live among them.'

In a few weeks from this that priest died, the husband of the good woman just named dropped an obituary notice in a paper which he edited, mentioning the conciliatory disposition of the priest and his exertions in the parish to keep peace. A nephew of this priest called a few days after and thanked the editor for the kind notice, saying, 'it was more than he could expect'. In two weeks from this an obituary of the nephew was inserted in the same paper. But mark the effects of simply carrying out the principle of Christian kindness! Was Christ dishonoured – was Christ offended?

PROSELYTISM

It requires the Irish language to provide suitable words for a suitable description of the spirit which is manifested in some parts to proselyte, by bribery, the obstinate Romans to the church which has been her instrument of oppression for centuries.[35] The English language is too meagre to delineate it in the true light. Rice, Indian meal, and black bread would, if they had tongues, tell sad and ludicrous tales. The artless children too, who had not become adepts in deceit, would and did sometimes by chance tell the story in short and pithy style. It was a practice by some of the zealous of this class to open a school or schools, and invite those children who were in deep want to attend, and instruction, clothes and food should be given, on the simple terms of reading the Scriptures and attending the church. The church catechism must be rehearsed as a substitute for the Romish, and though in substance a passage or two looked as if the hoof of the so-called 'beast' might have been over it and left a modest track, yet by its adherents it was thought to be the pure coin.[36]

The children flocked by scores and even hundreds: they were dying with hunger, and by going to these places they could 'keep the life in 'em', and that was what they most needed; they could go on the principle, 'if thou hast faith, have it to thyself before God', and when the hunger was appeased and the 'blessed potato' should come, they could say Mass at home again. When such children were interrogated, the answer would be, 'We are going back to our own chapel or our own religion when the stirabout times are over'; or when the 'bread's done', or the 'potatoes come again'.[37]

'But you are saying these prayers and learning this catechism.'

'We shan't say the prayers when we go back – we'll say our own then,' &c.

Now the more experienced father or mother would not have said this to a stranger, and such might have passed for a true convert while receiving the stirabout. The priests were very quiet while this kind of bantering was in progress; they knew its beginning, and by this 'concordance' could well trace the end; they held these favoured ones of their flock by a cord while the stomach was filling, as the traveller does his steed that he is watering, and turns it away when its thirst is assuaged, caring little at what fountain he drinks, if the water be wholesome. 'We had as lief they would be in that school as any,' said a priest, 'while they are so young; we can counteract all the bad or wrong impressions their lessons may have had on their minds.'

The priests of Ireland have had their wits well sharpened by the constant check held over them by penal laws, and a government church, and they have not been guilty of great proselyting, finding as much work as would keep them upon the alert continually to keep their own hold and the flock safe already in possession. The Episcopalians and Dissenters, on the other hand, knowing that they were the minority and that the power they held was not precisely 'just and equal', feared that some new king or minister, or some sudden government squall, might blow down their uncertain bamboo fabric, had to double their cries of priestcraft and popery, persecutions and murders to keep their citadels of self-defence well secured, with the stirring watchword of 'popery' ever stimulating the soldiery to ready action, in case of insurrection. Thus, as they first preached Christ through bullets, bombshells and fire, so they still hold Him up as the God of battles to all who would not receive Him through the breath of their mouths.

The soldiery stationed in Ireland are a living proof of this principle, and especially so as this army is required to show its warlike power in defense of the missionaries stationed there, being called out to display their banners when any new converts are to be added to the Protestant ranks from the Romish Church. An instance of this was related by a coast-guard officer stationed in the town of Dingle.[38] Some five or six years ago, a half-dozen or more of the Romans had concluded to unite with the Protestant mission establishment there, and the Sabbath that the union was to take place in the church the soldiery were called out to march under arms to protect this little band from the fearful persecutions that awaited them on their way thither. The coast-guard officer was summoned to be in readiness *cap à pie* for battle, if battle should be necessary. He remonstrated – he was a Methodist by profession, and though his occupation was something warlike, yet he did not see any need of carnal weapons in building up a spiritual church; but he was under government pay, and must do government work.

He accordingly obeyed, and, to use his own words substantially, 'We marched in battle array, with gun and bayonet, over a handful of peasantry – a spectacle to angels of our trust in a crucified Christ, and the ridicule and gratification of priests and their flocks who had discernment sufficient to see that with all the boasted pretensions of a purer faith and better object of worship, both were not enough to shield our heads against a handful of turf, which might have been thrown by some ragged urchin, with the shout of "turncoat" or "souper", as this was the bribe which the Romanist said was used to turn the poor to the church; and though this was before the Potato Famine, yet the virtues of soup were well known then in cases of hungry stomachs, and the Dingle Mission had one in boiling order for all who came to their prayers.' The coast-guard continues, 'We went safely to the church, and the next Mission paper, to my surprise and mortification, told a pitying world that so great were the persecutions in Dingle that the believing converts could not go to the house of God to profess their faith in Him without calling out the soldiery to protect them.'

This circumstance is quite in keeping with much of what is called persecution there; and though it cannot and should not be denied, but that in some cases there has been great opposition and much severity mani-fested by papists towards those who have left their church, yet a spirit of retaliation will never deaden the life of that persecuting spirit, nor bring any to see the benefit of a religion which bears the same impress which is stamped on theirs. These two contending powers have had so much to do to keep, one his own foot-hold, and the other his flock, that little time has been left for preaching Christ or carrying out his gospel; and I pray to be forgiven, if wrong, in saying, that in no place whatever where Christian-ity is preached, have the sad effects of a nominal one been more fatal. The letter without the spirit has shown emphatically what it can do. It can make men proud, covetous, vainly puffed-up, and it can make them oppressive too; it can make them feel, and it can make them act as did the Puritan in the early settlement of the New England colonies.

'The earth,' he said, 'was the Lord's, and the fullness thereof, and what is the Lord's belongs to the saints also. Therefore they [Puritans] had a right to drive out the savages and take their lands.' Accordingly they did.[39] The same spirit is literally carried out there in the tithe gather-ing; these 'saints' have a claim on what belongs to God, and consequent-ly the law covenant belonging to the Jewish priest, under Moses, is hand-ed over to them, and whatever barbarian, Scythian, Jebusite or Perizzite dwells in the land, must to them pay tribute.[40] The magistrates who col-lect this tribute sometimes do it in the face of spades and pitchforks, and stockings full of stones, which the brave women hurl; but having the 'inner man' well strengthened by both law and government gospel, they generally escape with the booty. These ludicrous and shameful scenes have measurably abated since the tithes are gathered in a form not quite so tangible, by merging them in or behind the landlord's tax, who puts this ministerial 'tenth' into an advanced rent on the tenant; but murder will out, and the blow is felt as severely, and by many traced as clearly, as when the hand was more tangible.

In the summer of 1848 in the city of Cork, one man belonging to the Society of Friends had a good set of chairs taken, which the owner affirmed was but a repetition of the same proceedings, the Church collectors having a peculiar fancy for his chairs; they had taken many sets in yearly succession. Now while all this is in progress in that country, talk not so loudly of popish heresy being the root of all the evil there. First, make the gospel tree, which was planted eighteen hundred years ago on the Mount of Olives, bear a little fruit, pluck a few fresh boughs from its neglected branches, and kindly present them to these popish-seared consciences, and see and mark well the result.

If the book called the Bible had been kept entirely out of sight, and its principles been fully exemplified in deed as well as in word, there can scarcely be a doubt but the prejudice which now exists against it would never have been known; and had the priests thundered their anathemas either from the confession box or the altar, louder and longer against reading or believing it, many of them would have defied all bulls of excommunication, as well as all purgatorial burnings, and have made their acquaintance with its pages. When any of these extortions are practised, the ready response is, 'This comes from the blessed book they're tachin' and prachin'. It is the substance that is wanting, not the shadow.

If popery have concealed Christ behind the Virgin, with her long retinue of sainted fathers and maids of honour, in the persons of St Bridgets, whose microscopic eyes can see Him any clearer through mitred bishops and surpliced gownsmen, fattened on the gatherings of the harvests of the poor and scanty savings of the widow and fatherless; if the incense from a Roman censer obscure the clear light of the Sun of Righteousness, think not to blow it away by the breath of alcohol, their smoke will only mingle together, and make the cloud still thicker. Some paste more adhesive than 'stirabout', and some stimulus more abiding than soup, will be required to keep the scrutinizing Paddy rooted and grounded in a new faith whose fresh lessons are only, 'Be patient, love, while I beat you, in true genteel and "royal style".' The Celt can quickly discern clean hands; and though his own may be filthy, yet he will content himself with the 'holy water' of his own church to cleanse them while he sees his neighbour's of the Protestant faith a little too smutty.

While speaking thus of proselytism and the errors of the church, the soup-shops should not be cast into entire contempt; for though they may, and undoubtedly have been, used for bribery there, yet they have been used for better purposes, and by the Protestant church too. The missionary stations in Dingle and Achill, so far as they adhered to their professed object in the beginning, which was partly to provide a retreat from persecution, and give labour as far as it was practicable to those who wished to renounce popery, did well. But have they acted entirely in accordance with these principles? Let the fruits be the judges. That there are real God-fearing Christians in those churches must be believed, but this is not the question. Were most of them made so by going there, or had they not been taught of the Holy Spirit before entering them? The heaven-taught Christian in Ireland in many places is driven to great straits to find a fold where the flock are fed with the true bread prepared by those who have really come out of the world, and they necessarily unite with any, where they can find a home. The Roman Catholic who turns to God with full purpose of heart, and has been really born of the Spirit, is indeed a spiritual Christian; he drinks deeply at the Fountain-head, and often exceeds those who had been in the path with the Scriptures in their hands for years. One Presbyterian clergyman observed, 'we must take large strides to keep up with them'.

I am not expecting, neither asking one pound of money, one good dinner, nor one blessing for these unsavoury statements, but they are the common sense observation of four years' practical experience among the strangely situated people who have been the gazing-stock of the world for so many ages; and though the remark of a Roman Catholic barrister, in the county of Mayo to his priest was somewhat severe, yet it might be well for the clergy of all denominations to look at it, and inquire whether they have not given cause for the people to feel that the benefits which have flowed from their ministrations are not on the whole a poor equivalent for the money which has been paid to them, and for the honour which has been bestowed upon their reverences.

This barrister observed that his occupation had led him to an acquaintance with the doings of the clergy of every denomination in Ireland; and he had settled on the firm belief that if every one of all classes, Priests, Protestants, and Dissenters, were put into a ship and driven out to sea, and the ship scuttled, it would be better for Ireland than it then was. 'Leave every man,' he added, 'to take care of his own soul, without being led hither and thither by men who worked either for money or party, or for both, and they would be in a better condition than they were at present.' The confounded priest uttered not one syllable in reply. It is somewhat amusing to a listener, who belongs to no one of them, to be present on any annual celebration of these clergymen and hear the reformations going on under their management.

The Established Church astonishes you with confirmations and the increase of communicants, and if the speaker be a missionary – why a few thousand pounds would bring half of popish Ireland into his net – could he build more cottages and dig more drains, mountain and bog for many a mile would be blossoming like the rose, and crooked things be made straight among the benighted Catholics, and Ireland in the Lord's time be a habitation for the righteous to dwell in. The number of converts from popery astonishes the credulous hearers, and the self-denials and persecution of the missionaries are second to none but Peter's or Paul's.

Next come the Presbyterians. They are a numerous, well-disciplined band, understanding precisely the tactics of their creed, and give you to understand that they are the true light that might lighten every man that cometh into Ireland. They have lengthened their cords and strengthened their stakes; and while many yet desire the 'leeks and garlics' a-growing in a government hot-house, yet some have nobly testified against making a hodge-podge church of Christ and Mammon. They are not idlers, and their Sabbath-schools train their children in the true faith of Presbyterianism as faithfully as does the Romish priest in his. They, like the Established Church, feel that the mammoth incubus that is weighing the godly of Ireland down is the Romish Church, and though they acknowledge that a state church is not precisely the best thing, yet that is not the mountain, but yet would gladly have it removed if by rooting up these tares the wheat should not be rooted up also; for if government should let go its hold, and say 'Stand on your own foundation, or stand not at all', they might be shaken in the fearful crash. The *regium donum* still lingers there, and if tithes should slip, why not draw after them this 'royal gift'?[41] Many are good preachers and eloquent platform speakers; some have advanced into the free air of anti-slavery principles, and an isolated one, here and there, may not approve of the practice of war; but few comparatively have abandoned the use of the good creature, in moderation, and doubtless they are fated to see more and suffer more, and dig deeper into their own hearts before they will believe, but that wisdom will die with them.

The Methodists have a standing in numbers among the ranks of Bible-Christians, and their zeal has provoked many. They pray on, and they sing on, through thick and through thin; they tell you that Methodism is the only salvo, and can never praise God enough that they stepped into her ranks. John Wesley echoes and re-echoes with loud amens, wherever there is a chapel to eulogize his name. They too abhor the 'beast', and have blunted, if not plucked, some of his horns; but not being quite so orthodox in the eyes of their more Calvinistic brethren, they go more on their 'own hook', working in their own way, than the two first named. Though it is to be feared they are drinking in and conforming more to the world than formerly, yet they keep well in their own ranks, and let the world rock to and fro, their motto is onward; they are not so prone to seek shelter from a storm in time of trouble; and to run over to the enemy till the danger is over, as some who are more in search of popularity, more timid and less self-denying. They are so undoubting in the truth of what they profess, that they spend less time in securing props to keep up their fabric; and consequently they have more space for preaching Christ. Those Catholics who are not afraid of entering into any chapel but their own are fond of listening to the enthusiastic manner of preaching which they find there, and are often seen standing about the doors of a chapel, with great reverence; occasionally some are drawn in by the gospel, and remain faithful to Christ.

The Independents are a worthy class, and have unostentatiously made a good impression on the minds of the humbler portion of the inhabitants. Their Bible readers have in general been men of untiring faithfulness, and by kindness have gained access to the hearts of the peasantry, who listen to the reading of the Scriptures without that opposition which must follow where a harsh course and abuse to the priests are manifested. One of their readers remarked that for more than twenty years he had visited the cabins, read the Scriptures, and held up Christ to them as the sinner's friend, and in no one case had he been rejected. Some of them speak and read Irish, which always gains access to the heart. The Independents in respect to government aid, reject all *regium donums,* and they stand on a firmer rock than an earthly royal treasure. They have funds gratuitously supplied by their own church, and their missionaries and Bible readers are mostly supported by them. Their pastors are men in general of plain common-sense, knowing how to adapt themselves and their preaching to the masses; and had they more of a proselyting spirit, would certainly make more noise, more money, and add more stony-ground hearers to their number.

The Baptists, humble in number as they are, should not be left out; they make their way slowly and softly, and show much patience in labouring in the destitute parts. Their flocks are increasing, and like the station at Ballina, many of their number are from the Romish Church. These, when they put on Christ by a new baptism, as they call immersion, the burial with him into his death, arise and walk in newness of life, and in general remain steadfast in their profession. It is a fact, which should be more noticed among all these denominations, that where Christ is the most faithfully preached, error falls silenced without that struggle of argument to maintain its hold, as when some object of contempt is held up to ridicule or to shun. All the enemy's forces are then rallied to the rescue, and often the conqueror in argument is the force most weakened in the best part.

The Plymouth Brethren, or Bible-Christians as they may call themselves, have a numerous body in Dublin, and worship Christ in a manner distinct from either which have been named. Acknowledging no head but Christ, they have no ministers to support, and like the Apostles' churches have all things in common so far as this – as when one member suffers, all suffer with it; and accordingly none are left in want. They were very active in the Famine, working efficiently, feeding and clothing many; and the Sabbath-school in which Christ and only Christ was taught was numerously attended by the poor, who were fed and clothed, not as a bribe, but as an act of Christian charity, due to the poor. 'Come, and we will tell you of Christ,' was the invitation, and not 'come and join us, and we will feed you'.

The Unitarians in Ireland are not numerous, but generally wealthy, intelligent and benevolent. They did much in the Famine to ameliorate the state of suffering, and to their honour they were many of them teeto-tallers. Their doctrine to the Catholic is more incomprehensible than any of the 'heresies' which they meet; for beside rejecting the Mother, they say they reject the Son likewise, and have neither Intercessor nor Saviour; and if they were disposed to proselyte, the Catholic chapels would not be the 'shops' in which to set up their stirabout boilers.

The Roman Catholics are peculiarly distinct in one noble practice, from all other professed Christians we meet. They will not in the least gape after, nor succumb to any man's religion because he is great and honourable, though they will crouch and call him 'yer honour' in matters of this world; but where their religious faith is concerned, they call no man master.

The Unitarians, therefore, collect into their ranks such as, being whole, need no physician, and the lamentation or confession seldom goes up of being 'miserable sinners' and going 'astray like lost sheep'. They are certainly a people in their influence over others, especially the lower classes, less to be dreaded than those who 'hold the truth in unrighteousness'. The heresy of needing no atonement by an infinite God is more shunned than sought after by all such as have been led to believe that man is in a lost state; for if he is lost, and finds himself so, he seeks to be found; but if no one is in the way sufficient to lead him, how is he bettered by the inquiry? On the other side, those who hold the truth in unrighteousness, in other words who bear no fruit, have not the power of it, and when the letter only is understood, he who professes Christ and knows him not in a fellowship of his sufferings, and a resurrection of life, is a more dangerous lure to the inquirer; for, in the first case, if there is no Saviour all powerful, there is nothing to embrace; but if there is one in word and not in deed, he is more to be dreaded than none at all, a false God is worse than none.

There is a society of Moravians, and it would be superfluous to say anything of them, they are so well known for their simplicity, sobriety, retirement and good order that they walk more unseen than any denomination whatever. They never say, 'Come and see my zeal for the Lord.' The Roman Catholics look upon them somewhat as they do upon the Society of Friends – a second 'blessed people,' wondering what the religion must be.

The Society of Friends in Ireland stand out as they do in other places, distinct. They meddle but little in the politics of the world around them; whatever government they may be under they sit quietly and let the world rock on. A Yearly Meeting of that denomination is more interesting in Ireland than elsewhere on one account, because they are entirely free from vain boasting and whining tales of persecution, or the great growth of their denomination, the downfall of error before their preaching, &c. You have solemn silence, or you have something uttered unvarnished with rhetorical flourishes or borrowed extracts from House of Commons or House of Lords. Their extracts are borrowed from the Holy Scriptures, their prayers are addressed to the Majesty of Heaven and not to men, they speak as if in his presence and sit as if in his presence, and if you are not particularly edified, you are solemnized, your heart if not melted is softened, and you go away feeling that for an hour or more you have been shut from a noisy, empty, gabbing world, from a party church which has not stimulated you to kill any priest, or down any chapel or convent. You feel to inquire, am I right? Is all well within? Have I the Spirit of Christ? if not, I am none of his. I have never heard that any Roman Catholic has ever turned to that Society in Ireland; but if they had proselyting agents in the field they would have their share, or if they had even that outward show in their meeting-houses which takes away all reserve from the stranger, and gives him to feel that the place is for all, many would be induced to go in; that now stay away.

When stopping in Cork, great surprise was expressed, even by some dissenters, that I should take such liberties as to go to a place of worship where none were wished to attend but their own; and the Catholics supposed that none could be allowed to enter, but such as have on the particular dress. The caution of these people in the time of famine to avoid the appearance of proselyting was carried to an extent almost unparalleled. It was said that a ministering Friend from England, who had been in the habit of attending or holding a meeting in the west part of Ireland when he visited them, declined doing so, in the year 1847, when in the same place, lest it should be construed as a desire to make converts by the liberality which his Society were showing.

The Catholics in Ireland are the Catholics everywhere in some respects; in others they may have some shades of difference. Having always been placed under restrictions, they could not always appear free; and yet when these restrictions have been removed they have not taken undue advantage, as their enemies supposed they would. The removal of the penal laws did not make them insolent but thankful that they again had the prospect of being ranked among the human family as human beings. That cord of fear by which they have been so long held is loosening, and they take liberties, that at times cause the priest to say that they are quite beyond his control, and he is often put down at the altar – that most sacred place, when he lays restrictions which are not congenial.

Their superstitions too are fast vanishing; fairies and banshees have not the hold on the imagination as in former days; the holy wells and bushes covered with rags and strings which had been dipped in the waters, to wash the believing diseased one, are now disappearing. This practice is not confined to the Catholics, either in Ireland or England, being practice in the latter place to some extent now; but there is still a most fearful practice in the west part of Ireland which a priest related in my hearing, and comforted our horror by saying that he had caned the man most faithfully that morning, and it would never be repeated. The practice has been in use for ages, and is called the 'Test of the Skull'.[42] It is this – when a person is suspected of crime he is placed kneeling, and made to swear over the Bible that he is innocent, and then laying his hand on the skull, he invokes heaven that the sins of the person that owned that skull in life, with those of the seventh generations before and after him, might be visited on his head if he were guilty, and if this swearing was false, the skull was to haunt him incessantly day and night to the end of his life. This horrid practice is so loudly spoken against that it is performed with the greatest secrecy when it is done. It has extorted many a confession that nothing else would do, and is found a very useful experiment in incorrigible cases. The skull used is always the skull of the father, if the father be dead, which makes it mere terrific to the suspected one.

Superstitions of these kinds are prevalent more upon the sea coasts and in the mountains, where the inhabitants are secluded from much intercourse; and sitting in their dark cabins, or climbing the crags upon the lofty mountains or cliffs hanging over the sea, they hear the constant roar of old ocean, or the hollow groaning of the wind as it winds through the defiles and caves; and having no intelligent intercourse and no books, they conjure up all that imagination is capable of doing, and when it is conjured up and brought a few times before the mind, it is reality which is difficult to efface. Their fairy superstitions are not frightful, and go to show a very poetic turn, of which the mind of the Celt is quite capable. Fairies are always pretty, 'light on the fut' and light on the wing, are pleasant and playful, particularly fond of children and babies, and often exchange them when the mother is gone or asleep, and many times she never knows the difference; frequently she has been heard to complain that a sicklier child has been put in her child's place, and sometimes blue eyes have been exchanged for grey.[43] They never like to displease one of these gentry, lest she should be disposed to kill or injure the child. I found these ideas still lingering among the mountains where some of them would not be willing to leave off red petticoats because they kept the fairies from doing any little mischief which otherwise they might do.[44] The Angel's Whisper, too, has a foundation in real truth. It has long been supposed that a sleeping infant hears some pleasant thing whispered in its ear by the ministering angel that is always hovering near; and it is noticeable that the superstitions of the peasantry are more poetical than frightful, and they generally turn all supernatural appearances to a favourable account.[45] But the Famine changed their poetical romance into such fearful realities that no time was left to bestow on imagination.

CHAPTER IX

'Shall I see thee no more, though lov d land of sorrow?'

The time had come when the last long adieu must be taken of a people and country, where four years and four months had been passed, and it would be impossible to put the last penciling upon a picture like this, and not pause before laying it aside, and look again at its 'Lights and Shades' as a whole. In doing so, the task is more painful than was the first labor – first, because these 'Lights and Shades' are imperfectly drawn; and second, because no future touch of the artist, however badly executed, can be put on; what is written is written, and what is done is done forever.

My feet shall never again make their untried way through some dark glen, or wade through a miry bog, or climb some slippery crag to reach the isolated mud cabin, and hear the kind 'God save ye kindly, lady; come in, come in, ye must be wairy'. Never again can the sweet words of eternal life be read to the listening wayside peasant, when he is breaking stones, or walking by the way; never will the potato be shared with the family group around the basket, or the bundle of straw be unbound and spread for my couch. Never will the nominal professor, who learned his Christ through respectability, without even the shadow of a cross, again coolly say, 'We do not understand your object, and do you go into the miserable cabins among the lower order'; and never, oh never! again will the ghastly stare of the starving idiot meet me upon the lonely mountains I have trod; never again will the emaciated fingers of a starving child be linked in supplication for a bit of bread, as I pass in the busy street; though the painful visions will forever haunt me, yet the privilege to relieve will never again be mine in that land of sorrow. It is over. Have I acted plainly? – have I spoken plainly? – have I written plainly? This is all right, – for this no apology is made. But have all these plain actions, plain speakings, and plain writings, been performed with an eye single to the glory of God? If so, all is as it should be; if not, 'Mene, Tekel' must be written.[1]

These pages speak plainly of Clergymen, of Landlords, of Relief Officers, of the waste of distributions, and of Drinking Habits. Are these things so? Glad should I be to know, that in all these statements a wrong judgment has been formed, and that they have been and are misrepresented. Yes, let me be proved even a prejudiced writer, an unjust writer, a partial writer, rather than that these things shall be living, acting truths. But alas! Ireland tells her own story, and every stranger reads it.

The landlords have a heavy burden, and if the burden cannot be removed, it is right that they should be heard. Even if by their own neglect or unskillfulness they are now where they feel the wave rolling over them, and this wave is like to swallow them entirely, what philanthropist would not throw out the life-boat and taken them to land? If they are not good steersmen, then place them not again at the helm; if they neither understand the laws of navigation, nor the duties of captains to the crew, assign them a place where with less power they can act without injuring the helpless, till they learn lessons of wisdom from past ages of recklessness and thoughtless improvidence. And while God says, 'What measure ye mete shall be measured to you again,' yet who shall presume to deal out this promise, nor let one retaliating lisp be encouraged to clothe the oppressive or careless landlord in like rags that his tenants have worn. Give him a second coat, and though his hands may not be adorned with rings, yet dress him in clean garments, and put shoes upon his feet. If you give him not the 'fatted calf', yet feed him not on the one root which his scanty pay has compelled the sower and reaper of his fields to eat, strip him not of the last vestige his habitation may possess of decency and comfort, and shut him not in the walls of a work-house, to lie down and rise up, go out and come in, at some surly master's bidding. Let him walk among men, as a man breathing free air on God's free earth that he has freely given to the children of men. Say not to him, when you see that his day has already come, 'Ah! I told you so.'

Conscience, if he have any, will tell him that, and if he have not any, you cannot furnish him with one. There are landlords in Ireland who have measurably rendered what is just and equal, if not wholly so. There are Crawfords and Hills, who have done nobly and outlived the storm, and there are many others, who like them have acted well, but could not, and have not, outlived it.[2] In one crumbling mass, they and their tenants are looking in despair on each other without cause or disposition to recriminate, and when they part, it is like the separation of kindly members of one family, united by one common interest. These are some of the bright spots, green and fresh, which still look out upon that stricken country, and leave a little hope that lingering mercy may yet return and bless her with the blessing that adds no sorrow.

The minister, too – shall his sacred name and calling be on the tongue and pen of every wayfaring traveler who may chance to pass through his parish, and tarry but for a night – who may hear but a passing sermon, and that a good one, too, and hasten away and denounce him as a hireling or unfaithful? Let candor, courtesy and Christianity forbid it!

The watchmen on Ireland's wall have had a stormy, bleak night to guard the city, and amid the roar of tumultuous tempests have scarcely known how to guide or to warn the lost traveler into a safe shelter – they may have seen danger through a false glare – they may have warned when no danger was nigh, and they may have wrapped their robes about them, and hid from an enemy when they were the only leaders that could have led to victory. Some have split on the fatal rock – love of gain; others are insnared by the deceitful, flattering word, 'respectability'. This above all others seems to be the hobby; nor is it confined to the Established Church: they as a body are so well paid and honored, that they have less need to keep up a struggle respecting the name, as most of them (the curates excepted) can and do hang out the indisputable sign – a carriage, and its accompaniments; and if the character of such an one be inquired after, however he may live, and how far removed from the vital principles of the gospel he may be, if not among the vilest, 'Oh! he is very respectable; if you should see his gardens, and grounds, and carriage, and then his glebe-house, and his wife and daughters – they're the ladies.'

The dissenting classes, who profess by their very dissenting, that they believe more fully that the regenerating spirit of the gospel calls for newness of life, and nonconformity to the world; yet to induce the world to follow them, to become members of their body, they must throw out the bait of 'respectability', to keep up an influence which conformity to the world alone can do; that part of the legacy which Christ left, they acknowledge is a good one when applied to real martyrdom. When the disciples were told if they hated me, they will hate you also, and that they must rejoice and be exceedingly glad, when all manner of evil should be said of them, for his sake; but for disciples in the nineteenth century the constitution of things is changed, and as 'a good name', the wise man tells us, 'is better than precious ointment', this good name must be obtained, even though a few circumstantials in the Christian creed should be modestly suspended.[3]

This good name is the last thing that the professed Christian will leave in the hands of Christ; he will intrust him often with his property, his indefatigable labors, and even life itself; but his reputation, ah! his reputation is too sacred to go out of his hands; and mark! this reputation is one acquired according to the customs of the world. Here is the fatal split, here it is, where he who purchases this article, purchases at the expense of that vitality, and indwelling principle of holiness, which, if nurtured and kept alive, by walking in the liberty of Christ, will go on from one degree of grace and glory, till the perfect man in Christ is attained.

The dissenting Christians of Ireland, many of them, are wealthy enough to be respectable; and though they are not in general as high as their Established brethren; yet those who have a *regium donum* can figure somewhat genteelly, and if they do not attain to the highest notch they do what they can; if they cannot keep a coach and four, they would not be inclined to ride meek and lowly, as their Master did through the streets of Jerusalem, and will get the best carriage their means will allow.

Now respectability is not to be despised; but seeking it at the expense of that humility, that condescending to men of low estate, that not only giving to the poor, but doing for the poor, and doing too at the expense of our own ease, and in face and eyes of the customs of a God-hating world, is reprehensible, and wholly and entirely aside from the precepts and examples of Christ and his followers; and though to the blameworthy this may appear severe, because true, yet I cannot be a faithful recorder of what I saw and experienced in Ireland without leaving this testimony, which I expect to meet at the judgment, that a proud, worldly, respectable Christianity is the first great deep evil that keeps that country in a virtual bondage, from which she never will escape till the evil be removed.

The awful gulf which is placed between the higher and the 'lower orders' there, is as great between professed Christians and the world, as between the estated gentleman or titled lord, who makes no pretensions, and in many cases much greater. There are lords, sirs, and esquires in Ireland, who would sooner admit a bare-foot into their back-door and hear his tale of woe, than would many of the dissenting classes, of so-called followers of the meek and lowly Jesus. Why is it so? Simply this, not because these lords and gentlemen were Christians, but because they were not in danger of losing a standing which a worldly government had given them, by so doing, while the Dissenter, a step lower in worldly honor, without sufficient vital piety to fall back upon, must keep the respectable standing that he had, or he was lost forever.

And before closing these pages, duty requires to correct statements which have been made by many of the misjudging class of Irish who read the first volume, and have said that I had no opportunity to give a true account of the character of the people there, because I mingled with none but the lower classes – I give the following illustrations: – This is a mistake wholly and entirely. I did not make long visits with the higher orders except in few cases, not because I was not treated with all the courtesy and attention that vanity would require by some of these, but because my message was to the poor; and the attentions of the great were not recorded for many reasons, among which some of the most prominent are, that many such persons do not wish to read their names on the random pages of an unpretending tourist, or a vain smattering one; and if their vanity could be fed, the greater caution should be used to withhold flattery, for they are in no need of compliments; and beside, they have only done what they could easily do without sacrifice, and are required by the common claims of civility to strangers, as well as by the higher requirements of the gospel, to do.

And, again, what traveler who has whirled through that island on a coach, and who, in his own country was scarcely known, beyond his humble seat in the church or chapel where he was wont to sit, but has carefully wrapped a complimentary card, given by a titled gentleman, to a dinner, to show to his family, to the third, and probably fourth generation, of the great honor bestowed on him. And in conclusion, on this part of the subject, let it be said, that access was gained to every class of people in Ireland, some 'by hook and by crook,' and others by an abundant entrance, and by a greater part of them was I treated with more courtesy than by those a notch or two below, in worldly standing.

The old hackneyed story of popery in Ireland has been so turned and twisted that every side has been seen – nothing new can be said about it. There it stands, its principles are well known, its superstitions and persecuting character, its idolatries, and all its trimming and trappings, are the same in essence, as when Queen Elizabeth put her anathemas forth against its creeds and practice; and with all her errors she maintains a few principles and practices which it would be well for her more Bible neighbors to imitate. Her great ones are more accessible; the poor of their own class, or of any other, are not kept at such an awful distance; the stranger is seldom frowned coolly from their door; to them there appears to be a sacredness in the very word with which they would not trifle; the question is not, is he or she 'respectable,' but is he a stranger; if so, then hospitality must be used without grudging. In the mountains, and sea-coast parts, it has ever been the custom to set the cabin door open at night, and keep up a fire on the hearth, that the wayfaring man, and the lone stranger, should he be benighted, could see by the light that there is welcome for him, and if they have but one bed, the family get up and give it to the stranger, sitting up, and having the fire kept bright through the night. This has been done for me, without knowing or asking whether I was Turk or Christian; and were I again to walk over that country, and be out at nightfall in storm or peril, as has been my lot, and come in sight of two castle-towers, one a Roman and the other a Protestant owner; and were the former a mile beyond, my difficult way would be made to that, knowing that when the porter should tell the master a stranger was at the gate, he would say, 'Welcome the stranger in for the night, or from the storm.' The Protestant might do the same, but there would be a doubt. His answer would probably be, 'A stranger! How comes a stranger here at this late hour? Tell him we do not admit persons into our house unless we know them'. Christian reader, this is one strong reason why you should admit them, because you do not know them.

The Catholics are much more humble in their demeanor, and certainly much more hospitable and obliging in all respects, as a people. They are more self-denying, will sacrifice their own comforts for the afflicted, more readily will they attend their places of worship, clothed or unclothed, and beggars take as high a place often in the chapel, as the rich man; the gold ring and costly apparel, is not honored here, as in the Protestant and dissenting churches; and it is remarked that when any turn to the Protestant faith, they never lose that condescension, nor put on those pretenses of worldly respectability, as their Protestant brethren do.

A little for the Relief Officers at parting. To those who have been intrusted with money for the poor, and have been bountifully paid for the care of the loan put in your hands, if you have done by the starving poor, as you would that they should do unto you in like circumstances – if you have given the same quality and quantity of bread, that you should be willing to receive and eat – if you have never sent a starving one empty away, when you had it by you, because the case would be disturbed – if dinners and toasts have not drained any money that belonged to the poor, then 'well done, good and faithful servant;' and if you have may you be forgiven, and never be left 'to feel the hunger.' My lot was to be once in a house where a sumptuous feast was held among this class of laborers, and that was in the midst of desolation and death. They 'tarried,' to speak modestly, a little too long at the wine that night, and drank toasts, which, if they honored the Queen, did little credit to men in their station, and in their responsible work. But I have seen and handled the 'black bread' for months, and have told the story. I have seen many sent from the relief, on days of giving it out, without a mouthful, and have not a doubt but many died in consequence of this, when they should and might have been fed.

Time will not allow of dwelling on these cases; but one which was vividly impressed, and particularly marked at the time, may serve as a specimen. Going out one cold day in a bleak waste on the coast, I met a pitiful old man in hunger and tatters, with a child on his back, almost entirely naked, and to appearance in the last stages of starvation; whether his naked legs had been scratched, or whether the cold had affected them I knew not, but the blood was in small streams in different places, and the sight was a horrid one. The old man was interrogated as to why he took such an object into sight, upon the street. He answered that he lived seven miles off, and was afraid the child would die in the cabin, with two little children he had left starving, and he had come to get the bit of meal, as it was the day he heard that the relief was giving out. The officer told him he had not time to enter his name on the book, and he was sent away in that condition; a penny or two was given him, for which he expressed the greatest gratitude; this was on Wednesday or Thursday. The case was mentioned to the officer, and he was entreated not to send such objects away, especially when the distance was so great.

The next Saturday, on my way from the house where the relieving-officer was stationed, we saw an old man creeping slowly in a bending posture upon the road, and the boy was asked to stop the car. The same old man looked up and recognized me. I did not know him, but his overwhelming thanks for the little that was given him that day, called to mind the circumstance; and, inquiring where the child was, he said the three were left in the cabin, and had not taken a 'sup nor a bit' since yesterday morning, and he was afraid some of them would be dead upon the hearth when he returned. The relieving-officer had told him to come on Saturday, and his name should be on the book, he had waited without scarcely eating a mouthful till then, and was so weak he could not carry the child, and had crept the seven miles to get the meal, and was sent away with a promise to wait till the next Tuesday, and come and have his name on the books. This poor man had not a penny nor a mouthful of food, and he said tremulously, 'I must go home and die on the hairth with the hungry ones.' The mother had starved to death. He was given money to purchase seven pounds of meal; he first clasped his old emaciated hands, fell upon his knees, looked up to heaven and thanked the good God, then me, when the boy was so struck with his glaring eyes, and painful looks, that he turned aside and said, 'let us get away.' The old man kept on his knees, walking on them, pausing and looking up to heaven; and thinking myself that seven pounds would not keep four scarcely in existence till Tuesday, we stopped till he came upon his knees to the car; he was given money enough to purchase as much more; when, for a few moments, I feared that he would die on the path. His age, exhaustion by hunger, and the feelings of a father, together with the sudden change, from despair to hope, all were so powerful, that with his hands clasped, clinching the pennies, and standing upon his knees, he fell upon his face, and for some time remained there; he was finally restored to his knees, and the last glimpse we had of this picture of living death, he was behind us on the path, descending a hill upon his knees.

What his destiny was, I never knew; but the relieving-officer expressed no feelings of compunction when told of it some time after, nor did he know whether he had applied again. 'If he died, what then?' was the answer. This solitary case is only a specimen of, to say the least, hundreds who might have been saved had these stewards applied the funds where most needed. Those who were obliged to walk miles, and lie out over night upon the highway-side, were sent back to come again, while those who lived nearest, had the most strength, and could clamor the loudest for their rights, were soonest supplied.

This relieving-officer was an Irishman, and though among some of these there was great compassion and long continued, yet as a whole the English were much more so; and had they, without being advised or influenced in the least by the Irish landlords and Irish relieving-officers, taken their own course, much better management of funds and better management for the suffering would have followed. The English were unused to such sights as Ireland in her best times presents, besides they never had oppressed these poor ones, while the rich, powerful Irish, like our slaveholders in the United States, had long held them writhing in their grasp, some of them beside had been too lavish, their means for sporting and pleasure were lessening, and why not take their share of what they wanted, while it was in their hands. The English officers, entirely unacquainted even with the location of distressed districts, till, for the first time, their eyes were saluted with these frightful sights, would certainly be led to apply means, when and where more experienced ones should direct.

The Irish landlords too, had another strong temptation. They had many comfortable farmers, who till the Famine, had not only paid them good rent, but had turned the worst soil into beautiful fields. They must either abide on the land and pay less rent, or none at all, till the Famine ceased, or they must emigrate. Now a few hundred pounds would keep these tenants on their feet, and pay the landlord. And if these landlords had not before been influenced by the grace of God to do justice, it cannot be expected in this peculiar crisis they should suddenly be transformed to act so against their own worldly good. Who would trust a dog with his dinner if the dog be hungry? These are not random strokes made to finish a book, nor to gratify a splenetic sourness – particular prejudices have not been the spring of motion in this work; but being flung into all and every position, how could I but see all and everything that fell in my way? In the worst districts my tarry was generally the longest, and in some cases I literally carried out the precept, 'Into whatever house ye enter there abide and thence depart,' where the most information could be gained, and the family who invited me were able to supply all needful things, and had urged the visit, however protracted it might be; and in the face and eyes of all sincerity on their part, they had been taken at their word, and though the blarney grew thinner and weaker, yet I had long since accustomed my palate to bread without butter or honey, and potatoes without gravy or salt.

Ireland possesses an ingredient in her composition, beyond all other nations – an elasticity of such strength, that however weighty the depressing power may be, she returns to her level with greater velocity than any people whatever, when the force is removed. Then arise to her help; let every Protestant and Dissenter put on the whole armor; let them together cast tithes and *regium donums* 'to the moles and to the bats,' and stand out in the whole panoply of the gospel; then indeed will they appear terrible as an army with banners; let their worldly respectability be laid aside for the honor that comes from God; let them do as Christ did, condescend to men of low estate.[4] Who can tell, if the professed church of Christ, of all denominations should do her first work there, but that a loophole would be made, through which government might look beyond the dark cloud that has covered her reign over that island, and joyfully say, 'Live, for I have found a ransom!' For though government now holds the church in her hands, could she do so if the church was moved by an Almighty power? God now suffers, but does he propel? Is not the machinery of the church there one of the sought-out-inventions, which never emanated from the uprightness of God?[5] See to it, see to it, and then talk with success of the idolatries of popery.

The dark night had come, my trunk was packed, and the vessel was in readiness that was to bear me away. When I entered that pretty isle in June, 1844, all was green and sunny without, water, earth, and sky all united to say this is indeed a pleasant spot, but why I had come to it I knew not, and what was my work had not been told me; step by step the voice had been 'onward,' trust and obey – obey and trust. The ground had been traversed, and in tempest and darkness my way was made to the packet, on the Liffey, with one solitary Quaker, who was compelled to hurry me among the tumultuous crowd without time to say Farewell.[6] A few friends had assembled to meet me there, who had been tried ones from the beginning, but so great was the crowd, and so dark was the night, they found me not.[7]

The spires of Dublin could not be seen, and I was glad – I was glad that no warm hands could greet me; and above all and over all, I was glad that the poor could not find me; for them I had labored, and their blessing was mine, that was a rich reward; and when my heart shall cease to feel for their sufferings may my tongue cleave to the roof of my mouth.[8]

THEY THAT SOW IN TEARS SHALL REAP IN JOY.[9]

Sow thy seed, there is need, never be weary,
Morning and evening withhold not thine hand;
By the side of all waters let faith and hope cheer thee,
Where the blessing may rest is not thine to command.

Do thy best, leave the rest, while the day serveth –
Night will assuredly overtake noon;
Work with thy brother, while he thine arm nerveth,
Without him, or for him, if holding back soon.

As the grain, oft in pain, doubt, care, and sadness,
The husbandman needs must commit to the soil,
Long to struggle with darkness and death, if in gladness
He may hope ere to reap the new harvest from toil.

Sow they seed, there is need, never mind sorrow,
Disappointment is not what it seems to thee now;
Tears, if but touched by one heavenly ray, borrow
A glory that spans all, – the bright promised bow!

NOTES

NOTES TO INTRODUCTION BY MAUREEN MURPHY

1. Nicholson received a grant of twelve testaments for distribution in the south and west in 1845. In 1846 she received a grant of one Bible and fourteen testaments. 'Grants to individuals'. *Hibernian Bible Society annual report (1842-1849)*. Dublin, 1849.

2. 'Warning out', apparently some sort of harassment, was declared illegal in 1817 (*Chelsea*, 8).

3. Nicholson may be referring to Paul's Letter to Titus 11:4-5. I Timothy 11:1-10 also speaks to the belief that a woman's salvation depends on her faithful discharge of her Christian duties to her family and to her home.

4. The Temperance Society of Chelsea was not organized until 1829 (*Chelsea*, 55); however, temperance might have been a feature of the 'Christian movement' of the Revd Frederick Plummer which reached Chelsea in 1811 (*Chelsea*, 59).

5. Nicholson's parents died in 1830 and 1837; Norman Nicholson died in 1841. While testimonies in *Nature's Own Book* speak of living with Mrs Nicholson and her family, and while she lamented the loss of a silver spoon which 'had an indenture made by an agonized child when in the act of taking medicine' (*Annals*, 171), there are no records of children born to Asenath and Norman Nicholson.

6. Nicholson is careful to point out that she did not alter her account of her 1844-45 travels in light of later events but that the facts themselves of that journey were enough to predict disaster (*Welcome*, vii).

7. A white coffin or coffin of white boards was the mark of a decent burial. Maurya's last speech in *Riders to the Sea* concludes 'Bartley will have a fine coffin out of the white boards and a deep grave surely. What more can we want than that?' (Synge, 27).

8. F.J. Davis's painting 'The State Ballroom, St Patrick's Hall, Dublin Castle', depicts a dance hosted by the Lord Lieutenant and Lady Clarendon. Christina Kennedy, in her notes about the picture in *America's Eye: Irish Paintings from the Collection of Brian P. Burns*, points out the difference between the Davis painting and an engraving published in *The Illustrated London News* (11 August 1849) indicating that there was extensive redecorating of the ballroom during the Famine years in preparation for the visit of Queen Victoria (Dalsimer, 102).

NOTES TO THE INTRODUCTION TO THE AMERICAN EDITION

1. The title of Nicholson's first book about Ireland was *Ireland's Welcome to the Stranger; or, An Excursion through Ireland in 1844 and 1845 for the purpose of personally investigating the condition of the poor*. Printed by Richard Webb

in Dublin in 1847, the book was published in London by Gilpin. Baker and Scribner published the American edition in the same year. A selection from *Ireland's Welcome to the Stranger* was published in the *Friends' Weekly Intelligencer* in 1847 (318).

2. Nicholson refers to money arriving from New York (*Annals*, 40) in December 1846 when she describes 'the man of the house' (James Webb) bringing her a parcel with cash. Nicholson does not identify her benefactor, nor is it clear whether the money came through the Central Relief Committee Office.

3. *Annals of the Famine in Ireland* appeared first as Part II of Nicholson's *Lights and Shades of Ireland*. See Editor's Note for the history of the text (p.18).

4. J. L. is probably Rev. Joshua Leavitt (1794-1873), editor of *The Emancipator.*

NOTES TO THE PREFACE

1. Nicholson arrived in Ireland for her first visit on 26 June 1844, and stayed until 9 August 1845, when she left for Scotland. She was back in Derry by May 1846 (*Lights*, 201) and stayed in Ireland until 4 September 1848. Her travels were unique not only for the length of time she spent in Ireland but also for her habit of staying among the poor in areas of the west seldom visited by travellers.

NOTES TO CHAPTER I

1. Nicholson alludes to the parable of the Good Samaritan, Luke 10:23-37.

2. While Nicholson is probably talking about accounting for one's stewardship at the Last Judgment, she is also warning landlords that their mortal day of reckoning was fast approaching, for she believed that a complete reform of the land system was both required and inevitable.

3. Nicholson's mention of a struggle could be a reference to one or another of two millenarian prophecies, the Prophecy of Columcille and Pastorini's Prophecy, that circulated in the Irish countryside in the nineteenth century telling of a final Armageddon at which time the Catholic Gaels would be victorious. S.J. Connolly describes the millenarian movement as the Catholic lower class counterpart to the middle class Repeal movement in his essay, 'The Great Famine and Irish Politics' (Póirtéir, *Echoes*, 38). Christopher Morash discusses the millenarian paradigm in his Introduction to *The Hungry Voice* (Morash, 22). Allusions to the prophecies appear in Antony Raftery's poems describing contemporary historical events: 'The White Boys', 'The Catholic Rent', 'The Galway Election', 'O'Connell's Victory', 'Barney Richards', 'The Dispute with the Bush', 'The Cause a Pleading', and 'How Long has it been Said?' In Raftery's poems, O'Connell's success is often linked with the fulfilment of the prophecies. While O'Connell rejected any form of violence, lines from 'The Galway Election' link him with a final apocalyptic victory:

Ach d'iompuigh an rota, ní sásadh dúinn aon rud, Gan seasamh [le] chéile 's na Sasanaigh 'claoidh (Hyde, 262) (But the wheel has turned, and there is no satisfying us without standing together and destroying the Sassanach.)

4. Nicholson travelled through Connemara and through western Mayo to Achill; however, her 1844-45 visit concentrated on conditions in rural Munster.

5. Nicholson visited Bantry in February 1845. Father Mathew had advised her: 'If you wish to seek out the poor, go to Bantry, there you will see misery in all and in every form.' I took his advice, went to Bantry, and there found a wild, dark, sea-port, with cabins built up on the rocks and hills, having the most antiquated and forlorn appearance of any town I had seen' (*Welcome*, 259).

   While in Bantry, Nicholson visited the home of poor Irish that she likened to an African *kraal*: 'Looking in, I saw a pile of dirty broken straw, which served for a bed for both family and pigs, not a chair, table or pane of glass, and no spot to sit except upon the straw in one corner, without sitting in mud and manure. On the whole, it was the most revolting picture my eyes ever beheld, and I prayed that they might never behold the like again' (*Welcome*, 260).

6. The travel writers Mr and Mrs Samuel Hall observed this 'hungry season' when they travelled in Ireland in 1841. 'A very limited portion of land, a few days of labour, and a small amount of manure, will create a stock upon which a family may exist for twelve months: too generally, indeed, the periods between exhausting the old stock and digging the new are seasons of great want, if not absolute famine' (Hall, I 82; Killen, 16).

7. Nicholson observed both stoic acceptance in the patient suffering of the Irish poor as well as their recognition that the present system would have to change.

8. Mary Helen Thuente, who studied the rise of Irish literary nationalism in *The Harp Restrung*, suggests that these unidentified lines were written in imitation of Thomas Moore.

9. Richard Webb wrote a similar observation from Erris in his letter of 15 May 1847 to the Central Relief Committee in Dublin: 'During my stay of about ten days in the barony of Erris – although it was not uncommon to hear of sheep, cows, and even horses being stolen, killed and eaten by the famishing people – I heard of no instance of highway robbery or personal violence upon land' (*Transactions*, 200). Webb did, however, report instances of boats being surrounded and crews being overpowered and robbed of provisions.

10. The image of a wheel reversing the positions of the strong and the weak was popular in the folk mind. It appears in Raftery's poems. Lady Gregory used it in her plays *The Rising of the Moon* and *The White Cockade*.

11. Nicholson's father was descended from Thomas and Grace Hatch of Dorchester, Yarmouth and Barnstable, Massachusetts (Hatch-Hale, 9).

NOTES TO CHAPTER II

1. Nicholson paraphrases Luke 22:42, 'Father, if You are willing, remove this cup from me, nevertheless, not my will but Yours be done.' Nicholson frequently describes herself as one on a divinely appointed mission.

2. Luke 24:31,32 describes the disciples after Jesus appeared at Emmaus.

3. In the 1846 Glasgow edition of *Nature's Own Book*, Nicholson praises Indian meal. 'There is no gruel that the taste and stomach will so long relish as that made of the American Indian meal' (*Nature*, 1846, 84). While Indian corn is

associated with the Great Famine, E. Margaret Crawford points out in her essay 'Food and Famine' that Indian meal had been introduced in Ireland before the Famine (Póirtéir, *Echoes*, 63). Charles E. Trevelyan, Assistant Secretary to the Treasury, explained in *The Irish Crisis*, his analysis of the Famine, that Indian corn was introduced because it was a food that would not interfere with the home markets (Trevelyan in Killen, 177).

4. Nicholson speaks about the need to properly prepare the Indian meal and explains for that reason she cooked the Indian meal herself for those she fed. In 'Food and Famine', E. Margaret Crawford describes the painful consequences of eating inadequately prepared Indian meal. 'The flint hard grain was sharp and irritating and capable of piercing the intestinal wall. Little wonder it was so unpopular with the Irish who called it "brimstone" on account of its bright yellow colour' (Póirtéir, *Echoes*, 64).

5. This staple of northern Italian cooking is prepared by stirring in one cup of corn meal to three cups of boiling water and simmering the mixture over low heat for about twenty minutes.

6. Nicholson returned to Ireland in the summer of 1846. For a time she stayed in Dublin with Richard Davis Webb and his family at 176 Great Brunswick Street, now Pearse Street. The house has been demolished. When Webb's brother, the linen draper James H. Webb, was out of town, Nicholson looked after his house De Vesci Lodge, which still stands at the corner of Carrick-brennan Road and Upper Mounttown Road (Harrison, 56).

7. Nicholson is probably referring to the seasonal hunger that occurred yearly during the period from when the old potato crop ran out till the new harvest came in. Beyond the 'hungry season' there were famines before the Great Famine. See the list in L.A. Clarkson, 'Conclusion: Famine and Irish History' (Crawford, 220-6).

8. Here Nicholson is picking up on the pejorative 'lazy' used to describe the Irish. In *Ireland's Welcome to the Stranger*, she frequently notices the irony of a people desperate for work called 'lazy'. Kevin Whelan indicates that potato cultivation was considered another mark of Irish laziness. 'There was a prevalent ideological antipathy to the potato as a "lazy root" grown in "lazy beds" by a "lazy people"' (Póirtéir, *Echoes*, 28).

9. Work on one of the public works projects created to provided famine relief, required a ticket from the local relief committee (Daly, 74).

10. This was likely to have been one of the road work projects that was a feature of Irish relief work in 1846.

11. Here, as elsewhere, Nicholson accurately describes the clinical symptoms of starvation (Best, 1408). See Lawrence Geary, 'Famine, Fever and the Bloody Flux' (Póirtéir, *Echoes*, 74-85) and Sir William P. MacArthur, 'Medical History of the Famine' (Edwards, 263-315).

12. Rooms at the back of De Vesci Lodge overlook the old graveyard at Carrick-brennan, Monkstown which is now on the grounds of the Christian Brothers School. Aside from this graveyard, there were no burial grounds in nineteenth-century Kingstown until Deansgrange was opened in 1863 (Pearson, 71).

13. James H. Webb, a linen draper, had premises at 10-12 Cornmarket (*Thom's*, 920).

14. Nicholson may have been reading about the New York Yearly Meeting of the Society of Friends which was held 6 January 1847, at which time money and food were asked for the Irish poor. The letter sent to Jacob Harvey was published in the *New York Tribune* on 4 February 1847. In her study of Quaker relief, *The Largest Amount of Good. Quaker Relief in Ireland 1654-1921,* Helen Hatton says Nicholson was the field agent for the New York Relief Society (Hatton, 136). There was a Friends New York Committee headed by Jacob Harvey and an Irish Relief Committee of New York which listed James Reyburn as Treasurer but there does not appear to be a New York Relief Society.

15. Mary Daly quotes from Elizabeth Smith's diary to demonstrate the rise in the price of food in 1846. Smith's notes give some idea of the worth of £100 in that year. In November 1846 she wrote, 'At present prices it would require 21s. (£1.05) a week to support a labourer and his family; he earns 6s. (30p), 7s. (35p) or 8s. (40p) at the highest.' (Daly, 60).

16. It was Joseph Bewley who wrote to Irish Quakers in the fall of 1846 suggesting that the Friends might organize some form of relief to deal with the Famine crisis (Goodbody, 4). His initiative led to the founding of the Central Relief Committee. The strain of Bewley's work with the Committee cost him his life. He died at fifty-six from an apparent heart attack (Goodbody, 78). On 23 January 1847 the Central Relief Committee opened a soup-shop in Charles Street, Upper Ormond Quay, Dublin. Soup sold for one penny a quart or one and a half pence with bread. Soup was purchased by ticket and tickets could be purchased for distribution. The Charles Street soup-shop produced, on average, 1000 quarts of soup per day (*Transactions*, 53). Charles Street was not the first Quaker soup-shop in Ireland. Friends opened soup-shops in Clonmel, Limerick, Youghal and Waterford by November, 1846 (Goodbody, 28).

17. Hatton contrasts the recipe for Quaker soup with the recipe for the notorious government or Soyer Soup provided for under the Soup Kitchen Act (Hatton, 139-40). See Nicholson's mock heroic description of the reception in Dublin for Soyer Soup (143-4).

18. Maria Waring wrote to her niece Lydia Shackleton warning her to protect herself against infection and not to handle the soup vessels directly when helping in the soup kitchen (Harrison, 43). See the *Illustrated London News* engraving of the Quaker soup-shop (16 January 1847) in Kissane, 81.

19. To convey the depths of her despair at the sight of the poor in line at the Charles Street soup kitchen, Nicholson may have alluded to the lines from *Paradise Lost*: 'Thrice he assay'd and thrice, in spite of scorn,/ Tears such as angels weep burst forth' (Milton, 23).

20. The duration of Nicholson's January – July soup-kitchen corresponded to the Central Relief Committee's Charles-Street operation which ran from 23 January until 15 August 1847.

21. Early in January bread carts were attacked by railway labourers at the corner of Summer Hill and Lower Gardiner Street, and bread shops in Marlborough Street and Eden Quay. *Illustrated London News* (16 January 1847; Kissane, 57). Nicholson avoided bread shops saying there was no fear of violence but 'dreadful importuning' (42, 45).

22. According to *Thom's Dublin Directory for 1847*, there were ten tenements and nine vacant houses in 1847 (672). There were sixteen coffin-makers or undertakers including two women undertakers: Anne Kenny and Mary Reed, and one woman coffin-maker, Elizabeth Connolly, at numbers 2, 22 and 44 Cook Street.

23. In his Journal, Alfred Webb recalled that Nicholson sometimes took his brother Richard and him around Dublin with her (Webb, 125-6). In his biography of Richard Webb, Richard Harrison suggests Nicholson visited the poor of the Liberties with the young Webbs (Harrison, 56).

24. Nicholson left Dublin on 4 September 1848.

25. Nicholson is describing one of the clinical stages of under-nutrition, lowered intellectual capacity (Best, 1408).

26. It is not clear where Nicholson moved when she left De Vesci Lodge. A letter to the Central Relief Committee dated 7 July 1847 gave 45 Hardwicke Street as the return address; however, she describes herself as living in 'a tall house overlooking the Liffey' three floors above the ground with gentlemen's offices below (52). A drawing of Lower Ormonde Quay in 1850 indicates that the tall narrow number 31, the premises of J.J. Clarke, a solicitor, may have been Nicholson's lodging in 1847.

27. Nicholson published an edition of *Nature's Own Book* for private circulation. Printed by Willaim Brown in Glasgow in 1846, this edition included Nicholson's observations about diet in Ireland made during her 1844-45 tour. In a letter to Lydia Shackleton, Maria Waring refers to an untitled second book which seems to have concerned household management or domestic economy (Harrison, 56).

28. Father Mathew used similar language in one of his charity sermons: 'Were I permitted to rouse the men of wealth from their dreams of avarice, the ladies of fashion from their silken lethargy, would they permit me to conduct them for one day where they ought to go every day and where they should esteem it a high privilege to be allowed to go – to the abode of pain and sorrow, to the squalid receptacle of the agonized and the dying – I would answer for their hearts' (Augustine, 452).

29. A Mrs Ethelinda Warren was listed in *Thom's* as owner of 45 Hardwicke Street. Nicholson was also friendly with an O'Dowda family (*Lights*, 52). The *Thom's* lists a John J. O'Dowda Esq. at 55 Lower Sackville Street (*Thom's*, 889). Her friend Peter Kelly, the Ballina solicitor, had premises at 36 Upper Dominick Street (*Thom's*, 861).

30. The Dublin Central Relief Committee and its London counterpart sent an 'address' to members of the Society of Friends in Ireland and England on 30 November 1846 (Goodbody, 8).

31. There were corresponding Committees to the Dublin Central Relief Committee in Cork, Limerick, Waterford and Clonmel.

32. Nicholson's access to the correspondence of the Central Relief Committee is a measure of her close relationship with Dublin Quakers. Extracts from the American correspondence, including Harvey's letter to Cope, were published in *Transactions of the Central Relief Committee of the Society of Friends During the Famine in Ireland in 1846 and 1847* (1852). The *Transactions* were

printed by Nicholson's friend Richard D. Webb. Nicholson quotes a letter from Cope and other Philadelphia members of the Society of Friends: 'In consequence of a letter addressed by Jacob Harvey of New York to Thomas P. Cope containing certain printed sheets in relation to the suffering poor of your island, and the proceedings of Friends in Dublin for their relief; a meeting of Friends of this city was held at the Mulberry Street House on the 29th instant, at which committees were appointed to make collections in aid of your benevolent efforts, and also a committee composed of ourselves to receive and forward such funds as might be collected and to correspond on the subject' (*Transactions*, 220).

According to the *Transactions*, the meeting was held on 29 December 1846 (220). The Mulberry Street House was not a Quaker meeting house; it was the African School which opened at 2 Mulberry Street in 1820. That the meeting was held at the African school and not at meeting house suggests this was not a Quaker activity though it had the support of individual Quakers.

33. The list printed in *The New York Tribune* for 18 January 1847 gives some idea of the range of response to the call for aid.

34. The British Association for the Relief of the Extreme Distress in the Remote Parishes of Ireland and Scotland was a private relief organization whose aim was to aid the poor '... who are beyond the reach of the government' with grants of food, fuel and clothing'. The Association was founded on 1 January 1847 by London businessmen; Thomas Baring was its first Chairman. They were advised by Irish Friends: Jonathan Pim, Secretary of the Dublin CRC, and J.J. Cummins of the Cork Committee (Woodham-Smith, 169).

35. This is probably the General Irish Relief Committee of the City of New York. Jacob Harvey's letter of 28 December 1846 to Jonathan Pim mentions printing a circular for New York Friends and sending notices to the papers calling for local subscriptions to the Relief Fund. Harvey worked with Bishop John Hughes who instructed his priests to ask for aid from the altar (*Transactions*, 217). By the middle of January money was coming in from New Yorkers. *The New York Tribune* for 18 January 1847 lists individual contributions by wards.

36. Nicholson refers to Exodus 41:1-28: Joseph's interpretation of Pharaoh's dream of an approaching famine.

37. The belief that the Famine was a judgment is called providentialism and, according to James S. Donnelly's essay, 'Mass Evictions and the Geat Famine', the belief that the Famine was sent by God to punish idolatrous Catholics was widespread among British politicians including Charles Trevelyan who was chiefly responsible for Famine relief policy. His *Irish Crisis* (1848) reflects the ideology of providentialism (Póirtéir, 171). Folklore accounts suggest that the Irish too regarded it as a judgment or punishment. See Edwards, 395; Póirtéir, *Echoes*, 34-49.

38. Nicholson's position was that the Famine was man-made and that better-managed relief efforts, more compassionate and timely government intervention, prohibition of food export and especially diversion of grain for distilling, would have saved thousands. For Nicholson, a permanent solution for Ireland's poor would be a reformed land system with peasant proprietorship and increased opportunities for employment.

NOTES TO CHAPTER III

1. These lines have the cadence of a hymn.

2. Nicholson quotes the well-known lines from Psalm 23:4: 'Yea, though I walk through the valley of the shadow of death, I will fear no evil.'

3. Nicholson was critical of government relief agencies that insisted that paperwork be completed before the poor could be fed (51). Other contemporary reports support Nicholson's charges. The *Freeman's Journal* (24 April 1847) reported that the First Report of the Irish Poor Relief Commissioners indicated since the Temporary Relief Act became law, that they had distributed not food but fourteen tons of paper (Killen, 135). A year later, the *Dublin Weekly Register* (29 April 1848) carried an account of the Revd Mr Henry of Bunenadden, Sligo, indicting the Guardians of the Poor-law in Boyle for neglect in the deaths of a Mrs Kilkenny and her child after several unsuccessful applications for relief (Killen, 186).

4. Nicholson credits Catholicism with inculcating a spirit of patient suffering among the Irish poor. At the same time here, as in other passages, Nicholson accurately describes the clinical symptoms of starvation which include apathy.

5. In January 1847 a half crown (2s. 6 or $12\frac{1}{2}$p) bought one stone of Indian meal or wheaten meal.

6. See the text of Nicholson's letter in the Introduction (p. 15).

7. Nicholson may refer to the designation of the Messiah as 'Comforter' and to the passage from the Beatitudes (Matthew 5:4) that promises comfort to those who mourn: 'Happy are those who mourn for they shall be comforted'.

8. Rules about cleanliness including frequent bathing were a feature of Nicholson's Grahamite boarding-houses (*Nature's Own Book*, 19-20).

9. Richard Webb was printing the sheets for *Ireland's Welcome to the Stranger*. The Preface is dated 10 June 1847, Dublin.

10. Among the Famine legends collected by the Irish Folklore Commision and quoted in Roger McHugh's 'The Famine in Irish Oral Tradition' are versions of the legend of hospitality rewarded with an inexhaustible supply of food: meal, potatoes or milk (Edwards, 404-06). See also Póirtéir, *Echoes* 260-79.

11. William Forster volunteered his services to the London Committee at their 25 November 1846 meeting. His experience working with soup kitchens among the poor of Norwich made him a valuable adviser to Irish and English Quakers working with Famine relief. Forster went on a four and a half month fact-finding tour of the west. At different times he was joined by other Quakers such as James Tuke and Joseph Crosfield. See excerpts of his report in *Transactions*, 153-60, and Flood's discussion of the Foster family and the Famine. Joseph Crosfield, a Liverpool Quaker, travelled with Forster (Goodbody, 17). Part of Crosfield's report appear in Appendix III of *Transactions*, 145-7.

12. James Hack Tuke, a Quaker from York whose family pioneered in the humane treatment of the insane, worked with the Central Relief Committee for relief of the poor and later for emigration reform (Hatton, 138). Tuke travelled in the west of Ireland with William Forster during 1846-47 and returned later for a second tour that was the subject of his *A Visit to Connaught in the Autumn of 1847*. The book was controversial because Tuke condemned the evictions on

Achill on lands which belonged to Sir Richard O'Donnell of Newport. Jonathan Pim defended O'Donnell who was working with the CRC saying that the land had been in the Chancery Court for nineteen years and that O'Donnell was not responsible. The CRC dissociated themselves from Tuke's book (Hatton, 187). Nicholson took Tuke's side. When she met Tuke at Samuel Bourne's home in Rosport and travelled with him from Rosport to Ballina in September or October of 1847, she characterized his report as a 'candid recital' and predicted that it would 'live despite all opposition' (96). See *Transactions*, 147-53, 204-07. Marcus Goodbody, a corresponding member of the CRC, was a miller from Clara. He told the govenment that government-purchased food sold at a reduced price to the poor did not interfere with private enterprise. He warned that the demand for food was underestimated by the government and that it was necesssary to provide food for the poor 'on any terms' (Woodham-Smith, 167). William Dillwyn Sims's report was published by the London Friends in 1847 (Goodbody, 25). William Todhunter headed two Famine-related projects for the CRC: the distribution of seeds (*Transactions*, 385-6) and the revitalization of the fishing industry (*Transactions*, 406-14). His work for the fishing involved spending three months on the trawler *Erne* off the west coast as far north as Blacksod Bay and south to the bays of Kerry and west Cork. Another victim of overwork in the cause of Famine relief, Todhunter died at forty-six (Goodbody, 28).

13. We have William Bennett's *Narrative of a recent journey of Six Weeks in Ireland in connexion with the subject of supplying small seed to some of the remoter districts with current observations of the depressed circumstances of the people, and the means presented for the permanent improvement of their social condition* to thank for a rare contemporary account of Nicholson. Part of Bennett's account appears in *Transactions*, 160-8.

14. The lack of provision for outdoor relief under the terms of the 1847 Temporary Relief Act sent the poor to the union workhouses which were not designed to serve as the major relief provider, so they were inadequate to meet the demand. See map in Kissane (91) for the number of workhouses in 1847, 1849.

15. Nicholson does not further identify the school. There is a donation of $1.34 from the boys of a School No. 3 in New York's Tenth Ward on the lower east side in the *Report of the general Irish relief committee* (1849). The few barrels were the five barrels of meal that arrived for Nicholson on the *Macedonia* in July 1847. See the *Illustrated London News* (7 August 1847) for an engraving of the *Macedonia*.

16. Nicholson's allusion is to Mark 12:42: 'And there came a certain poor widow, and she threw in two mites.' This is one of a number of instances where Nicholson praises the real generosity of the poor to the suffering Irish.

17. It is likely that this school was the Presentation School at George's Hill founded in 1789.

18. Nicholson was not the only one to complain about the arbitrary decisions of the CRC. Father Mathew's biographer suggests that the CRC's Cork counterpart, the Cork Relief Committee, was not always cooperative with Father Mathew's relief efforts (Augustine, 416).

19. Having investigated claims of misappropriations of relief funds for the CRC in

Mayo in May 1847, Richard Webb would have been well-placed to represent Nicholson's application to the CRC.

20. *Thom's* lists Mrs Phepoe as the Mother Superior of the George's Hill Presentation convent in 1847 (*Thom's*, 47).

21. *Thom's* lists the City of Dublin Steam Packet Company's Belfast service as departing every Tuesday and returning from Belfast every Thursday (442). July 6th fell on Tuesday in 1847.

22. *Thom's* lists a Revd John Gregg, 67 Lower Gardiner Street, as chaplain of Trinity Church (*Thom's*, 302).

23. The Belfast Ladies' Relief Association for Connaught was organized by Dr John Edgar, the Belfast temperance advocate (Luddy, 187).

24. Nicholson may be referring to the Ladies' Industrial School founded in 1847 (McNeill, 292). They also started infants' school in the Belfast poor-house (McNeill, 265).

25. Dr Edgar established the Connaught Industrial Schools with the support of the Belfast Ladies' Association for Connaught. He received a grant for 500 pounds from the CRC in response to a Ladies' Association application for aid made in May 1848 (*Transactions*, 436). By 1850 thirty-two Connaught schools earned 1000 pounds per year (Hatton, 186). There were thirty-two schoolmistresses who employed more than 2000 poor girls and women (Luddy, 187). Nicholson mentions that she visited one of these schools on Samuel Bourne's estate in Rosport, Mayo, in 1848 (98).

26. The phrase 'hewing of wood and drawing of water' is from Joshua 9:21: 'But all the princes said unto them, Let them live; but let them be hewers of wood and drawers of water unto all the congregation; as the princes had promised them.'

27. Maria Webb was Richard Davis Webb's cousin. He described her to the American abolitionist Maria Weston Chapman in his letter of 13 October 1846 as 'a very good woman, intensely evangelical' (Webb, MA 1.2.v.16.p.109).

28. Mary Ann McCracken (1770-1860) was a member of a distinguished Belfast family. Her grandfather founded the *Belfast Newsletter* in 1737; her brother Henry Joy McCracken was hanged for his part in the 1798 Rising in Antrim. Her life involved social causes and the preservation of Irish cultural tradition: Irish music and the Irish language. She would have been seventy-seven in 1847 when Nicholson was in Belfast.

29. William Butler was the Inspecting Officer of the Electoral District of Belmullet and Binghamstown between May 1846 and September 1847. The 'Address of Thanks' from the Erris Relief Committee, published in the *Trawley Herald and Sligo Intelligencer* (16 September 1847), praised Butler's temper, energy and intelligence. This is not the same William Butler that Woodham-Smith describes witnessing the evictions in Kilrush (368).

30. Nicholas Grimshaw built a mill in Whitehouse in 1779 for spinning cotton thread (McNeill, 29).

31. Mrs Susan Hewetson received a grant of ten pounds for female employment from the CRC on 13 January 1847 (*Extracts*, 53).

32. Nicholson reports that Mr Hewetson had been an overseer in the Board of Works during the first season of the Famine. It does not appear that he was the

same Hewetson as Deputy Commissary General Hewetson who was responsible for the Indian meal depot at Cork. Deputy Hewetson's correspondence with Trevelyan warned of starvation if the government allowed grain to leave the country to pay rent and if they permitted speculation in grain by merchants (Woodham-Smith, 477; Augustine, 394, 412).

33. Proverbs 3:10-31 speaks of the virtuous prudent wife. Nicholson refers to Proverbs 31:15: 'She riseth also while it is yet night, and giveth meat to her household, and a portion to her maidens.'

34. Nicholson's description recalls Edmund Spenser's description of the starving Irish in *A View of the Present State of Ireland* (1596): 'Out of every corner of the woods and glens they came creeping forth upon their hands, for their legs could not bear them. They looked anatomies of death, they spake like ghosts crying out of their graves' (Spenser, 104). Both Spenser and Nicholson describe a condition in the severely undernourished when the loss of fat is partially replaced by water causing edema or anascarca, dropsy. In addition, lower calcium absorption results in osteoporosis or osteomalacia (Best, 1408). See also Laurence M. Geary, 'Famine, Fever and the Bloody Flux,' Póirtéir, *Echoes*, 74-85; Sir William P. MacArthur, 'Medical History of the Famine,' Edwards, 263-315.

35. Nicholson refers to the Bishop of the Diocese of Raphoe the Rt Revd Patrick McGettigan. She would have had more in common with the neighbouring Bishop of Derry, the Rt Revd Edward Maginn, who was a strong advocate of temperance.

36. George Augustus, Lord Hill (1801-79) was generally regarded as an improving landlord. His *Facts from Gweedore* went to three editions: 1845, 1846, 1854. Tuke contrasts Hill's efforts to improve conditions for his tenants with the neglect of the neighbouring estate by the Marquis of Conynham (Tuke, 54-55).

37. Rundale is a method of distributing land within a townland so that holders shared different qualities of land equally. In practical terms, it meant landholders cultivated small scattered plots. Lord Hill believed that there could be no improvement in the condition of the tenants in rural Ireland as long as the Rundale system existed and he took measures to eradicate the Rundale tradition at Gweedore. He included a map in *Facts from Gweedore* showing the land with the Rundale system and after their consolidation.

38. Mary Daly has pointed out that resident landlords were essential to local relief. Their ability to propose projects, to apply and to lobby for government grants were key factors in securing public works funds for local employment (Daly, 84).

39. Hill described the practice in Mayo (Hill, 17). Kevin Danaher mentions the custom of fastening the harrow to the pony's tail in his study of rural life, *In Ireland Long Ago*: 'there evidence to show that, in backward places, horses were tackled to plows and harrows by the simple expedient of tying a trace to their tails. This was forbidded by law and gradually died out' (Danaher, 85).

40. M'Kye's list appears in *Facts from Gweedore* (Hill, 12). See Killen, 29. In Hill's 1854 edition of *Facts*, he supplies a list of supplies available through his store in Bunbeg, Gweedore.

NOTES TO CHAPTER IV

1. Nicholson quotes from James MacPherson's *Poems of Ossian* (1765), a telling of the story of Oisín based on Scottish Fenian ballad tradition, which influenced early nineteenth century British poets.

2. David, the son of Jesse, was sent by his father to the army where he accepted the challenge to fight Goliath (1Samuel 17:15).

3. Nicholson's quote reflects the attitude on the part of some that Irish was a language of poverty.

4. Elizabeth Malcolm discusses the well-organized poitín trade in nineteenth century Donegal in *Ireland Sober, Ireland Free* (Malcolm 34-35). See also Connell, 'Illicit Distillation: a Peasant Industry'.

5. Nicholson realized that to break up the Rundale clachan or village was to destroy the social fabric of Irish rural life. The passage about dancing at intervals is quoted directly from Hill's *Facts from Gweedore* (Hill, 40-1).

6. Matthew 9:16. Jesus said when he was rebuked for eating with the publicans and sinners, 'And indeed I did not come to call the righteous.'

7. Bennett gave Charlotte Forster five pounds from the Ladies' Association, London (Bennett, 81). He identified her husband Frances Forster as Lord Hill's 'able intelligent agent'. The Forsters lived four miles from Dungloe at Roshine Lodge (Bennett, 82).

8. Nicholson stayed with Valentine Pole Griffith and his family (77). See a letter about Arranmore signed by Griffith and dated Templecrone Glebe, Dungloe, 19 January 1847 (*Transactions*, 189). Bennett said Griffith's residence was Maghery (64).

9. See Nicholson's story of the body of an orphan girl on Achill devoured by dogs (87). The most horrific Famine image, similar accounts appear in other Famine episodes (Hatton, 136; Killen, 148) and in Jeremiah O'Ryan's Famine ballad 'Ireland's Lament: A Poem': 'Shroudless and coffinless they thickly lie / The famish'd dogs devour'd them in their graves' (Morash, 69).

10. According to *Thom's,* James McGhee was the parish priest of Lettermacaward (*Thom's*, 302). He may have been responsible for Arranmore.

11. Nicholson is probably referring to Griffith's curate.

12. This is a paraphrase of Job 3:3, 'May the day perish when I was born'.

13. R.K. Thompson was the Inspecting Chief Officer of the coast guard stationed at Rutland, Donegal (Bennett, 75). Coast guardsmen were often the local relief agents for the Quakers and other charitable organizations.

14. William Bennett proposed to the CRC that he distribute seeds to small farmers in the west (*Transactions*, 40).

15. Nicholson describes Crohy Head near Maghery which has cliffs and caves that are accessible by boat.

16. The lines from Zechariah 8:5 'And the streets of the city shall be full of boys and girls playing in the street thereof' offers the hopeful prospect of a restored Jerusalem that would be stable enough for children to play in its streets.

17. The lines are similar to those in the Ossianic 'Fragments': 'They came on the foe like two rocks falling from the brows of Ardven.'

18. In the spring of 1849 Nicholson was in Herefordshire, England, or on the Isle of Man.

19. The Letter of Paul to Titus 2:5 counselled women 'to be discreet, chaste, keepers of home'.

20. Belfast's Linenhall Library, founded in 1788 by the Belfast Society for Promoting Knowledge, had the United Irishman Thomas Russell as its first librarian. While Nicholson praises the Linenhall for having no fiction, she read Scott with enjoyment (*Loose Papers*, 67).

21. O'Connell was opposed to any Poor-law provision for the able-bodied, but modified his position in view of clergy support for some relief. During debate on the framing of the Poor-law, his slogan 'Repeal of the Union or a Poor-law' reflected his belief that a Parliament dominated by landowner interest would not cripple itself with poor rates (Macintyre, 217).

22. Nicholson also speaks about the burden of the Poor-law rates on the middle class of Ballina (125). Mary Daly describes the increased rates as almost an 'academic exercise' because the relief burden had driven many landholders, particularly small farmers, to bankruptcy or near bankruptcy (Daly, 95).

23. Bishop John MacHale (1791-1881), the 'Lion of the West,' was appointed Archbishop of Tuam in 1834. A nationalist, he advocated land reform and was a staunch supporter of the Irish language. His publications in Irish included a translation of the *Iliad*. In later years, MacHale's differences with Cardinal Cullen weakened his position with the Irish hierarchy.

24. Nicholson stayed with Mrs Margaret Arthur in Newport during her first visit to Ireland (*Welcome*, 430).

25. Nicholson records other episodes of the poor staring through windows: Mrs Hewiston's kitchen, the home of Richard Savage at Achill Sound and another, unidentified, place where the bodies of a mother and child were found under a window (63, 85, 90).

26. By 1849 there was a work-house in Newport, but in 1847 the nearest work-house was the already overcrowded work-house at Castlebar. See Kissane 94-5;100-01.

27. Slater's *Directory of Ireland* (March 1846) lists three Protestant schools in Newport run by the Established Church, the Presbyterians and the Darbyite Conventicle (Ó Móráin, 125).

28. Nicholson stopped at Savage's Hotel at Achill Sound during her first visit to Achill. She received great hospitality from Mrs Savage and stayed two nights before continuing on to Achill. When she was rebuffed by the Nangles, Mrs Savage invited her to stay again (*Welcome*, 416, 429). Everyone seemed to have a good word for Savage. The Halls described him as a former coastguard turned hotel-keeper who was an 'intelligent guide, counselor to sportsmen' (Hall, III, 394). In his letter from Erris to the CRC, Richard Webb called Savage 'the intelligent hotel keeper at Achill Sound' (*Transactions*, 199).

29. This is likely an allusion to Genesis 49:14 'Issacher is a strong ass crouching down between two burdens.'

30. The Irish-born Protestant evangelist Edward Nangle (1799-1883) visited Achill first in 1831 when he went with a shipment of meal for the starving people of the island. He returned to lease the island from Sir Richard O'Donnell to found a mission. The colony was always controversial. The Halls visited Nangle's mission and indicted him for his lack of charity toward the islanders.

It was the place Nicholson most wanted to visit in Ireland and she devoted her last two chapters of *Ireland's Welcome to the Stranger* to the mission. Like the Halls, she found the Nangles lacking in charity and respect for the dignity of those among whom they worked. Her persistent questions and frank views resulted in a hostile account of her visit in Nangle's mission paper *The Achill Herald and Western Witness*.

31. Nicholson suggests that the old couple were named Abraham and Sara but it is likely she named the pair after the Abraham and Sara of Genesis.

32. The region around Mount Ephraim is an open plain.

33. Father Theobald Mathew began his temperance crusade on 10 April 1838. He was encouraged to begin his campaign by the Quaker Cork baker William Martin who has been called 'the Grandfather of Teetotal Cause' (Harrison, Cork 54). Martin was also a friend of Nicholson's.

34. The full title of the pamphlet is *Irish improvidence encouraged by English bounty being a remonstrance against the government projects for Irish relief and suggestions of measures by which the Irish poor can speedily and effectively [be] fed, relieved, employed and elevated above their present degraded position without taxing English industry for this purpose* by an ex-member of British Parliament.

35. Elizabeth Malcolm says little about alcohol and the Famine except to note that the duty on spirits increased and that in 1847, with the grain prices sky high, the consumption of legal spirits fell only about twenty-five percent, from approximately 8,000,000 gallons to about 6,000,000 gallons (Malcolm, 144). The 60,000,000 pounds of grain or 30,000 tons of grain to distill 6,000,000 gallons of eighty proof spirits could have provided more than 300,000,000 servings of grain-based cereal.

36. Matthew 5: 28,30. 'And if thy right eye offend thee, pluck it out and cast it from thee. And if thy right hand offend thee, cut it off.'

37. Nicholson describes an experience in Scotland when she was invited to drink whiskey by some ministers and she refused. 'Timothy's stomach (1 Timothy 4: 1-5, a criticism of false asceticism) and the marriage at Cana were spread out most religiously and I was warned not to treat with lightness the Word of God' (*Loose Papers*, 55).

NOTES TO CHAPTER V

1. William Paul Dawson, the Rector of Kilmore Erris, was a member of the Erris Relief Committee in 1847. He received a grant for fifteen pounds from the CRC in that year (*Transactions*, 59).

2. The lines come from an unidentified poem in Tuke (27): 'Who shall enumerate the crazy huts/ And tottering hovels, whence do issue forth/ A ragged offspring, with their upright hair/ Crowned like the image of fantastic Fear?/ Shrivelled are their lips;/ Naked and coloured like the soil, the feet/ On which they stand, as if thereby they drew/ Some nourishment, as trees do by their roots,/ From earth the common mother of us all./ Figure and mien, complexion and attire,/ Are lengthened to strike dismay; but outstretched hand/ And whining voice denote them suppliants/ For the least boon that pity can bestow.'

3. Critical as he was of the landlord system, Tuke was sympathetic to those resident landlords who tried to relieve the suffering of their tenants: 'It would be utterly unjust to blame a great portion of the present landlords for not discharging the duties of ownership when their circumstances entirely disable them from doing so. I bear a most willing testimony to the kind-hearted and zealous efforts of not a few of this class during the late season of trial (*Transactions*, 207).

4. The poor-house was a distance of forty miles. Tuke argued that the Erris Poor-law district should be divided (*Transactions*, 204). Later, the district was divided and there was a temporary work-house at Binghamstown, *Transactions*, 204n).

5. Hugh Dorian's manuscript describes coastal salvaging (251-5). Gerald Griffin's 'Hand and Word' and Mrs Hall's 'The Wrecker' describe coastal people misleading ships to cause wrecks and then salvaging. In John Messenger's ethnology of Inishere in the 1960s, *Inis Beag. Isle of Ireland* (1969), he describes the traditional 'law of wrack' which recognizes the right of islanders to objects which wash ashore, including a cargo of Scotch whisky in 1960 (48).

6. Mrs D may have been the wife of George John Darcy (*Transactions*, 198).

7. Webb wrote about this in his 'Letter from Erris': 'In the barony of Erris, living trees are unknown; although the bogs contain abundant remains of timber, which show that this district must once have been profusely wooded. There are probably many thousands of the present inhabitants who have never seen a living tree larger than a shrub. R.R. Savage, the intelligent keeper of the hotel at Achill Sound, told me that when his daughter, then a child of five years old, first visited Westport, she was afraid the trees would fall upon her as they waved over head across the road' (*Transactions*, 199). Nicholson also commented on the lack of trees in Galway (*Welcome*, 386).

8. The abbey is Cross Abbey, two miles west of Binghamstown, where tradition tells that those buried in the Kilmore graveyard were buried standing.

9. The Belmullet coast could be treacherous for ships. The *Tyrawly Herald* (14 October 1847) describes the wreck of the brig *Claudine* en route from Trinidad to Greenock.

10. In 1842 Nicholson was listed as the widowed proprietor of a boarding house at 26 Beekman Street. 90 Beekman Street, the corner of Cliff Street, was the premises of John Bigley, grocer. Cliff is the next street that crosses Beekman.

11. The image is as startling as John Donne's 'A bracelet of bright haire about the bone' in 'The Funerall'.

12. This is misleading. Nicholson did not get as far as Erris in her 1845 visit to Mayo.

13. This is likely the 49th Regiment who not only guarded the meal supply in Belmullet but also helped evict a number of tenants (Woodham-Smith, 319).

14. Bournes had a small estate of about seventy families (Bennett, 35). He was remembered in local oral tradition as a charitable landlord who not only saved his own tenants from the Famine but the tenants on other estates in the Rosport-Ballina area (Póirtéir, *Echoes* 205-06).

15. James Perry and Jonathan Pim consulted Cary when they visited Mayo in April 1847 (*Transactions*, 197). Inspecting Chief Officer Frederick Carey was sta-

tioned at Dunkeehan, Belmullet in 1847 (*Thom's*, 236).

16. Local folklore records that people on the Mayo coast ate sea birds and their eggs during hungry times, and there were famous cliff walkers who were known for their prowess at robbing eggs (Póirtéir, *Echoes* 56, 62). The practice continued on Aran down through the 1930s. Tom O'Flaherty describes cliff walkers in 'The Dwellers in the Cliffs' (99-109).

17. Sloke is edible; however, one can not subsist on a diet of seaweed. Local accounts of the Famine describe Arranmore islanders and coastal people around Louisburgh living on seaweed in 1847. See Edwards, 401.

18. Bowen suggests that W.P. Dawson was the curate who had the breakdown but there is no other evidence to suggest that was so (190).

19. John Greene was curate of Kilcommon-Erris in 1847 (*Thom's*, 299-300).

20. Afraid of Esau's anger, Jacob divided his people and his flocks so that if one group were attacked the others could escape (Genesis 32). Nicholson might have been suggesting a similar strategy for the tenants facing the 'driver.'

21. Nicholson's letter was published in the *Tyrawly Herald and Sligo Intelligencer* on 2 December 1847 with the headline 'DISTRESS IN ERRIS' and the note, 'The following letter from that philanthropic lady Asenath Nicholson, addressed to a friend, will give a frightful picture of the conditions of the poor of Erris.'

22. Nicholson is probably referring to James Tuke.

23. George Thompson (1804-48) was the English abolitionist associated with William Lloyd Garrison and the American abolitionists. Thompson converted Richard Webb to abolitionism (Garrison, 2, 684; Harrison, 23).

24. Samuel Stock (d.1866), the Rector of Kilcommon-Erris, was the Chair of the Erris Relief Committee and the chief organizer of relief efforts in the Rossport area (*Transactions*, 200-01). He was the grand-nephew of Bishop Joseph Stock of Killala who left an account of the 1798 French invasion, *What Passed at Killala* (1800). Stock was transferred to Castleconnor in 1849. James O'Donnell was a local landlord who received aid from the CRC: forty pounds for relief expenses in various parts of Erris and four bushels of Indian meal (*Extracts*, 58).

25. Nicholson refers to the belief in Puritan New England, including the Congregationalism of her youth in Chelsea, that man was 'lost.'

26. Phineas slayed Zimri and Cozbi who brought on plague by intermarrying with Midiamite women (Numbers 25:6-18).

27. The 'young, indefatigable, kind-hearted and poor' curate who never engaged in proselytism was probably Samuel Stock's curate John Greene.

28. Mrs Stock manned a soup kitchen in her rectory and set up a clothing industry with local women till an outbreak of fever interrupted their work (Bowen, 192). See Clothing App. 2157 (1848) from Mrs Stock to the CRC who noted that the Stocks were 'active parties ' in relief.

29. Nicholson is probably referring to the Gospel of Luke 21 which tells of 'the seas and waves roaring' (25) and Christ appearing for the Last Judgment. 'And then they shall see the Son of man coming in a cloud with power and great glory' (25).

30. A story in the *The Tyrawly Herald* for 18 November 1847 describes the storm:

'Monday the 8th of November, will be a memorable day to the inhabitants of the sea coast in the county of Mayo. The morning had been cloudy, and the ocean a little disturbed till about three o'clock pm, a dead calm succeeded, leaving the water like a molten looking-glass. The winds seemed as if holding their breaths to collect fresh strength – and suddenly, as if pressed from some mighty engine – the maddening tempest lashed the ocean into a fury – the Almighty came out of his pavillion, and, in awful majesty rode upon the whirl-wind. A company of fishermen on the Island of Achill, at Bowford, were preparing to go out with their nets, and two boats, and three curraghs had got upon the waters, when the tempest rushed upon them; they struggled in vain – in a few moments one boat disappeared and was seen no more; the second became a wreck upon the shore – three men escaped from it and succeeded in ascending the cliffs but perished upon the mountains of Ashley; one was washed up on the shore dead, another was under the wreck of the boat the next morning. These two boats contained ten men and all were lost. It is reported that one of the curraghs has been seen near Newport floating uninjured, but not a man has been found belonging to the three curraghs. Nineteen persons were lost, fourteen of these had families whose wives and children are cast upon poor hapless Ireland for bread.'

31. Nicholson was trying to make peace with Nangle after he had published an account of her visit in his *Achill Missionary Herald and Western Witness* which concluded that she was '... the emissary of some democratic and revolutionary society' (*Welcome*, 438). On her first visit to Achill, Nicholson was sent off to Moll Vesey's shebeen.

32. The Achill Mission was the first to use the Irish language in its proselytizing efforts. William Neilson's *Introduction to the Irish Language* was published by the Mission Press at Achill in 1845.

33. The author of the 'Irish Crisis' was Charles E. Trevelyan (1807-86), Assistant Secretary of the Treasury, who was the person most responsible for the Famine relief programme. He was knighted for his work in 1848.

34. Jeremiah 9:1. 'Oh, that my head were waters and mine eyes a fountain of tears, that I might weep day and night for the slain daughters of my people.'

NOTES TO CHAPTER VI

1. Webb wrote from Bemullet on 8 May 1847 that '... a large proportion of sufferers only apply for admission [to the Ballina work-house] in the hope that they should be provided with a coffin when dead, which is more than could be expected if they died outside the work-house wall' (*Transactions*, 190).

2. Nicholson visited Westport in 1845 but she does not mention the work-house (*Welcome*, 405-14).

3. Thomas Carlyle also observed the 'make work' project, some '5 or 600 boys and lads pretending to break stone' in the Westport Work-house. He asked, 'Can it be *charity* to keep men alive on these terms?' (Carlyle, 202). That there was little difference between a work-house and a prison can be demonstrated by the same stone-breaking activities which occupied the prisoners that

Nicholson observed when she visited the Spike Island in Cove Harbour (152).

4. Nicholson refers to the notorious Quarter Acre or Gregory Clause in the 1847 Relief Act that stipulated that a person who occupied more than a quarter of an acre would be ineligible for relief. Cormac Ó Gráda has commented, 'By depriving those on relief of supplementary income for the land, this measure and the clearances inspired by it were probably responsible for thousands of deaths' (110).

5. This is an ironic reference to the Tudor conquest and the land confiscations of the sixteenth and seventeenth centuries.

6. The Irish became as numerous as the frogs of the second plague of Exodus (8:1-15).

7. 'a man for a' that' is a line from Robert Burns's poem 'For A' That and A' That,' a poem probably inspired by the French Revolution.

8. Queen Victoria (1819-1901) ruled from 1837-1901. John Russell (1792-1878) served as Prime Minister between 1846-52, and in 1865-6.

NOTES TO CHAPTER VII

1. Charles Wilson was the incumbent of Achill in 1847 (*Thom's*, 299). A Rose Willson died in the rectory at Newport in 1873 at the age of seventy. She is buried in the Newport churchyard.

2. Sir Richard Annesley O'Donnell, Bart., of Newport House was considered an improving landlord and worked with the CRC. O'Donnell alleged that he did not know his driver was evicting tenants. Nicholson's view was that ignorance was no excuse and that landlords were responsible for those they employed.

3. The Dublin solicitor John Walshe, a land speculator with property in Erris, had the villages of Tiraun, Mullaroghoe and Clogher in the Mullet cleared shortly before Christmas, 1847. *Dublin Evening Post* (8 February 1847). See Bowen, 191. Walshe protested his bad press and there was an exchange of letters about the evictions in the *Tyrawly Herald*. When Webb visited the Mullet in February, 1848, he reported to the CRC that there were probably 200 cabins destroyed leaving at least 400 homeless (*Transactions*, 208). See Tuke's Postscript 'Evictions in Erris' 61.

4. Job 31. Job maintains his innocence regarding sins of oppression including failure in his obligations to widows and children.

5. The Epistles of James 5:1-6 warn the rich who exploit the poor that the 'coming of the Lord draweth near.' The well-known lines 'Father, forgive them ...' are from Luke 23:34.

6. Nicholson met Patrick Pounden, Rector of Westport or Aughaval, on her first visit to Ireland and called him 'benevolent' (*Welcome*, 406). Pounden received a grant of one ton of Indian meal for 'present relief' from the CRC (*Extracts*, 1847, 58).

7. Tuke reported that O'Donnell employed nearly 1000, principally women, at flax. 'Even at this miserable rate of wages (four pence a day for women and eight pence a day for men), I have seldom seen more cheerful or industrious labourers' (Tuke, 9). In 1848 Father Mathew sought advice from the Flax Cultivation Society of Belfast about the advisability of beginning a flax indus-

try, but he received no encouragement and abandoned the idea (Augustine, 474).

8. Mr Gildea's cotton factory at Belcarra near Westport had twenty-six looms. He employed a considerable number of women and children (Lewis, II, 700). In 1847 he employed nearly 700 women in hand-scutching and spinning flax (Tuke, 10).

9. Tuke described this tragic practice. 'In some cases, it is well-known, where all other members of a family have perished, the last survivor had earthed up the door of his miserable cabin to prevent the ingress of pigs and dogs, and then laid himself down to die in this fearful family vault' (Tuke, 8). See Gabriel Rosenstock's letter 'The Famine' in *The Irish Times*, 8 January 1996.

10. There was some Molly Maguire activity in Mayo. *The Tyrawly Herald* (9 March 1848) reported a brutal double murder where the defendants alleged that the victims had come as Molly Maguires to attack their house when they, in fact, had demolished their own house as a cover for their actions.

11. For his part in the 1848 Rising John Mitchel was sentenced to fourteen years' transportation and William Smith O'Brien was sentenced first to death and then to transportation for life. Both were sent to Van Diemen's Land (Tasmania). Mitchel escaped to America in 1853 and returned to Ireland in 1875 when he was elected MP for Tipperary. O'Brien was unconditionally pardoned in 1856.

12. William Hamilton Maxwell (1792-1850) published *Wild Sports of the West* in 1832.

13. Webb visited Ballycroy in February 1848, perhaps just after Nicholson, and commented that '... the people were exerting themselves with much energy and that there was a prospect of a good deal of land being sown' (*Transactions*, 210). The 'Practical Instructor' Thomas Martin who was engaged to give agricultural advice in Erris reported in *The Tyrawly Herald*, (16 December 1847), that there were large tracts of land around Ballycroy worth reclaiming.

14. A reticule is a small bag, often woven, that can be carrried over the arm.

15. Nicholson may be referring especially to 1 Timothy 5:14. 'I will therefore that the younger women marry, bear children, guide the house, give no occasion for the adversary to speak reproachfully.' See also Proverbs 31:10-31.

16. Webb visited Ballycroy first in May 1847. He spoke of the water guards at Tullaghan. Nicholson may have gone there for the church service that she describes. A.T. Hamilton was the Inspecting Lieutenant at Mullaghmore in 1847 (*Thom's*, 236).

17. In 1996 there were still driftwood tree trunks on the Daly land next to the ruins of the Granuaile castle.

18. The castle known variously as Fahy or Doona Castle is still associated with Granuaile (Gráinne ní Mháille). Nicholson mentions visiting another one of her castles, Carrigahooley (Carraig an Chabhlaigh), two miles from Newport in her essay 'Grana-uille and her Castle' (*Loose Papers*, 20-28). She describes her castles scattered along the coast in ruins and concludes,'They have the impress of the owner in their want of taste and coarseness of look' (28). See also Halls' description and engraving of Carrigahooley (III 390).

19. Nicholson may have met Kelly, the Ballina solicitor, through her Dublin

friends the O'Dowdas. In Part 2 of *Lights and Shades*, she mentions that Peter Kelly of Ballina had married the daughter of Thaddeus O'Dowda (*Lights*, 183).

20. Francis Kinkead was one of two Church of Ireland curates in Ballina (*Thom's*, 197). When he died on 28 January 1847, Catholics as well as Protestants contributed to his memorial tablet (Bowen, 219-220). A tribute to Kinkead in *The Tyrawly Herald* (10 April 1847) spoke of his great charity, '... his memory is enshrined in the hearts of the poor of the neighbourhood.'

21. One of the last things Kinkead accomplished was the founding of the Ballina Ladies' Institution on 11 January 1847. *The Tyrawly Herald* (17 February 1848) carried the First Report of the Ballina Ladies' Institution showing the organization a little in the red: 287.17 collected and 289.17.9 expended.

22. Bowen describes Ballina as a centre for missionaries including the Baptists (217). The Baptist minister in Ballina in 1847 was William Hamilton (*Thom's*, 350).

23. This may have been Peter Kelly's sister-in-law. Nicholson mentions in *Lights and Shades* that she had access to the volumes of the archaeological society through a member of the O'Dowda family (52). Henry Shaw (1850) lists John T. O'Dowda at 42 Lower Ormonde Quay.

24. The view from the one-arched bridge at Pontoon looks toward Illannaglashy Island. The Halls said that Lord Lucan built the bridge to replace the dangerous ferry (III 382).

25. G.C. Otway inspected the Castlebar Work-house to investigate the claims in Revd Richard Gibbon's description of the Work-house. His report concluded, 'I regret to have to report that the statements in Mr Gibbon's letter are true and so far from being exaggerated, hardly come up to the facts of the case' (Kissane, 94-95). From correspondence relating to the State of the Union Workhouses in Ireland, 49-50, P.P.1847 (766) LV. A letter from G.C. Otway, Assistant Poor-law Commissioner, regarding the Castlebar Work-house said that Lord Lucan, through his agent, supplied meal (Kissane, 94). Castlebar was founded by John Bingham, ancestor of the Earls of Lucan (Duignan, 151).

26. Nicholson may be talking about the reprisals taken against the rebels involved in the French invasion of 1798.

27. Walter Bourke, QC of Carrowkeel, joined the Connaught Bar in 1838 (Burke, 284).

28. Conciliation Hall, built for the headquarters of the Repeal Association, was opened 22 October 1843.

29. William Baker Stoney was Rector of Newport in 1831, Rector of Burrishoole, Newport-Pratt in 1837 and Rector of Castlebar in 1847 when Asenath Nicholson visited (*Thom's*, 299). An evangelical Protestant, Stoney disputed with James Hughes in the pages of the *Mayo Telegraph* in 1836, 1837 (Bowen, 131). Nicholson praised Stoney for giving employment. He wrote very sympathetically about the Famine poor: 'Never has such a calamity befallen our country. The whole staff of life is swept away; the emaciated multitudes are and have been seen looking in vain for food with hunger depicted on the countenance' (Killen, 75).

30. There is no Protestant curate for Castlebar listed in *Thom's Directory of 1847*.

31. The parish priest of Partry in 1847 was Peter Ward; the curate was Peter Conway (*Thom's*, 356).

32. Nicholson did not visit Skibbereen, but by the spring of 1847, after the Cork artist James Mahony did a number of engravings for the *Illustrated London News* of the conditions in the town and its surroundings, Skibbereen became a metaphor for Famine suffering.

33. It was probably Kilkeeran which is situated near the shore of Lough Mask.

34. Nicholson does not refer to what Desmond Bowen describes as a war in Partry between Peter Ward and the Church of Ireland Bishop Plunket of Tuam and his sister Catherine because they set up a Protestant school in the Partry Mountains at Tourmakeady. The CRC gave Catherine Plunket thirty pounds for 'present relief' for those along the western shore of Lough Mask. See Póirtéir, *Echoes*, 174-5 for a Galway story about another Plunket sister's soup-shop.

35. Nicholson refers to the river Robe. One of the ruins is the fourteenth century Augustinian friary.

36. The abbey at Cong has been described by the Halls and other travellers. One of the more extensive accounts, with engravings and drawings is found in Sir William Wilde's *Lough Corrib, its Shores and its Island with Notices of Lough Mask* (1872).

37. The Cong legend of the fish was retold by Samuel Lover as 'The White Trout: A Legend of Cong.' He claimed to have heard the tale in 1825 from a woman, a great-grandmother, at the Pigeon-hole (Yeats, 36-40).

38. The Ashford demesne which included Cong was held by Lord Oranmore in 1837; by 1872, it was the property of Sir B.L. Guinness MP.

39. Nicholson seems to be talking about two people; Dr Rafe, a Protestant clergyman of Ballinrobe, and the local Roman Catholic curate.

40. John Bunyan (1628-88) violated the Restoration ban on noncomformist worship and spent twelve years in prison where he wrote *Pilgrim's Progress* (1679).

41. Peter Kelly's sister may have been the Julia Kelly who married Edmund Francis Garvey of Fallduff, Old Head (Garvey, 193). Edmund Francis was arrested and tried for treason on the strength of a letter found on the person of a French officer at Ballinamuck (Garvey, 43-55). There was a National School at Fallduff in 1835 which enrolled about fifty children; the master was Anthony Egan (Lyons, 41).

42. Patrick MacManus, parish priest of Kilgeever (near Louisburgh), wrote in 1847, 'There is but one resident gentleman in the parish Mr James Garvey of Tully' (Kissane, 35).

43. A mile from Louisburgh, in Kilgeever Graveyard, are the remains of Kilgeever Church and Tobar Rí an Domhnaigh where some Croagh Patrick pilgrims complete their penitential exercises. Despite Nicholson's approving note that priests had forbidden the practice and the custom was discontinued, pilgrims were completing rounds in 1996. One of Frederick William Burton's (1816-1900) early paintings was 'The Blind Girl at the Holy Well'.

44. Nicholson describes a woman making a *caoine* or lament for her husband. A traditional form of folk poetry are spontaneous laments performed in Irish by women. The most famous of the *caointe* is 'Caoine Airt Uí Laoghaire'.

45. The Garveys of Tully were Catholic.

46. The active priest in 1848 was Thomas McCaffrey; the faithful Protestant curate was Patrick James Callanan (Lyons, 36, 35).

47. Robert Potter and his wife worked tirelessly for all the poor of Louisburgh.
Potter died of famine fever probably in 1847 (Lyons, 35).

48. Nicholson travelled with Mrs Callanan and either Dr Durkin or Dr Fergus.

49. Mrs Garvey's cousin 'of the same name' was either Jane Garvey, wife of John
Christopher Garvey of Murrisk (Garvey, 194), or the wife (widow?) of James
Garvey of Tully who would have more likely held lands in the valley between
Louisburgh and Delphi.

50. The present Louisburgh-Leenane road goes through the Doolough Pass that
Nicholson travelled with the Garveys. The following year the route was the
scene of a tragic Famine walk. Four hundred starving people set off from
Louisburgh to Delphi Lodge where the Board of Guardians were meeting. The
Guardians said they could do nothing to relieve their suffering and the people
started back to Louisburgh. A storm came up and some, weakened by hunger
and exhaustion, were blown over the cliff into Doolough, others died of expo-
sure (Berry, 39-42). There is an annual Famine walk through the Pass. In 1991
the walk was led by Archbishop Desmond Tutu whose words, 'In 1991 we
walked AFRI's great "Famine" walk at Doolough and soon afterwards we
walked the road to freedom in South Africa' are inscribed on one of the two
monuments that mark the site.

51. The 'pretty river' is the Bunowen that rises in the Sheeffry Hills and empties
into Clew Bay.

52. The sweet lake is Doolough.

53. Adelphi Lodge was owned by Lord Altamont, Marquis of Sligo, the major
landowner in the Louisburgh area.

54. The conical heath mountain is Bengorm.

55. The Bundorragha River flows from Doolough into Killary Harbour.

56. Nicholson would have been looking back from the top of the Doolough Pass
on a view of mountains rising from the water.

57. The good landlady was probably Mrs Garvey of Tully, though all of the
Garveys were remembered as generous to their tenants.

58. The John Christopher Garveys lived near Murrisk Abbey where there is monument to John Christopher to the right of altar: 'Erected by his/ afflicted widow/
to the memory of/ her beloved husband/ John Christopher Garvey JPBL/
whose mortal remains/ repose near the altar/ of Murrisk/ He died April 5 AD
1856/ aged 48 years/ Blessed are the dead which/ die in the Lord.'

59. The Very Revd B. Burke of Westport was Dean, Chapter of Tuam, Archdiocese
of Tuam in 1847 (*Thom's*, 300).

60. Alexis Benoit Soyer (1809-58) was the French chef at the Reform Club in
London. He was engaged by the government to set up a model soup-kitchen in
Phoenix Park. See engraving in Kissane, 84 from *The Illustrated London News*
(16 April 1847). See Hatton, 139 for the contrast between Soyer Soup and
Quaker Soup.

61. Christopher Morash includes a Soyer Soup ballad called 'Another Version of
Soyer's Soup' in *The Hungry Voice*. This street ballad is from the White
Collection at Trinity College Dublin. Nicholson's Swiftian satire is very much

in the spirit of the public reaction to the Soyer Soup scheme.

62. In William Cowper's (1731-1800) comic ballad, 'The Diverting History of John Gilpin' (1782), Gilpin loses control of a borrowed horse. Nicholson also alluded to the ballad in *Loose Papers*: 'The coachman now had fresh horses and he plied fresh skill; indeed, "John Gilpin" fell quite in the rear' (81).

63. This is probably a reference to a line in one of the Soyer Soup street ballads.

64. Nicholson refers to the comic relief, really gallows humour, provided by the Soyer Soup ballad. It is not clear whether these lines are from a contemporary Famine poem.

65. The text suggests Murry and Jordan worked in Castlebar. Edward Dill lists the Irish Evangelical Society as one of the agencies whose work would 'cure' Ireland's miseries (Bowen, 110).

66. Nicholson visited the Presentation Convent in Tuam.

67. The Quakers worked especially hard to revitalize the fishing industry (see *Transactions*, 390-414). Hatton discusses the Quakers' work with Claddagh fishermen (216). See also Tuke, 35-7, and Goodbody, 48-58.

68. The Jesuits had the school in the Claddagh which was called the Jesuit Piscatorial School (Hatton, 216).

69. Nicholson had a lot of trouble with Bianconi cars in *Welcome*. Nicholson's experience with Bianconi's carmen was at odds with the praise of the system in 'Individual Exertions: Mr Bianconi' in the *Dublin Penny Journal* (8 September 1832). According to the article, Bianconi directed his drivers'... to pick up, free of charge, all pedestrians who evidently can not pay for a whirl and who seem to be travelling with pain to themselves.' It concluded '... the drivers of Bianconi's cars are as civil a set of fellows as you would see handle a whip.'

70. The Father Mathew Tower stands on private grounds on Mount Patrick, about a mile north-east of the Drumkettle Railway Station. The Penrose family were wealthy Quakers with a home called Woodhill on Middle Glanmire Road overlooking the River Lee. The house was demolished in 1989. In 1798 Cooper Penrose encouraged Cork Quakers to protest against the slave trade (Harrison, Cork 52). He was also the friend of Curran's who took in Curran's daughter Sarah (Barry, 96). Curran did not attend the wedding of his daughter to Henry Sturgeon, a member of the Royal Staff Corps, who was stationed in Cork in 1805. The couple were married in the parish church in Glanmire, County Cork. The bride was given away by Cooper Penrose.

71. The first lines of Thomas Moore's song 'She is Far from the Land' was written in memory of Sarah Curran who died on 5 May 1808 at Hythe-on-Kent. She is buried in Newmarket, County Cork. Her headstone, erected by the people of Newmarket, has a verse from Moore's song (Barry, 127).

72. There were four convents in Cork including two of the Presentation order. Nicholson refers to the South Presentation Convent whose Douglas Street location would put them closest to Father Mathew's house. Father Mathew was Father Superior for fourteen years (1835-49) to the South Presentations and to the Ursulines. Nicholson went with Father Mathew to the Golden Jubilee of Mother Clare Callaghan at the South Presentation Convent on the eighth of January 1845 (*Welcome*, 380, *Annals*, 259). Nicholson also visited the Ursulines.

73. J. Windell could be John Windle of the Crown Office and Blair's Castle

(Aldwell, 200) or perhaps Father Mathew's American correspondent named Waddell (Augustine, 415).

74. 'Father Mathew was among the first to call the attention of the government to the catastrophe and for information given and suggestions offered, was thanked by Mr Richard Pennefather who was then Under-Secretary in Dublin Castle' (Augustine, 394). Starting in the summer of 1846, Father Mathew ran a soup depot for the starving (Augustine, 413). Like their Dublin counterparts, the CRC closed at the end of May 1847; however, Father Mathew kept up the Southern depot where they fed 5000-6000 with Indian meal (Augustine, 416).

75. There were no Catholic burial grounds until one was provided by Father Mathew (McNamara, 108). Father Mathew's St Joseph's Cemetery was established on the grounds of the former Botanical Gardens (Lincoln, 90). From 1 September 1846 to 1 June 1847, 10,000 bodies were buried at St Joseph's. Fr Mathew had to close the cemetery for a while in the summer of 1847 for public health reasons (Augustine, 432).

76. Abraham Beale, who had an iron works at 6-7 Patrick's Quay, Cork, died of typhus in August 1847 at the age of fifty-four (Hatton, 204; Goodbody, 78).

77. Nicholson alludes to John 14:1-2. 'In my Father's house are many mansions: if it were not so, I would have told you, I go to prepare a place for you.'

78. Abraham Beale's sisters lived at 7 Myrtle Hill Terrace near Woodhill. Sarah Beale had a school at her home for fifteen pupils (Harrison, *Cork* 70).

79. Sliding coffins had a hinged bottom that worked as a trap door to drop a body into a grave. It could be used over and over again. (See Póirtéir, *Echoes* 183).

80. The South Presentations worked closely with Father Mathew. Nicholson's record of their work is a valuable addition to their history, for they say modestly in their Annals only: 'During the years of 1846-47 when God visited this Cork City by Famine, Father Mathew spent nearly every half-penny of which he was possessed in relieving the poor starving children. He had a host of friends who gladly opened their purses to him. By this means he was able to feed and keep the spark of life in them. We experienced his generosity more than others. Flour and meal came to us from America which we dispensed for a lengthened period among the poor children until God sent brighter times and removed the Scourge' (*Annals*, 300).

81. A Gothic mansion was attached to the fifteenth century McCarthy Keep at Blarney by the Jefferyes family who landscaped the gardens known as Rock Close (Lincoln, 90). Nicholson also visited Blarney in 1845.

82. The Song of Solomon 2:15. 'The little foxes spoil the vines.'

83. William Martin urged Father Mathew to take up the cause of temperance.

84. The belief that the Famine was a punishment no doubt added to the sensitivity and silence. See Póirtéir, 'Abundance Abused and Blight' (*Echoes*, 34-49).

85. Castlemartyr had a turbulent history in the last half of the seventeenth century when it was taken from the Fitzgeralds by Murrough the Burner, returned to the Boyles after the Cromwellians and besieged and wrecked by the Jacobites in 1688 before the Battle of the Boyne in 1690.

86. Castlemartyr House is now a Carmelite Priory.

87. The *Cork Directory* (1844-45) lists a Cork magistrate called Maurice Kelly living at Ringaboltig Cove (461). Nicholson visited the Powers in 1845 in their

'cottage near Cork.' She had a letter of introduction from Mrs Powers' brother. Mrs Powers, an American, was the daughter of Judge Livingston. Spike Island was a prison between 1847 and 1883 (Lincoln, 123).

88. Mitchel was held at Spike Island before he was transported to Bermuda and later to Van Diemen's Land.

89. Nicholson was not so reticent about talking politics the following year in Inverness. When another guest at a dinner party criticized Americans for slavery and for the love of money, she said: 'To the first I bowed a mortified but *hearty* assent, and thanked him as sincerely as though a guilty conscience had accused me of being an accessory to the whole trade. On this question, we Americans in a foreign land may blush that he calls himself a republican. I frankly acknowledge that republicanism was a solemn mocker in that country, for though there were some *free* men and some *free* women, they did not constitute the majority, and as the majority must do and stamp the character of a nation, we must, by all usages of law and custom, be a tyrannical, despotic nation' (*Loose Papers*, 24).

90. The foundation stone of the Mathew Tower was laid on 30 October 1843; it was formally opened on 10 November 1846 (Holland, 133).

91. O'Connor built the Tower not only to celebrate the work of Father Mathew but also to express his thanks for Mathew's London reception and to create a symbol of friendship between the two peoples (Holland, 132).

92. The cottage and its contents have disappeared. The Tower has been restored by its present owner.

93. In 1848 Louis Philippe (1773-1850), who was King of France between 1830 and 1848, fled to England when his failure to accept parliamentary reforms resulted in the 1848 Rising, in Paris.

94. The statue of Father Mathew was the work of John Hogan (1818-74). The statue survives, but the top of the head and the right arm are missing.

95. The Right Revd Dr John Murphy (1772-1847) was the Bishop of Cork.

96. The carved chimney piece still exists, but the heads of the figures have been mutilated.

97. Father Mathew planned to go to the United States but postponed his trip when the country was in political turmoil leading up to the Rising of 1848. He finally left for America via Liverpool on 14 May 1849; he reached Staten Island on 1 July (Augustine, 486). He visited twenty-five states and over 300 cities giving the pledge to 500,000 people before leaving for Ireland on 8 November 1851.

98. Between the time Nicholson left Cork in September 1848 and 1850 when she was writing *Lights and Shade*, O'Connor died of cholera.

99. The article appeared in *The Cork Examiner*, 30 August 1848.

100. Nicholson actually went to England and later to the continent; she did not return to the United States for another three years.

101. Nicholson's letter, dated 4 September 1848, was printed in *The Cork Examiner* on Wednesday 6 September 1848 under the title 'The Mathew Tower – Mrs Nicholson' with the note 'This amiable lady has forwarded the following to Mr O'Connor.'

NOTES FOR CHAPTER VIII

1. Nicholson suggests that Charles Wolfe's 'The Burial of Sir John Moore' was set to the air 'Soldier's Grave'. Like John Moore, Wolfe was buried where he died, in Cobh in 1823. There is a memorial tablet to Wolfe in St Patrick's Cathedral in Dublin.

2. C. Litton Falkiner's 1909 'Introductory Memoir' to *The Burial of Sir John Moore' and other Poems* says that Wolfe was buried in Clonmel, County Tipperary (xix); however, Wolfe is buried in the graveyard at the ruined church of Clonmel, County Cork which is located about one mile north of Cobh (Duignan, 177). Many of the *Lusitania* victims are buried at Clonmel.

3. Falkiner says that Wolfe's poem on Moore circulated among friends and was finally published in *Blackwood's Magazine* (xxvi-xxvii); O'Donoghue says the poem appeared first in the *Newry Telegraph* and was claimed by several imposters (488).

4. The lines are the third and fourth of the third stanza of 'The Burial of Sir John Moore': 'No useless coffin enclosed his breast, / Not in a sheet or in shroud we wound him; / But he lay like a warrior taking his rest, / With his martial cloak around him' (Wolfe, 1).

5. Wolfe was appointed curate of Ballyclog, County Tyrone. After a few weeks he moved on to be curate of Donaghmore, County Tyrone, where he served until the year of his death, 1823 (Falkiner, xxviii).

6. Wolfe travelled to Bordeaux and then to Cobh for reasons of health. There was no improvment and Wolfe died in Cobh on 21 February 1823 (Falkiner, xix).

7. The lines are the first four lines from Thomas Moore's 'Oh! Breathe not his Name' (Moore, 243).

8. This was Charles Mathew of Lehenagh.

9. Psalms 46:10: 'Be still, and know that I *am* God: I will be exalted by the heathen, I will be exalted in the earth.'

10. Job 13:15: 'Though he slay me, yet will I trust in Him.'

11. The Munster poet Eoghan Rua O'Súilleabháin's (1748-84) witty poem 'A Chara mo Chléibh' to his friend the smith, James Fitzgerald, asking him to refit a shaft to his spade tells him that since his learning does not pay, O'Suilleabháin must take to the road as a *spailpín*, an itinerant labourer.

12. The Epistle of Paul to the Galatians 6:7: 'Be not deceived; God is not mocked; for whatsoever a man soweth, that shall he also reap.'

13. Acts of the Apostles 17:24-26: 'And hath made of one blood all nations of men for to dwell on the face of the earth.'

14. John Bright (1811-89) was an English orator and Member of Parliament almost continuously from 1843-89. Bright refers to the housing classification system adopted by the 1841 Census Commissioners which assigned householders to one of four categories based on the condition of the dwelling. The third and fourth classes were mud cabins of one room (Leadam, 4) or two to four rooms and windows (Leadam, 3). See Kissane, 8.

15. Nicholson would have shared a number of Bright's reforming views which included the disestablishment of the Irish Church, the sale of encumbered estates, increased tenant occupancy and other measures directed to attack the cause of famine rather than simply to provide famine relief (Leadam, 278).

16. Dr Richard Barter (1802-90) opened a very posh spa at St Anne's Hill near Cork in 1842 '... to restore good health, to provide cheerfulness and good temper' (Lincoln, 88). Nicholson visited Barter on her first trip and and pronounced herself satisfied (*Welcome*, 242). By her second visit, Barter was allowing his patients meat more than once a day. There are two photographs of Barter's St Anne's Hydro in Lincoln (88, 89).

17. In 1844-45 William Martin had a bakery and provisions store at 12 and at 57 Patrick Street, Cork; there are William Martins listed at 8 Waterloo Place and at 47 Pope's Quay (Aldwell, 200).

18. Nicholson is observing the Irish custom of walking, even a few steps, with a funeral.

19. Luke 7:11-17, A widow of Nain loses her only son and he is restored to her by Jesus.

20. Revelations 14:13: 'Blessed are the dead which die in the Lord that they may rest from their labours.' The text is also found in the Rite for the Burial of the Dead in the *Book of Common Prayer.*

21. The *Cork Directory* for 1844-45 offers two possibilities for the hospitable Mrs Fisher. One Mrs. Fisher is listed as living at 40 Victoria Terrace. There is no number 40 Victoria Terrace. There is a number 4 Victoria Terrace, a three-storey house at the end of a terrace of four houses not far from Middle Glanmire Road. There is a second Victoria Terrace off Alexandra Road, but there is no number 40. The second Mrs Fisher is Mrs Ellen Fisher who owned a hotel and livery stable-keeper at 1 Caroline Street in the centre of the city. Thomas Fisher Esq., a Quaker, is listed as living on Caroline Street as well (Aldwell, 174). That Nicholson said she had the use of a drawing-room suggests she boarded in a private house and not at a hotel.

22. In 1848 the *Report of the General Relief Committee of the City of New York* was published, which suggests that the American Committee had concluded its work for famine relief.

23. Nicholson must have stayed with Richard and Hannah Webb at 176 Great Brunswick Street in September 1848 when she returned to Dublin briefly before leaving for London.

24. Matthew 6:19-20: 'Lay not up for yourselves treasures upon earth, where moth and rust do corrupt, and where thieves break through and steal: But lay up for yourselves treasures in heaven.'

25. Nicholson may be refering to 1 John 3:19-20: 'By this we shall know that we are of the truth, and reassure our hearts before him whenever our hearts condemn us; for God is greater than our hearts, and he knows everything.'

26. This appears to be a pastiche of lines from the Bible that speak to Paul's First Letter to the Corinthians which addresses the qualifications for good stewardship. Nicholson seems to be speaking of 4:2: 'Moreover it is required in stewards, that a man is found faithful.'

27. Father Mathew's 'blasted hopes' may have been his hope of succeeding Bishop Murphy who died 1 April 1847. The parish priests of the Diocese of Cork supported Mathew, but Mathew had two opponents: the General of the Capuchins who was unhappy that Mathew had not been to Rome (Augustine, 427), and closer to home, Archbishop Slattery of Cashel. According to the Rescript of 1829, the Bishops of a province could overturn the vote of the

parish priests. Slattery used the proxies of the Bishops of Waterford and Kilfenora to elect the Very Revd Dr Delany (Augustine, 442-443). When Father Mathew returned from America in 1852 he was offered the Vicariate Apostolic to Jamaica, but he declined for reasons of health (Augustine, 523).

28. Numbers 25:6-18. Phineas slayed Zimri and Cozbi for offences that brought on the plague. See Chapter V, note 26.

29. Father Mathew's work with temperance and with famine relief brought him financial troubles. There was a public subscription and John Russell tried for a Civil Pension for Father Mathew. The Queen declined in 1846 but later, in 1847, approved a 300 pound pension for Father Mathew's work with temperance (Augustine, 438).

30. This misunderstanding may have had to do with an insurance policy on Father Mathew's life that was meant to cover the balance of his debt.

31. In addition to his business worries and misunderstandings, there were three other issues connected with his American trip: *The Freeman's Journal* accused him of making the journey as a secret emissary of the British government; there was a complaint that he visited districts without ecclesiastical permission and, what was probably most distressing, his American supporters who were Abolitionists pressed him to appear at a public meeting in Boston to denounce slavery. Father Mathew refused to appear and further alienated the Abolitionists by taking his temperance crusade to the southern states (Augustine, 493-7). Nicholson, as was her fashion, had only compassion for Father Mathew. Both had to compromise in order to do their work in a cultural setting other than their own. Nicholson had to put her suspicion of Catholics aside to work with the clergy to aid the poor; Father Mathew had to set the cause of abolitionism aside to pursue the cause of temperance.

32. The letter from the English Prime Minister John Russell in the *Protestant Watchman* (12 May 1848) takes Hosea 6 as his text to make the curate's wife's point. The people starve because they are idolatrous. See Killen, 189.

33. Oral tradition, which is always a valuable record of attitudes, beliefs and stereotypes, preserves stories and songs about proselytism. See Edwards, 410-11; O'Gráda, 67; Póirtéir, *Echoes*, 166-81. See also Varian's 'Proselytism', Morash, 216-217. Desmond Bowen's study of proselytism in the dioceses of Killala and Achonry, *Souperism: Myth or Reality?*, argues that Souperism did occur on the part of some of the proselytizing Protestant agencies, the charge could not be proven against the Established Church (229). Irene Whelan's 'The Stigma of Souperism' examines the bitter 'Souper' legacy and concludes that the evidence indicates that the reputation of the Church of Ireland did suffer because of some evangelical zealots and henceforth all Protestants, laymen or clergy who involved themselves in social welfare were suspect (Póirtéir, 152-3).

34. Dr Carlisle, Presbyterian Scholar to Birr, was a National Board of Education Commissioner who worked with William Crotty from 1838 till his death in 1854 to nurture the Presbyterian community in Birr (Bowen, 113).

35. The Irish words included *cat breac* (speckled cat), a word for a Protestant convert so called because of the cover of the book used by the proselytizers. Jumper came from the Irish word *iompú*, to change.

36. The Beast was the Antichrist. See Revelations 13:1-18. See Whelan's discussion of the Revd Alexander Dallas and his Society for Irish Church Missions. Dallas believed that the conditions for the millenium included the destruction of the Antichrist which he charged was the Roman Catholic Church (Póirtéir, 143).

37. In his study of famine folklore, Roger McHugh supported the Nicholson position that most conversions were temporary and were the result of hunger. Those who remained Protestant were called 'soupers' or 'jumpers' (Edwards, 410-11).

38. See Nicholson's account in *Welcome,* 354. Revd Charles Gayer, Lord Ventry's private chaplain, founded a Protestant colony at Dingle. It attracted some notoriety when Gayer sued the Editor of the *Kerry Examiner* for slander (Bowen, 85). Nicholson was thrown out of the Dingle colony by Mrs Gayer when she accused the Gayers of oppression (*Welcome*, 352).

39. Nicholson appears to be critical of the Puritan doctrine of the elect which justified their taking land from the Native Americans whom they regarded as savages who posed the threats of massacre and captivity to the settlers (Miller, 256). The early settlers did try to bring the Gospel to the Indians, provided they were '... good Indians and would accept the whites as superiors and entitled to rule' (Atkins, 265).

40. The Jebusites inhabited Jerusalem (Numbers 13:29); the Perizzites lived in unwalled villages between Bethel and Hai (Genesis XIII:7) and the Scythians invaded Assyria from the north *c*.627 BC.

41. A *regium donum* would be a gift to a ruling authority.

42. There is a version of this legend, 'The Clearing from Guilt' in Lady Wilde's *Ancient Legends of Ireland*, 69-70.

43. Nicholson describes the 'changeling', a well-documented folk legend. See Yeats, 50-64.

44. The petticoat tradition for little boys survived into the 1920s in the west.

45. The belief that when a child smiles in its sleep it is talking with the angels is the subject of Samuel Lover's poem 'The Angel's Whisper'.

NOTES TO CHAPTER IX

1. Daniel 5:26-27: 'This is the interpretation of the thing: *Mene,* God hath numbered thy kingdom and finished it. *Tekel*, Thou art weighed in the balance and found wanting.'

2. Sharman Crawford, like George Hill, was an improving landlord. His letter in the *Downpatrick Recorder* (2 March 1850) arguing to farmers at Killinchy that it was in landlords' own interests that tenants' rights be legalized gives some insight into Crawford. See Killen, 235.

3. Matthew 10:22: 'Ye shall be hated of all men for my name's sake.'. Ecclesiastes 7:1: 'A good name is better than precious ointment; and the day of death than the day of one's birth.'

4. Isaiah 2:20: 'In that day a man shall cast his idols ... to the moles and to the bats.'

5. This appears to be a reference to the question of the disestablishment of the Church, a move Nicholson favoured. The Church of Ireland was disestablished in 1869.

6. The one solitary Quaker was bound to have been Richard Davis Webb.

7. Nicholson said that she saw Mary, a young woman she had befriended, on the day that she left Ireland. The man from Kingstown walked seven miles to give Nicholson his blessing but she was out (45).

8. Psalm 137: 'If I do not remember thee, let my tongue cleave to the roof of my mouth.'

9. Psalm 126:5: 'They that sow in tears shall reap in joy.'

WORKS CITED

Aldwell, Alexander. *Cork Directory. 1844-1845*. Cork: 1846.

Atkins, Gaius and Frederick L. Fagley. *The History of American Congregationalism*. Boston: The Pilgrim Press, 1942.

Augustine, Revd Father. *Footprints of Father Theobald Mathew, O.F.M. Cap.* Dublin: Gill, 1947.

Barry, Michael. *The Romance of Sarah Curran*. Fermoy: Éigse Books, 1985.

Bennett, William. *Narrative of a recent journey of Six Weeks in Ireland in connexion with the subject of supplying small seed to some of the remoter districts with current observations on the depressed circumstances of the people, and the means presented for the permanent improvement of their social conditions*. London: Gilpin 1847.

Berry, James. 'Death at Doolough' *Tales of the West of Ireland*. Gertrude M. Horgan (ed.). Dublin: Dolmen Press, 1966, pp. 39-42.

Best, Charles and Norman B. Taylor. *The Physiological Basis of Medical Practice*. 8th (ed.) Baltimore: Williams and Wilkins, 1966.

Bowen, Desmond. *Souperism: Myth or Reality? A Study in Souperism*. Cork: Mercier, 1970.

Burke, Oliver J. *Anecdotes of the Connacht Circuit*. Dublin: Hodges Figgis 1885.

Carlyle, Thomas. *Reminiscence of my Irish Journey in 1849*. London: Sampson Low, 1882.

Chelsea Historical Society. *A History of Chelsea, Vermont. 1784-1984*. Barre: Chelsea Historical Society, 1984.

Clarkson, L.A. 'Conclusion: Famine and Irish History' in E.M. Crawford (ed.), *Famine: the Irish Experience*. Edinburgh: John Donald 1989.

Connell, K.H. 'Illicit Distillation: a Peasant Industry' *Irish Historical Studies* III. London: Bowes and Bowes, 1961, pp. 58-91.

Dalsimer, Adele M and Vera Kreilkamp (eds). *America's Eye: Irish Paintings from the Collection of Brian P. Burns*. Boston: Boston College Museum of Art, 1996.

Daly, Mary E. *The Famine in Ireland*. Dundalk: Dublin Historical Association, 1986.

Danaher, Kevin. *In Ireland Long Ago*. Cork: Mercier, 1962.

Edwards, R. Dudley and T. Desmond Williams (eds). *The Great Famine. Studies in Irish History 1845-52*. Dublin: Brown and Nolan, 1956; Lilliput Press, 1994.

Flood, Jeanne A. 'The Forster Family and the Irish Famine' *Quaker History*, 84, 2 (Fall, 1995), pp. 116-30.

Garvey, Rosemary. *Kilkenny to Murrisk. A Garvey Family History*. Westport: Berry, 1992.

Goodbody, Rob. *A Suitable Channel. Quaker Relief in the Great Famine*. Bray: Pale Publishing, 1995.

Griffith, Gerald. 'Hand and Word' *Tales of the Munster Festivals*. Dublin: Maxwell 1827.

Hale, Thomas. 'Historical Address' *Centennial Celebration of the Settlement of Chelsea, Vermont*. Keene, N.H.: Sentinel, 1884, pp. 28-98.

Hall, Samuel C. and Anna. *Ireland. Its Scenery and Character*. Vol. 3. London: Hall, Virtue and Co, 1842.

Harrison, Richard. *Cork City Quakers 1655-1939: A Brief History*. Cork: 1991. *Richard Davis Webb: Dublin Quaker Printer (1895-1872)*. Skibbereen: Red Barn, 1993.

Hatch-Hale, Ruth. *Genealogy and History of the Hatch Family*. Salt Lake City: The Hatch Genealogical Society, n.d.

Hatton, Helen E. *The Largest Amount of Good. Quaker Relief in Ireland 1658-1921*. Montreal: McGill-Queen's University Press, 1993.

Holland, M. 'A Forgotten Mathew Memorial' *Journal of the Cork Historical and Archaeological Society*, XIX, 99 (July-September, 1913), pp. 131-4.

Hill, George Augustus. *Facts from Gweedore*. 3rd edn. Dublin: Philip Dixon Hardy, 1854.

Hyde, Douglas. *Abhráin atá Leagtha ar an Reachtúire. Songs Ascribed to Raftery*. Dublin: Gill, 1903.

'Individual Exertions: Mr Bianconi' *Dublin Penny Journal* (8 September 1832), p. 7.

In Memorian. William Goodell, Born in Coventry, New York, October 27, 1792. Died in Janesville, Wisconsin, February 14, 1875. Guilbert and Winchell, 1879.

Killanin, Lord and Michael V. Duignan, *The Shell Guide to Ireland*. London: Ebury Press, 1967.

Killen, John (ed.). *The Famine Decade. Contemporary Accounts. 1841-1851*. Belfast: The Blackstaff Press, 1995.

Kissane, Noel. *The Irish Famine. A Documentary History*. Dublin: National Library of Ireland, 1995.

Leadam, Isaac Saunders. 'John Bright' *Dictionary of National Biography* XXII, Supplement. Sir Leslie Stephens and Sir Sidney Lee (eds). London: Oxford University Press, 1922.

Le Duc, Thomas. 'Grahamites and Garrisonians' in *New York State History*, 20 (1939), p. 190.

Lewis, Samuel. *A Topographical Dictionary of Ireland*. London: S. Lewis, 1837.

Lincoln, Colm. *Steps and Steeples. Cork at the Turn of the Century*. Dublin: O'Brien, 1980.

Luddy, Maria. *Women and Philanthropy in Nineteenth-Century Ireland*. London: Cambridge University Press, 1995.

Lyons, John. *Louisburgh. A History*. Louisburgh: Louisburgh Traders Association, 1995.

McNamara, T.F. *Portrait of Cork*. Cork: Waterman, 1981.

McNeill, Mary. *The Life and Times of Mary Ann McCracken 1770-1866. A Belfast Panorama*. Dublin: Allen Figgis, 1960.

Macintyre, Angus. *The Liberator. Daniel O'Connell and the Irish Party 1830-1847*. New York: Macmillan, 1965.

Malcolm, Elizabeth. *'Ireland Sober, Ireland Free.' Drink and Temperance in Nineteenth-Century Ireland*. Syracuse: Syracuse University Press, 1986.

'The Mathew Tower' *Journal of the Cork Historical and Archaeological Society* XXXII, 135 (January-June 1927), p. 5.

Messenger, John C. *Inis Beag. Isle of Ireland*. New York: Holt Rhinehardt and Winston, 1969.

Miller, Perry (ed.). *The American Puritans. Their Prose and Poetry*. Garden City: Doubleday, 1956.

Milton, John. *Paradise Lost*. Scott Elledge (ed.). New York: Norton, 1975.

Moore, Thomas. *The Poetical Works of Thomas Moore*. New York: Worthington, 1888.

Morash, Chris (ed.). *The Hungry Voice. The Poetry of the Irish Famine*. Dublin: Irish Academic Press, 1989.

Nicholson, Asenath. *Ireland's Welcome to the Stranger; or, An Excursion through Ireland in 1844 and 1845 for the purpose of personally investigating the condition of the poor*. London: Gilpin, 1847. *Lights and Shades of Ireland*. London: Houlston and Stoneman, 1850. *Loose Papers or Facts Gathered During Eight Years' Residence in Ireland, Scotland, England, France, and Germany*. New York: The Anti-Slavery Office,1853. *Nature's Own Book*. 2nd edn. New York: Wilbur and Whipple, 1835; Glasgow: William Brown, 1846.

O'Donoghue, D.J. *The Poets of Ireland*. Dublin: Hodges Figgis & Co, 1912.

O'Flaherty, Tom. *Aranmen All*. Dublin: The Sign of the Three Candles, 1934.

O'Gráda, Cormac. *An Drochshaol Béaloideas agus Amhráin*. Baile Atha Cliath: Coiscéim, 1994. *Ireland before and after the Famine*. Manchester: Manchester University Press, 1988.

O'Suilleabháin, Eoghan Rua. 'A Chara Mo Chléibh' *An Duanaire. 1600-1900. Poems of the Dispossessed*. Seán O'Tuama and Thomas Kinsella (eds). Dublin: Dolmen, 1981.

Pearson, Peter. *Dun Laoghaire. Kingston*. Dublin: O'Brien Press, 1991.

Perry, Lewis. *Childhood, Marriage and Reform. Henry Clarke Wright 1797-1870*. Chicago: University of Chicago Press, 1980.

Póirtéir, Cathal (ed.). *Famine Echoes*. Dublin: Gill and Macmillan, 1995. *The Great Irish Famine*. Dublin: Mercier Press, 1995.

The Report of the General Relief Committee. New York: General Relief Committee, 1849.

Shaw, Henry. *The Dublin Pictorial Guide and Directory of 1850*. Belfast: The Friar's Bush Press, 1988.

Sheppard, Alfred Tressider. 'Asenath Nicholson and the Howitt Circle' *The Bookman* (November, 1926), pp. 103-05. Introduction to *The Bible in Ireland* (an edition of *Ireland's Welcome to the Stranger* by Asenath Nicholson). London: Hodder & Stoughton, 1925.

Shyrock, Richard H. 'Sylvester Graham and the Popular Health Movement, 1830-1870' *Mississippi Valley Historical Review*, 18 (1931-1932), p. 174.

Spenser, Edmund. *A View of the Present State of Ireland.* W.L. Renwick (ed.). Oxford: Clarendon Press, 1970.

Synge, John M. *Collected Works. III. Plays. Book I.* Ann Saddlemyer (ed.). London: Oxford University Press, 1968.

Thom's Dublin Directory for 1847. Dublin: Thom's, 1848.

Thuente, Mary Helen. *The Harp Unstrung, The United Irishmen and the Rise and Fall of Literary Nationalism.* Syracuse: Syracuse University Press, 1994.

Transactions of the Central Relief Committee of the Society of Friends During the Famine in Ireland in 1846 and 1847. Dublin: Hodges and Smith, 1852.

Trevelyan, Charles E. 'The Irish Crisis' *Edinburgh Review* (January 1848).

Tuke, James H. *A Visit to Connaught in the Autumn of 1847.* 2nd edn. London: Charles Gilpin, 1848.

Valiulis, Maryann Gialanella, and O'Dowd, Mary (eds). *Women & Irish History. Essays in Honour of Margaret MacCurtain.* Dublin: Wolfhound Press, 1997.

Wilde, Lady Jane. *Ancient Legends, Mystical Charms and Superstitions of Ireland.* London: Ward and Downey, 1890.

Wolfe, Charles. *'The Burial of Sir John Moore' and Other Poems.* London: Sidgwick and Jackson, 1909.

Yeats, W.B. *Irish Fairy and Folk Tales.* New York: Modern Library ,n.d. [1888]

MANUSCRIPT SOURCES

The Annals of the South Presentation Convent, Cork. 1771-1892.

Chelsea Archives. *Folktales Incident to Chelsea.* Unsigned typescript. Town of Chelsea Library, Vermont.

Dorian, Hugh. Donegal Sixty Years Ago. St Columba's Library, Derry.

Fitz McCarthy, Connie. Asenath Hatch Nicholson: An Unknown American Author. unpublished thesis. Southern Connecticut State College, 1975.

Nicholson, Asenath. Letter, 7 July 1847, Famine Papers, National Archives of Ireland.

Russell, Ernest. Founder's File (1789-1858). Typescript. Records, Town of Chelsea, Vermont.

Webb, Alfred. Journal. Quaker Archives, Swanbrook House, Dublin.

Webb, Richard. Letters to Maria Weston Chapman: 13 October 1846 and 30 October 1847. Manuscript Division. Boston Public Library. 16 September 1847. Ms A.9.2.23 p. 43. Manuscript Division. Boston Public Library.

INDEX

INDEX OF PLACES

Achill, Co. Mayo, 8, 12, 16, 85, 105, 112
Achill Sound, Co. Mayo, 12, 85, 103
Antrim coast, Co. Antrim, 79-80
Arranmore, Co. Donegal, 73-7
Ballina, Co. Mayo, 12, 98, 124-5, 127-8
Ballinrobe, Co. Mayo, 133-5
Ballycroy, Co. Mayo, (Croy Lodge), 120-3
Bangor, Co. Mayo, 124
Bandon, Co. Cork, 147
Bantry, Co. Cork, 26
Belfast, Co. Antrim, 57-8, 60, 78-9, 82, 149
Belmullet, Co. Mayo, 6, 14, 91, 98-9, 121, 123
Binghamstown, Co. Mayo, 14, 93, 102
Blarney, Co. Cork 150
Bunbeg, Co. Donegal, 71
Cape Clear, Co. Cork, 160
Castlebar, Co. Mayo, 12, 84, 128-130, 133, 142, 145
Castlemartyr, Co. Cork, 151-2
Chelsea, VT, 5, 8
Cong, Co. Mayo 133-4
Connaught, 8, 82, 84, 98, 122, 125, 130, 153, 171
Cork, Co. Cork, 17, 89, 146-7, 148-151, 157, 168-170, 174, 184
Coney Island, Co. Cork, 148
Cove (Cobh) also Queenstown, Co. Cork, 147-8, 158
Croagh Patrick, Co. Mayo, 136, 142
Cross, Co. Mayo, 92-3
Crossmolina, Co. Mayo, 124
Derry, Co. Londonderry, 61-2, 69, 72, 78
Donegal (County), 7, 61, 63, 106
Donegal Sea, 160
Doona, Co. Mayo, 123
Down (County), 72
Dublin, Co. Dublin, 5-7, 12, 26, 36, 40-1, 51, 53-55, 57, 82, 103-4, 143-4, 145, 200
Dunfanaghy, Co. Donegal, 63
Dungloe, Co. Donegal, 72, 77
Edinburgh, Scotland, 174
Erris, Co. Mayo, 12, 91, 92, 93-5, 98-9, 100, 102, 112, 116, 125

Fermoy, Co. Cork, 146
France, 129
Galway, Co. Galway, 145-6
Glengarriff, Co. Cork, 26, 127
Gweedore, Co. Donegal, 64-5, 78
Haulbowline, Co. Cork, 148
Isle of Wight, England, 130
Jersey City, New Jersey USA, 17
Joyce Country, 131
Kerry (County), 26, 110, 159, 171
Killery mountains, 138, 160
Kingstown, Co. Dublin, 36, 38, 45
Kinsale, Co. Cork, 147
Larne, Co. Antrim, 79
Letterkenny, Co. Donegal, 63-4, 69
Limerick (County), 85, 146
London, England, 114, 143, 150, 154, 172-3
Lough Carra, Co. Mayo, 133
Lough Conn, Co. Mayo, 127
Lough Cullen, Co. Galway, 127
Lough Mask, Co. Galway, 130
Louisburgh, Co. Mayo, 137
M'Sweeney's Gun, Co. Donegal, 63
Mayo (County), 15, 110, 112, 142, 185
Milford, Co. Donegal, 63
Monkstown, Co. Cork, 148
Mount Patrick, Co. Cork, 148, 154-160
Mulranny, Co. Mayo, 120
Murrisk, Co. Mayo, 142
Newport, Co. Mayo, 8, 13, 82-3, 85, 112, 115
New York, NY, 9-11, 40, 48, 51, 93, 170
Old Head, Co. Mayo, 136-7
Parsonstown, Co. Offaly (King's Co.), 180
Partry, Co. Mayo, 130, 132, 140
Passage, Co. Cork, 148
Pontoon, Co. Mayo, 127, 133
Rathmelton, Co. Donegal, 63
Rocky Island, Co. Cork, 148
Rosport, Co. Mayo, 96-8
Rossgarrow, Co. Donegal, 7, 62
Skibbereen, Co. Cork, 130
Spike Island, Co. Cork, 8, 148, 152-3
Tipperary (County), 8, 101, 119
Tuam, Co. Galway, 82, 145
Tullaghobegly, Co. Donegal, 64-8
Ventry, Co. Kerry, 6

Westport, Co. Mayo, 11, 116, 142
Wicklow (County), 110, 160
Youghal, Co. Cork, 147

INDEX OF PERSONS

Abraham and Sara, eldery famine
   victims, Achill Sound, 85-7
Anderson, Mr, Pontoon landlord, 127
Arthur, Margaret, Postmistress of Newport,
   Co. Mayo, 12-13, 83-4
Barter, Dr. Richard, hydropathic cure, St
   Anne's, Cork, 166-7
Beale, Abraham, Cork Quaker and relief
   worker, 7, 149-150
Beale sisters, sisters of Abraham, AN
   friends, 150-1, 170
Bennett, William, English Quaker relief
   worker, 12, 55, 61, 76
Bewley, Joseph, Dublin Quaker, proposes
   soup shop relief, 41
Bianconi, Charles, public transportation
   pioneer, 146
Bourke, Walter, Q.C., Carrowkeel, Co.
   Mayo, 128
Bourke, Mrs, AN friend, Co. Mayo, 127
Bourne, Samuel, landlord, relief work,
   Rosport, Co. Mayo, 13, 97, 98, 100, 102
Bright, John M.P., industrialist, reformer,
   14, 165-6
Bunyan, John, English preacher and writer,
   135
Butler, Hon. William, Inspecting Officer of
   Belmullet and Binghamstown, Co.
   Mayo, 61, 91, 103
Carey, Miss, schoolmistress, Rosport, Co.
   Mayo, 98
Carey, Chief Officer Frederick, coast
   guardsman, relief worker, Rosport, Co.
   Mayo, 96
Carlisle, Mr, National Board of Education
   Commissioner, Birr Mission, 180
Chapman, Maria Weston, American aboli-
   tionist, 6
Cope, Thomas P., American Quaker, orga-
   nized relief efforts in Philadelphia, 47
Cowper, William, English poet, 144
Cromwell, Oliver, 110
Crosfield, Joseph, English Quaker, relief
   worker, 54
Curran, Sarah, Robert Emmet's fiancè, 148
Daly family, Doona, Co. Mayo, 123
Edgar, Dr John, educator, industrial
   schools, 8, 58, 98
Edgeworth, Maria, 11

Elizabeth I, Queen, 110, 196
Emerson, Ralph Waldo, American essayist
   and poet, 9
Fisher, Mrs. Ellen, Cork hotel-keeper 170
Fitzgerald, Widow, AN friend, Castlebar,
   Co. Mayo, 130
Forster, Frances, Lord Hill's agent,
   Dungloe, Co. Donegal, 72, 77
Forster, Mrs Frances, AN friend, 77-8
Forster, William, English Quaker, relief
   worker, 12, 55
Fox, Miss, AN friend, Ballina, Co. Mayo,
   126
Garrison, William Lloyd, American aboli-
   tionist and editor, 10
Garvey, Mrs James(?), Tully, Co. Mayo,
   landowner, AN friend, 136-140
Garveys of Murrisk Abbey, Co. Mayo, 142
Gildea, Mr, linen-factory owner, famine
   work, Belcarra, Co. Mayo, 117
Goodbody, Marcus, Clara miller, Quaker
   relief worker, 54
Goodell, William, American reformer, 9
Graham, Sylvester, American health
   reformer, 9-10
Granuaile, legendary sea captain, Doona
   Castle, Co. Mayo, 124
Greely, Horace, editor *New York Tribune*, 9,
   10
Greene, Rev. John, Curate of
   Binghamstown, 99, 102
Gregg, Rev. John, Chaplain, Trinity
   Church, Dublin, 57
Griffith, Rev.Valentine, Rector of
   Templecrone, Co. Donegal, 73, 74, 75,
   76, 77
Griffith, Mrs., AN friend, 78
Grimshaw family, millers, White House,
   Belfast, 61
Hale, Thomas, AN former pupil, 8
Hamilton, Inspecting Lieutenant A.T.,
   coastguardsman, Mullaghmore, Co.
   Mayo, 123
Hamilton, Rev. William, Baptist minister,
   Ballina, 126
Harvey, Jacob, American Quaker, organized
   Irish relief in New York, 47
Hatch, Benjamin, AN's brother, 6
Hatch, David, AN's brother, 6
Hatch, Martha, AN's mother, 5-7, 53
Hatch, Michael, AN's father, 5-6
Hewitson, Susan, relief worker, Rossgar-
   row, Co. Donegal, 7, 62-3, 78-9, 82
Hewitson, Miss, Susan's daughter, 61
Hill, Lord, George, landlord, Gweedore,
   Co. Donegal, 7, 64-5, 69-72

Ireland, Mary, Belfast Ladies' Association leader, 60

Jackson, Andrew, American president, 14

James I, King, 110

Kelly, Peter, Ballina and Dublin solicitor, 124, 126, 136

Kelly family, Ballina, Co. Mayo, 126, 136

Kinkead, Rev. Francis, Curate of Ballina, relief worker, 124

Lucan, Lord Richard, landowner, Castlebar, Co. Mayo, 127

McCracken, Mary Ann, Belfast Ladies' Association leader, sister of Henry Joy, 7, 60

McHale, Bishop J., Tuam, Co. Galway, 82

M'Kye, Patrick, teacher, West Tullaghobegly, Co. Donegal, 65-8

Martin, William, Cork Quaker, temperance reformer, 151, 168

Mathew, Charles, brother of Fr. Theobald, 163

Mathew, Father Theobald, temperance reformer, Cork relief worker, 17, 88, 148-160, 170, 174-5

Maxwell, William, novelist, 120, 124

Mitchel, John, 15, 119, 153

Mitchell, highwayman, 131

Moore, Sir John, English general, 162

Moore, Thomas, 148

Morash, Christopher, 13

Murphy, Bishop John, Cork, 156

Murry, Mr and Jordan, Independent Church of Irish Evangelical Society, 144

Nangle, Rev. Edward, founder, Protestant Missionary Colony, Achill, Co. Mayo, 8, 105, 107

Nicholson, Asenath Hatch, *early life*: family, childhood, teaching in Vermont, 5-6, 8; moves to New York, 9; Graham boarding-houses, 9-10, 23; meets the Irish poor in New York, 11; first visit to Ireland, 11; Dublin famine work, 38-57, 82, 142, 170-1, 195; Cook Street, 5, 12, 82, 144; *Mayo famine work:* Newport, 82-85, 115; Achill Sound, 85-8, 91, 103-5; Belmullet, 91-6, 98-100; Rosport, 96-8; Achill, 105; Ballycroy, 120-123; Ballina, 125-6, 128; Castlebar, 128-9, 142; Partry, 130-132; 142; Ballinrobe, 133-136; Westport, 142; visit to Cork, 144-170, 174, 183; return to Dublin and departure, 171, 192-3; *Annals of the Famine*, 17; *Ireland's Welcome to the Stranger*, 5-6, 11, 15, 17, 18; *Lights and Shades of Ireland*, 18, 192; Loose Papers, 8; *Nature's Own Book*, 6, 8-9

Nicholson, Norman, merchant, AN's husband, 9

O'Brien, William Smith, 15, 119

O'Connell, Daniel, 15, 26, 80

O'Connor, Roderick (Rory), King of Connaught, 133

O'Connor, William, Cork tailor and benefactor, 154-160

O'Donnell, James, landlord, relief worker, Erris, Co. Mayo, 102,

O'Donnell, Sir Richard, landlord, Newport, Co. Mayo, 115, 117

O'Dowda, Miss, AN friend, Ballina, Co. Mayo, 126

Ossian, 69, 77

Penrose, Cooper, Cork Quaker merchant, befriended Sarah Curran, 148

Pounden, Rev. P., Rector of Westport, 116

Power, Dr Maurice, M.P., 152-4, 161

Queen of Erris, 99

Rafe, Rev. D., Rector of Ballinrobe, 133, 134

Russell, Lord John, 36, 114, 165

St. Finbar, 148

St. Patrick, 137

Savage, R.R., coastguardsman, hotel-keeper, relief worker, Achill Sound, Co. Mayo, 12, 85-8, 91, 103

Savage, Mrs. R.R., relief worker, 12, 85-8, 105

Shackleton, Lydia, Dublin Quaker relief worker, 7

Shannon, Lord, Castlemartyr, Co. Cork, 152

Short, Widow, Ballina, AN friend, Ballina, Co. Mayo, 125

Sligo, Marquess, Lord Altamont, major landowner in Louisburgh, Co. Mayo, built Adelphi Lodge, 141

Sims, William Dillwyn, Quaker relief worker, 54

Soyer, Alexis Benoit, chef, Soyer soup, 143-4, 150

Stock, Rev. Samuel, Rector of Kilcommon-Erris, Chairman of the Erris Relief Committee, 100

Stock, Mrs Samuel, relief worker, 103

Stoney, Rev. W., Rector of Castlebar, 130

Sturge, Joseph, English corn factor, philanthropist, reformer, 14

Synge, John Millington, 13

Tappan, Arthur, American abolitionist, 9-10

Tappan, Lewis, American abolitionist, 9-10

Thompson, George, English abolitionist, 14, 100, 101

Todhunter, William, relief worker, 54

Trevelyan, Sir Charles, *Irish Crisis*, 13, 106, 109

Tuke, James Hack, English Quaker relief worker, 12, 54, 91, 98

Tyler, William, American classicist, Amherst College, 10

Vernon, Mr., owner of Croy Lodge, Ballycroy, Co. Mayo, 121

Victoria, Queen, 106, 114, 147, 155, 165, 197

Walshe, John, Dublin solicitor, landlord, evictions, Erris, Co. Mayo, 116

Ward, Peter, Pastor of Partry, 132

Waring, Maria, Dublin Quaker, 7

Webb, Alfred, Dublin Quaker, biographer, 9

Webb, Maria, Belfast Ladies' Association worker, 60

Webb, Richard Davis, Dublin Quaker, printer, temperance advocate, abolitionist, relief worker, 6, 7, 11, 17, 57, 173

Wesley, John, English evangelist, 186

Whelan, Irene, 16

William III, King, 151

Wilson, Rev. Charles, Rector of Newport, Co. Mayo, 115

Wilson, Mr., manager, Croy Lodge, Ballycroy, Co. Mayo, 121

Windell, John, Crown officer(?), Cork, 149

Wolfe, Rev. Charles, Curate of Donaghmore, Co. Tyrone, poet, 161-3

Wolfe, Major General James, English military hero, 161

Wright, Henry Clarke, American reformer, 10

INDEX OF SUBJECTS

abolitionists, 6, 9, 13, 100, 101, 102

Achill missionary colony, AN and mission 6, 105, 185; schools, 8, mission before the famine, 11; lack of charity 15; workmen poorly paid, 105

agents, agents killed 28, 81; Lord Russell as an agent 114

American Anti-Slavery Society, 9, 10

American famine relief, aid to AN, 40-1, 47, 82, 149, 172; New York meeting on behalf of the Irish 40-1, 47; meal from New York, 51; children's donation, 55; American clothing, 82, 84, 105, 107; American grain to Ireland, 89, 105; England and American relief, 102; difficulties of getting American relief to the poor, 106; relief to Father Mathew, 149; American Quakers, 159

American Indians, 91, 183

American Tract Society, 9

Battle of the Boyne, 152

banshees, 190

Baptists, in Ballina, 125-6, 187; AN, 181

beggars, 37, 41, 85, 108, 121, 125, 128, 132, 138, 142, 172, 192

Belfast Ladies' Association for the Relief of Irish Destitution, 7; origin, 58; support of industrial schools, 59

Bible readers, 11, 12, 14, 16, 187

Birr Mission, 180

Black bread, 8, 22, 108, 112-4, 136, 145, 150, 165, 181, 197

British Relief Assocation, 47, 56, 149

burial of famine dead, 38, 40, 75, 86-7, 94, 96, 109, 133; scarcity of coffins, 75-6, 86-7, 93-4, 95; poor concern with own coffin 86, 94, 119; poor carry corpses, 88, 94, 117, 164; dead buried in ruins of cabins 38, 92, 118; girl's hair above the stones, 94; families bringing their dead, 96, 104; woman comes to coffin husband, 104; uncoffined dead, 75, 87, 94, 115, 149; rich and poor burials, 117, *caoineadh* (keening), 137; sliding coffins, 149, 150; mass graves, 149; Irish attitude to dead, 142

burial grounds, Arranmore, 75; Cross 92; Binghamstown, 93; Rosport, 96

cattle seizure for debt, 99-100, 118

Central and Spring Street Presbyterian Mission (NY), 11

Central Relief Committee (Irish Society of Friends), begin soup shop, 12, 46-7; AN and, 16, 51-2, 56-7; Dublin soup shop, 41-2; New York committee, 55-6; grants, 63, 77, 85; Cork Committee, 149-50

Church of Ireland, AN indictment for failure of stewardship, 15; generosity to poor, 116, 125, 130, 137, 176; disestablishment, 166, 195; attitude toward the poor 176-7; bigotry, 173, 178; and Roman Catholics, 177-8; converts, 186; well-paid clergy, 194; AN on Church of Ireland, 194

class, gulf between classes in Connaught, 195-6

cleanliness, 60

convents, Tuam, 145; Cork, 149

convicts, 152; Spike Island prison, 152-3

crime, Catholics blamed, 28; absence of crime during famine, 38, 77-8; agrarian crime, 118; AN sees trial, 128; imprisonment for stealing food, 153; suspects and 'test of the skull', 190; Dublin servant pawns AN's clothes, 171-2 diet, middle class, 33

Dingle Mission, 182-3, 185

Dissenters, AN's evaluation, 182, 185, 194-5, 197

distilling (legal), grain diverted to alcohol, 89-90

distilling (illegal), 69

dogs: dogs as food, 37; dogs stop barking during famine, 63; dogs eat the dead, 73, 76, 87, 133, 137

drivers, 99-100, 115-6

education (see schools), middle class girls, 34

emigration, Irish to New York, 56; choice to emigrate, 142, 199

employment: AN and need for employment, 15, 33, 37, 102, 117, 125, 151, 154; AN provides employment, 44, 82; children taught skills for employment, 58, 71; children's work saves family, 79-80; local clergy and work schemes, 125, 137, 145

England, AN about England's relationship with Ireland, 110, 165-6, 176-7

English: English workers for Irish relief, 72, 126, 130, 199; grants to local relief workers 75, 77; privately organized relief, 106, 195

eviction, 27, 108, 115, 128, 132, 193; Mayo evictions, 92, 110, 114, 115-6

fairies, 81, 147, 190-1

famine: peculiarities of this famine, 38, 163-4; famine and lack of employment, 38, 145; AN's mission, 39, 44-5, 50, 56-7, 76, 105-6, 157-8; could have been avoided, 48-9, 173, 176-7, 194; famine and irresponsible landlords, 53; famine workers, 60-1, 75-6, 145-6, 187; clergy and famine relief, 64, 130-2, 135; responsible landlords and famine relief, 71-2, 98, 139-40; private relief funds, 78; schools during the famine, 80; generosity of the poor to the poor, 83; famine and alcohol consumption, 89; famine effect on Irish affect, 77, 92, 145; poorhouse as relief measure, 108-11; evictions, 114; famine and the 1848 rebellion, 117; soupshops as government relief measure, 143-4; prayer of the poor for the potato to end the famine, 163; famine as judgment, 163-4, 177

fever, 38, 132; typhus in Cork, 150

fishing, 145-6

holy wells, 137, 190

hunting, AN's disapproval, 69, 110, 121-3, 152

independent churches, 144, 180; AN's evaluation 187

Indian corn (meal), 7-8, 35-6, 39, 51, 52, 62, 75, 95, 100-1, 105-6, 108, 143, 165, 181 See also stirabout

Irish characterized as idle, 33, 35, 37, 59, 60, 76, 101, 137, 177

Irish Evangelical Society, 144-5

Irish language, 16; Lord Hill as Irish-speaker, 69; Protestant clergy and Irish, 75, 105, 175, 187

landlords, absentees, 11, 67; kind landlords, 43, 96, 139-40, 193; landlords' salvation and famine 116, 193; landlords and tenants' conditions, 66-8; landlords and drink, 89, 193; landlords give Indian meal to livestock, 90; lack of resident landlords, 91, 102; landlords as slave-holders, 96, 114, 199; landlords claim no knowledge of evictions, 115; attitudes toward tenants, 142, 177; landlords exploit poor, 165, 193; honesty of landlords, 176; difference improving landlords would make, 78; landlords' burden, 193

Methodists, in Ballina 125; good woman mourned, 180; hostility toward converts, 182; AN's evaluation, 186-7; coastguard in Dingle, 182

Moravians, AN's evaluation, 186-7, 189,

New York and Brooklyn Foreign Missionary Society, 9

Plymouth Brethren, AN's evaluation, 188

Poor Laws, 80, 111, 171; impoverishing the middle class, 80, 102, 115, 125, 193

Poor Law Guardians, 136

Poor rates, 80, 102, 118

potatoes, AN shares meals of potatoes, 11, 26, 159, 171, 192; dependence on potatoes, 33, 37, 48, 110, 163-5, 177; servants' food, 33, 38; destruction of the potato, 37, 48-9, 163, 181; woman tried for gleaning potatoes, 37; potatoes as a curse 48, 74; potatoes fed to livestock, 67; potatoes return to Arranmore, 78; blight, 102, 108, 163; potato diet, 110; planting potatoes, 136, 138-9, 163; hope for return of the potato 136, 163-4, 181; silence about the potato crop, 151, potato and spade, 164-5

Presbyterians, Ballina, 125; clergy praise faith of Catholics, 186; Presbyterian abolitionists, 186; AN, 186

Presentation nuns, Cork, 7, 17, 145; George's Hill, Dublin, 8, 55-6; Tuam, Co. Galway, 8, 145 proselytism, 11, 16, 177-9, 181-4; soupers, 16, 185; food based on creed, 178; use of the Irish language, 105, 181; schools, 181; temporary converts, 181-2, priests on proselytes, 182; soldiers protect converts, 182-3

Quakers (Irish Society of Friends), 7, 10, 11-12, 13, 14, 17, 29-30, 41-2, 54, 141, 149, 154, 178-9, 189-90; Quakers' accounts of the famine, 13, 54; Quaker recruitment of local relief workers, 17; praise for Quakers, 145, 178; Cork Quakers, 151, 184; Quaker funeral, 168-9; schools, 179; Irish curiosity about Quaker beliefs, 179-80, 189; AN's evaluation of Quakers, 189-190; Quakers scrupulous about appearance of proselytism, 189-90

rebellions, 119; 1848, 119-20; O'Connellites and '48, 120

relief officers (government), 15, 50-1, 60-1, 73, 75, 101, 106, 112-13, 118, 125,136,139, 188, 197-9; integrity of government relief agents, 101, 106, 176; drink, 90, 193, 197

relief officers (volunteer), 17, 60-1, 75, 78-9, 96

Repeal, 15, 26, 27, 119, 129

Roman Catholics, AN's view of Catholics as superstitious, 16, 131, 137, 181, 184, 186, 190, 197, 200; AN and the charity of the Catholic poor, 17, 83, 185; capacity to endure suffering, 26, 51, 77, 82-3, 120; Catholics blamed for crime, 28; cooperation between Catholics and Protestants, 60, 137, 178-9, 180-1, 189; Bishop entertains AN, 64; clergy and relief work, 64, 74, 137; priest and 1848 Rising, 119; Ballina, 125; influence of priests, 129, 131, 132, 190; baptism, 131; extreme unction, 131; zeal of laity, 135; AN on spiritual darkness of Catholics, 137, 184; education of poor, ; children, 149; most famine sufferers, 177; taunt soupers, 183; generosity of Catholics, 179, 197; AN's evaluation, 184-5, 188, 190, 197

rundale system, 65, 70

St Patrick's Day (1848), 129

schools, schools visited: George's Hill, 8; Achill mission schools, 8, 105; Newport, 8, 85; industrial schools, 8, 58, 79, 98; Mayo schools, 8, 112-3; Spike Island, 8, 153; Tuam, 8, 145; Donegal, 65; Larne, 79-80; Partry, 130; Rosport,

98; Ballycroy, 121; pauper school, Louisburgh, 136, 138; Cork, 149; Quakers, 179; decrease in school attendance, 68; spoiled black bread to school-children, 113; proselytism, 105, 181-2

seaweed as food, 94, 97; fertilizer, 139

shipwrecks, Mayo, 92, 93, 102; ship-wrecked sailors buried, 93, 98

Sisters of Mercy, 154

slavery, Dublin Quakers debate whether to accept aid from slave states, 15; some kind slaveholders, 43; government relief officers as slaveholders, 75; some tenants more degraded than slaves, 91, 96; cattle drivers as slavedrivers, 114; slave owners' and landlords' pleas of ignorance about conditions, 114, 115; Irish poor compared with slaves, 199

soldiers, Belmullet, 95-6; English soldiers and the 1848 Rising, 119; soldiers defend Protestant missionaries, 182;

soup, Joseph Bewley's, 41; soup shops, 41-2, 60, 143-4, 184; Soyer soup, 143, 150

Soupers, 183

starvation, 39, 45, 54,55, 58, 94, 112, 117-18, 130, 136, 172, 185, 192, 197; stages of starvation, 39, 43; description of the starving, 63, 72, 74, 85, 90, 99, 132; spoiled bread to the starving, 113

stirabout, stirabout times, 16, 150,181-2; food source, 35; food for labourers, 39; food for schoolchildren, 98, 145; stirabout boilers, 100; workhouse food, 110; proselytism, 181-2, 184

seeds, 76

temperance, 8, 9; clergy and drink, 88, 90, 173, 186, 188; diverting grain to distilling, 89; relief officers and drink, 106; Father Mathew, 151, 159, 160

Temperance Union, 9

Temporary Relief Act, 12

tithes, 28, 184

Tithe-gatherer, 81, 164, 183-4

turnips, 15, 76, 94; as substitute for pota-toes, 153

Unitarians, AN's evaluation, 188-9

vegetarianism, 9, 158

water-cure, 166-7

workhouse (also poorhouse, Union), 14, 35, 80, 84, 91, 108-11, 119, 128, 136, 143, 193; Galway, 7, 145; Castlebar, 84, 128; Ballina, 91; Westport, 108, 143; Ballinrobe, 133, 137; Tuam, 145; Limerick, 146; Cork, 149-50

Young Irelanders, 14, 119